Trump: The Wannabe Dictator

TRUMP
THE WANNABE
DICTATOR

HOW WE GOT TO THIS DIRE STATE OF AFFAIRS

ALON BEN-MEIR

Westphalia Press
An Imprint of the Policy Studies Organization
Washington, DC
2020

Westphalia Press
An imprint of Policy Studies Organization
1527 New Hampshire Ave., NW
Washington, D.C. 20036
info@ipsonet.org

ISBN: 978-1-941472-43-9

Cover and interior design by Jeffrey Barnes
jbarnesbook.design

Daniel Gutierrez-Sandoval, Executive Director
PSO and Westphalia Press

Updated material and comments on this edition
can be found at the Westphalia Press website:
www.westphaliapress.org

I dedicate this book to the children
who were separated from their parents at the Mexican border
who suffered unimaginable fear, agony, and pain
locked in cages unfit even for stray animals

Acknowledgments

I want to acknowledge Kim Hurley, for her skillful editing and significant input in the formulation of the book

Arbana Xharra, for her superb investigative journalism and research

Sam Ben-Meir, for his astute observations and constructive critique

Images

2018

2019

2020

Conclusion

INTRODUCTION

L ike many Americans, I have been observing Trump's rise to power with some perplexity, often asking myself how and why a man of his character became the President of the United States, which is viewed as the most powerful political office in the world. But out of a sense of fairness, I thought that he should be given a chance, as he might have been able to rise to the occasion and prove me and others wrong.

Indeed, for someone who seeks adulation, reverence, admiration of his "genius," respect, and appreciation of his "unlimited talents and expertise" on just about every subject, I wondered: why would he not use the power of the presidency to earn all that he desperately wants to be recognized for?

After all, despite his character flaws, he made it to the White House. And yet having reached the pinnacle of power, he still wants more, when in fact the presidency, regardless of constitutional constraints, provides him with all the power he needs to effect revolutionary constructive change—if he only willed it.

Over the past four years, I devoted over fifty of my weekly articles and essays to the Trump presidency, in some way chronologizing some of his statements, the issues he tackled, his policy initiatives, his ideological leanings, and certainly his appetite for making false statements, misrepresenting facts, and creating his own alternate reality.

Before long, I realized that this man is simply irredeemable. He has shown that he is plainly unfit to hold the office of the presidency, which carries an awesome power both domestically and internationally. He did not "make America great again"; he tarnished America's greatness for much of the world to see.

Many psychiatrists and psychologists who have analyzed his behavior, public utterances, and tweets have unanimously concluded that Trump is a psychopath, a pathological liar, uncompassionate, a narcissist, greedy, and shallow. He sees things only in black and white, and never cares to understand the nuances of any issue before him.

Here lies Trump's sickness. In his world, the presidency is not enough to satisfy his ego and make up for his dismal failures and complete lack of self-confidence. He needs unchecked power—dictatorial power—so that no one can question his actions, motives, or agenda, however skewed or criminal they may be.

Sooner than later, Trump will leave office disgracefully, leaving behind the wreckage of a century, the extent of which none of his predecessors have remotely left in their wake. He has stained the office of the presidency, as he has brought nothing but shame and disdain to the most prestigious office in the land, which is looked upon with awe and admiration around the world.

It will take years, and in some cases decades, to repair the extensive damage he inflicted on our country. We must now attend to healing our deep wounds that tore us apart before we can realize, once again, the American dream.

2016

TRUMP'S DAUNTING FOREIGN CHALLENGES

November 10, 2016

If nothing else, the 2016 elections reaffirmed America's solid democratic system. Without any major incidents, tens of millions of Americans went to polling stations across the land, voted for the candidate of their choice, and readied themselves, as always, for the peaceful transfer of power. I believe that even those who were deeply disappointed with the results of the election will sooner than later rise above the fray, put the nation's interests first, and work to build a more wholesome union.

Notwithstanding the post-election trauma that many Americans are experiencing and the time the Trump administration will need to sort out a host of domestic and foreign policy issues, the US faces numerous foreign crises, and it does not have the luxury of time to pause in dealing with them. America's leadership role and responsibility remain pivotal to mitigate, if not end, many of these violent conflicts sweeping the Middle East in particular. Although President-elect Trump is inexperienced and lacks the nuanced knowledge of the complex crises America is confronted with, he must now navigate his own way and develop new strategies, particularly in the areas where Obama fell short, including the Israeli-Palestinian conflict, the Sunni-Shiite war, and the civil war in Syria.

The Israeli-Palestinian conflict: There is no doubt that President Obama made supreme efforts to solve the seven-decades old Israeli-Palestinian conflict. However admirable his efforts were, the president and his chief mediator Secretary of State John Kerry failed to take into account the psychological dimension of the conflict, which has been and remains the core impediment to resolving the conflict, especially from religious, historic, and ideological perspectives.

Throughout the two sets of intensive negotiations in 2009–2010 and 2013–2014, and in spite of the progress made on various conflicting issues such as the Palestinian refugees, the future of Jerusalem, and borders, the failure to mitigate the psychological aspect connected to these issues made it impossible for either side to deliver what they agreed upon.

At this juncture, the gulf between the two sides has become even deeper and wider, and no amount of mediation, compensation, or coercion can persuade either side to make the significant concessions needed to make peace possible.

The Trump administration must first focus on a process of reconciliation (people-to-people activity) that would mitigate the profound mutual distrust, instill a sense of mutual security, and disabuse the strong constituencies on both sides that they can have it all.

During this process of reconciliation between the two sides, which should last for about two years, the US, with the support of the EU (led by France), should promote the Arab Peace Initiative (API) to provide the overall framework for peace based on a two-state solution.

Although many Israelis celebrated the election of Trump, believing that he would not pressure Israel to accept a two-state solution, the Trump administration will make a mistake of historical proportions if it leaves Israelis and Palestinians to their own devices.

The current relative calm should not be taken for granted, as the simmering tension can explode any time if the Palestinians see no prospect of ending the occupation in the foreseeable future.

Only by creating a social, political, and psychological atmosphere conducive to peace, and with the support of the Arab states, the EU, and other major powers, can the negotiations be resumed with a far better prospect of success. If Trump is concerned about Israel's future security and political integrity, he must not hesitate to pressure Israel now to seek a solution and save it from its own destructive path.

The Sunni-Shiite war: ISIS came to being in the wake of the Iraq war, which instigated a renewed violent conflict between the Sunnis and Shiites. Although the eventual defeat of ISIS is inevitable, it will not bring an end to the Sunni-Shiite conflict as long as Shiite Iran and Sunni Saudi Arabia fight for regional hegemony; they will continue to wage a proxy war in Iraq, Syria, and Yemen to secure their goal.

The key to settling this conflict is to revisit the Iraq war and its repercussions on the Sunnis in Iraq. After eighty-one years of continuous rule, Iraqi Sunnis now find themselves at the mercy of the Shiite governing majority, which has systematically discriminated against and marginalized them from the first day the Maliki-led Shiite government came to power.

The Trump administration must now understand that maintaining the unity of Iraq as a single country is no longer a viable option. Although the Sunni Iraqis loathe ISIS, they despise and detest the Shiite government in Bagdad even more. To help bring a swifter end to the civil war in Iraq, Sunnis need to be granted autonomy along the line of the Iraqi Kurds.

The US must now begin the dialogue between Sunni and Shiite leadership in Iraq to reach an amicable agreement with which both can live. The three Sunni provinces that include the city of Mosul should constitute the contours of such an entity, but given the lack of natural resources (i.e., oil) in these areas, an equitable distribution of oil revenue should be established between them and the central government.

In the final analysis, only a long period of peaceful coexistence between the two sides will allow them over time to develop a closer, more trusting, and friendlier relationship. This will greatly satisfy the Saudis, as the Sunnis will maintain a strong foothold in Iraq, while Iran will still be in a position to exert some influence on the Shiite government.

This would also bring an end to the bloodshed between Sunnis and Shiites that will otherwise further escalate in the wake of ISIS's inevitable defeat.

The civil war in Syria: The civil war in Syria will not end unless the US changes its approach to the war by putting both Putin and Assad on notice that the slaughter of Syrian civilians must immediately come to an end.

The US cannot assert its commanding regional role and at the same time save the Syrian people from near-complete destruction by leading from behind and merely providing military equipment and material to the rebels.

That said, the US must recognize that Russia has been for decades and will remain a permanent fixture in Syria, and Iran will not relinquish its long-standing interest and influence in Damascus as Tehran views Syria as the linchpin to the Shiite-dominated crescent of land between the Mediterranean and the Gulf. However unorthodox this may seem, the US has little choice but to work with these two powers to find a solution.

While recognizing the importance of Russia's role and its willingness to cooperate with Putin to find a permanent solution, the Trump administration must also convey in unequivocal terms to Putin and Assad that they must stop the indiscriminate bombing and killing of tens of thousands of innocent Syrians while erasing one neighborhood after another.

Given Putin's desire to work closely with Trump, he is likely to be more receptive in finding a solution to the conflict. But if he does not, the US must assert itself and be prepared to bomb and destroy all of Assad's air force fields, hangars, and munitions depots.

The cessation of hostilities in Syria will not, in and of itself, bring an end to the civil war, but it remains a prerequisite to open up diplomatic channels in the search for a permanent peaceful solution.

In any future solution, the US should not object to Assad remaining president throughout an agreed-upon transitional period if his participation keeps intact the bureaucracy, military, and internal security apparatus to prevent a replay of what happened in Iraq following the US invasion.

The US cannot escape its responsibility, and it must now confront head-on the three most urgent and intractable conflicts before they further escalate out of control.

Given that Trump is all about "America First"—and that America has significant geopolitical interests in the region—it is imperative that a Trump administration addresses these conflicts in a serious and consistent manner. Trump's first test will be his choices of advisors, who can assist him to navigate through the thicket of these conflicts.

Whom he chooses and how soon he will act after the inauguration will send a clear message to America's foes and friends alike where this nation is heading and its resolve to assert its global leadership role.

2017

TRUMP: "CLOSE THE OPEN HAND OUT OF LOVE"

January 11, 2017

President-elect Trump's appointment of David Friedman (known for his support of the settlements) to be the US ambassador to Israel, his appointment of Walid Phares (a Maronite Christian known for his pro-Israel track record and distaste for the Palestinians) as his Middle East advisor, and charging his son-in-law Jared Kushner (a staunch supporter of Israel who was recently appointed as Senior Advisor to the President) to take the lead in the search for a solution to the Israeli-Palestinian conflict, all suggest there could be a major change in US policy toward the conflict.

These appointments, coupled with Trump's campaign promise to relocate the American embassy from Tel Aviv to Jerusalem, may well translate to unfettered support for settlements and the annexation of more Palestinian territory. Should this come to pass, it will jeopardize the prospect of a two-state solution and the future of Israel as a viable Jewish state, not to mention the endless violence that will ensue.

We are already hearing the alarm bells from various Arab capitals. The victory of the Palestinians on the passage of UN Resolution 2334 that condemns the Israeli settlements has now been overshadowed by a sense of deep trepidation, while stirring major concerns among moderate Israelis and Europeans who don't know what to expect and how troublesome the situation may become.

Many members of the Israeli government feel emboldened by these developments. Education Minister Naftali Bennett has called for the annexation of the third largest settlement Ma'ale Adumim,[1] a few minutes' drive from East Jerusalem, which would virtually cut the West Bank in half and prevent the rise of a viable and contiguous Palestinian state. He further implored Netanyahu to rule out the establishment of a Palestinian state during his first meeting with President Trump, stating, "The next few weeks present a unique window of opportunity for Israel."[2]

For Netanyahu, Trump as president is simply heaven-sent. He believes that even though he won't succeed in convincing Trump to shred the Iran deal because of the international repercussions that Trump cannot dismiss, the

Trump administration will leave him to his own devices to expand the settlements and gradually render the prospect of a Palestinian state unfeasible by creating irreversible facts on the ground.

The irony here is that many of those who claim to care about Israel's future security and wellbeing do not want to acknowledge that the Palestinians in the West Bank and Gaza are not a fading phenomenon. Yes, Israel can build another hundred settlements and annex much of the West Bank, but what then? Will the Palestinians, the Arab world, and the international community simply sit on their hands and do nothing?

Those unflinching supporters of Israel should be true to themselves and answer—where will Israel be in ten or fifteen years? Will it be a Jewish state? A democratic state? An apartheid state? A bi-national state? What legal system will be in place to govern the West Bank? Will it be civilian or military? Will there be two different laws, one for Palestinians and one for settlers?

What is the vision of the detractors who oppose the creation of a Palestinian state about the relationship between Israel and the Palestinians? What does Netanyahu mean when he repeatedly invokes the Jews' claim to the entire "land of Israel?" Does Bennett have any clue what will happen following the annexation of Ma'ale Adumim, or the annexation of Area C, which represents 61 percent of the West Bank?

What will the reaction of the Arab states be? Can Netanyahu count on their cooperation during the next Palestinian uprising, which is bound to erupt once their hope for a state is dashed completely? What will be the outcome of the next Gaza war, and what will be the extent of the collateral damage?

Yes, Israel can reoccupy Gaza and decapitate Hamas' leaders, but is Israel willing to govern over 1.8 million Palestinians? At what cost, in both blood and treasure? If not, what happens when the next round of rockets rains down daily, terrifying every Israeli?

Can Israeli technology and anti-terror capabilities that Netanyahu boasts about bring peace? How, one might ask? Will the Arab states simply forget about the Palestinians' plight only because they are currently collaborating with Israel on matters of security and intelligence sharing to lessen Iranian threats?

Finally, have Netanyahu, Bennett, and their like considered the international outcry, condemnation, and sanctions that would ensue, and how isolated Israel would be? Have they thought about what Jews around the world would be subjected to? Antisemitism will intensify and Jewish businesses and organizations will be seen as "fair targets" for terrorism.

The young generation of Jews will be further alienated, whose immigration to Israel is already in decline. They will no longer view Israel as a safe haven for Jews but as a major liability, and will not want to enlist in the Israeli Defense Forces and be assigned to oppress the Palestinians and deny them the right to be free.

What many Israeli madmen and madwomen in and out of the government (like Netanyahu, Bennett, Lieberman, Justice Minister Ayelet Shaked, Culture Minister Miri Regev, and their cohorts) refuse to realize is that they can manipulate, maneuver, manage, or mar the Palestinians only up to a point—but they cannot control them indefinitely. Netanyahu in particular skillfully uses fear tactics and takes advantage of Palestinian incitement to justify his claim that they are not interested in peace.

Their most blatant lie is the contention that once Israel evacuates the West Bank, the territories will become just another Gaza (a "Hamastan"), a launching pad for rockets and terrorism, when in fact the withdrawal from Gaza was unilateral without any coordination with the Palestinian Authority (PA), which was in charge of Gaza at the time.

The economic dependency of the Palestinians in the West Bank on Israel and security cooperation will not end once there is a peace agreement. Israel is and will remain the economic lifeline for the Palestinians for decades. The Palestinians seek political independence, but they cannot (nor do they want to) simply divorce themselves from Israel completely because of these ties. They know about Egypt and Jordan's extensive collaboration with Israel in these areas and how much they benefit from having peace with Israel.

I do not, however, exempt the Palestinians for one moment from responsibility. It is time they stop living in the past; violence and incitement against Israel will do nothing but deprive them of the very thing they want to achieve—a state of their own. They must be prepared to pay the price for being free.

They must learn how to shoulder their responsibility, clean up their corrupt political system, and focus on building the infrastructure and institutions of a state. Above all, they must stop poisoning the next generation of Palestinians against Israel, as doing so only victimizes these young boys and girls and deprives them of a better and more promising future.

Before Friedman, Phares, and Kushner advise the president on how to deal with the Israeli-Palestinian conflict, they must answer all of these questions that have a major bearing on Israel's very future. I absolutely believe they all genuinely care about Israel and want to do everything they can to ensure its security and prosperity, to live in peace with its neighbors. But here is where tough love is needed. As Nietzsche succinctly put it, "This is the hardest of all: to close the open hand out of love, and keep modest as a giver."

This is precisely the point. Because of their commitment to Israel's wellbeing, they must carefully think about the ramifications if they recommend that the president fulfill his campaign promise to relocate the US embassy to Jerusalem without simultaneously acknowledging the right of the Palestinians to establish their own capital in East Jerusalem once a peace agreement is achieved.

They must warily consider the implications if Israel were to annex Ma'ale Adumim without agreed-upon land swaps that ensure a future Palestinian state maintains land contiguity. They must be extraordinarily cautious not to give Netanyahu a blank check to expand the settlements, which will scuttle the two-state solution and put Israel's future in peril.

As a dealmaker, Trump knows that no unilateral action by one party can seal a deal. An agreement between Israel and the Palestinians must be equitable—a non-zero-sum approach that answers to the aspirations of both people, especially because they have no choice but to coexist. Their destiny, like it or not, is intertwined—either they live in peace and harmony, or in perpetual violence, death, and destruction. Neither can have it their way only.

Here is where you, Mr. Trump, can play a historic role. As a dealmaker, I implore you, do not give Netanyahu what he wants. If you do, you will rob the vast majority of Israelis and Palestinians of everything they aspire to and set in motion an unrelenting cycle of violence that will spare neither side decades of more pain, agony, death, or destruction. A good and sustainable deal requires give and take; each side must make the necessary concessions and create a mutuality of vested interests to ensure its durability.

Kushner is the least zealous; he knows the Israeli scene well and understands that anything short of evenhanded peace will be to Israel's detriment. We can only hope that he will use his influence as a senior advisor and pave the way for President Trump to make the deal that all of his predecessors failed to achieve.

To sum up the thoughts of the visionary David Ben-Gurion, who was the leading founder of the state of Israel and its first Prime Minister, better a Jewish state on part of the land than all of the land without a state.

RELOCATING THE AMERICAN
EMBASSY TO JERUSALEM

Attaining a major breakthrough from a potentially disastrous fallout

February 8, 2017

Should President Trump fulfill his campaign promise to relocate the American embassy from Tel Aviv to Jerusalem, it would have major regional and international repercussions. The Trump administration is currently reevaluating the implications of such a move and no final decision has been made. Given the sensitivity and far-reaching consequences, if he nevertheless decides to relocate the embassy it is critical that **he concurrently takes a balancing act** to prevent the potentially disastrous fallout. This could profoundly change the dynamic of the Israeli-Palestinian conflict for the better, while preserving the two-state solution.

Trump should use the occasion of Prime Minister Netanyahu's visit to Washington on February 15 to make it clear that relocating the American Embassy to Jerusalem has a price tag: a) it cannot infringe on the prospect of a two-state solution, b) the US will recognize that East Jerusalem will be the capital of the future state of Palestine, c) the expansion of the settlements cannot continue unabated, and d) Israel must not begin the implementation of the new law that retroactively legalizes scores of illegal settlements built on private Palestinian land, which in any case, the Israeli Supreme Court will more than likely overturn.

Relocating the American embassy from Tel Aviv to Jerusalem unconditionally will be a *de facto* recognition of Jerusalem, east and west, as the capital of Israel. Since the Israeli government insists that Jerusalem is the eternal united capital of the state, the move suggests that the United States recognizes the Israeli position.

To put things in perspective, it is necessary to **first assess the fallout** of such a unilateral move on the part of the Trump administration.

First, the Arab states led by the Hashemite Kingdom of Jordan—the custodian of the holy Muslim shrines, the al-Aqsa Mosque, and the Dome of the Rock—will view such a move as a flagrant assault on Islam itself. Even though the Israelis will make a special provision that will allow Jordan to continue to administer its custodianship over these holy places, under no circumstances would the Arab states allow Israel to have sovereignty over Haram Al-Sharif (the Temple Mount), with the exception of the Wailing Wall (a part of the outer wall of the Second Temple).

Second, such a move will, for all intents and purposes, put an end to the prospect of peace based on a two-state solution. Indeed, for the Palestinians, the establishment of an independent state with its capital in East Jerusalem is non-negotiable. This is not merely a symbolic demand; it is a requirement at the heart of the Israeli-Palestinian conflict. No one should dismiss the potential breakout of ferocious violence between Israel and the Palestinians joined by other Arab extremist groups if the Palestinians are denied the establishment of their capital in East Jerusalem. Such violence would be incomparable to any such conflagration that we have witnessed in the past.

Third, the United States' standing and credibility in the Middle East, which has eroded since the Iraq War, would suffer another major setback in its relations with its Arab allies in the region. The US must reassert its position and lead with the support of its European and Arab partners to bring about an end to the many conflicts sweeping the region. The US cannot simply provide more openings for Russia, which is eager to capitalize on US setbacks as President Putin is poised to take full advantage of the prevailing chaotic conditions throughout the region.

Fourth, the move could have an extraordinarily adverse effect on Israel's future, as this would foreclose any prospect of an Arab-Israeli peace. The move would also embolden the right-wing Netanyahu government to annex more Palestinian territories and further expand settlements, scuttling any prospect of peaceful Israeli-Palestinian coexistence. While the Trump move appears on the surface to help Israel realize its long-held dream, it will in fact severely undermine Israel's relations with Egypt and Jordan and jeopardize their peace treaties, which is central to containing regional instability and limiting the threat against Israel's national security.

Fifth, the move would further alienate the European community, which feels the most affected by continuing turmoil in the Middle East and views the Israeli-Palestinian conflict as a major contributor to the upsurge of extremism. They view the rise of Hamas, Hezbollah, and other extremist groups as a direct result of the Israeli occupation. For the EU, relocating the

American embassy to Jerusalem is another, if not the final, nail in the coffin of a two-state solution, which would instigate increasing regional violence from which Europe will continue to suffer.

Attaining breakthrough from the potentially disastrous outcome

Should President Trump still decide to relocate the American embassy, he can convert the prospective disastrous consequences of such a move into a historic breakthrough that could change the nature of the Israeli-Palestinian conflict and cement the prospect of peace based on a two-state solution.

Given that the US **purchased land in West Jerusalem** on which to build the American embassy, which has been postponed by successive American administrations, Trump can announce that the US will soon begin the building of the new embassy in the western part of the city.

In conjunction with that, Trump must reemphasize the United States' traditional support for a two-state solution and the establishment of the Palestinian capital in East Jerusalem, provided that the Palestinians move quickly and steadily toward negotiating peace with Israel. The US ought to make it clear that relocating the American embassy to West Jerusalem does not constitute recognition of Israel's sovereignty over East Jerusalem.

That said, the US needs to reaffirm its position that Jerusalem must remain under any circumstances an undivided city and that the rights of every religious and ethnic group are secured. To assure the Palestinians of its intention, the US could purchase land or a building in East Jerusalem for future use for the American embassy in Palestine, because in any case there will be no Israeli-Palestinian peace unless East Jerusalem becomes the capital of the state of Palestine.

There is no doubt that the Netanyahu government would vehemently object to such a move, but due to the fact that US military and political support is indispensable for Israel, no Israeli government can ignore the US position. Indeed, if Trump is concerned (as I believe he is) about Israel's national security and its future wellbeing, the only way to safeguard that is by insisting that the two-state solution remains a viable option.

The implications of such a move alone will be far and wide:

1. Notwithstanding Israel's stern objection, it will breathe new life into a two-state solution;

2. It will prompt the Palestinians to change their approach to the conflict by ending incitement and violence, as they will begin to see the prospect of establishing a Palestinian state could soon become a reality, which they do not want to jeopardize;

3. It will dramatically enhance the United States' overall position among its Arab allies and restore its credibility as the ultimate guarantor of regional stability;

4. It will prompt Arab states to support the American initiative and pressure Palestinian extremists to accept the inevitable;

5. It will strengthen the hand of Israel's opposition parties, who will be in a better position to develop alternate policies to that of Netanyahu, while weakening the hand of extremist Israelis.

To be sure, President Trump can keep his promise to relocate the American embassy and at the same time, instead of torpedoing any prospect for peace between Israel and the Palestinians, inject new life into it and perhaps put an end to the most debilitating conflict since World War II.

TRUMP AND NETANYAHU: EMBRACING ILLUSIONS, IGNORING REALITY

"Catch'm, Bibi! He's all yours!"

February 21, 2017

President Trump remained true to his customary flip-flopping on just about every issue when he stated during a joint press conference with Prime Minister Netanyahu that he is "looking at two-state and one-state, and I like the one that both parties like ... I can live with either one."[3] By stating this, Trump gave Netanyahu what he was hoping to get—a departure from a two-state solution. To achieve that, Trump is reportedly looking at other options that would enlist the Arab states—who presently share mutual strategic interests with Israel to form a united front against their common enemy, Iran—to help broker a solution to the Palestinian problem.

To be sure, the two leaders who are both in trouble—Netanyahu is under multiple criminal investigations for corruption, and Trump is being attacked from just about every corner for his outrageous statements, contradictions, and self-indulgence—found comfort with one another.

Netanyahu went back home feeling triumphant, as he seemingly managed to sway Trump from the idea of two states, while Trump presented himself as a statesman thinking out of the box by looking at an Israeli-Arab comprehensive peace through which to fashion a solution to the Palestinian conflict.

Although CIA Director Mike Pompeo met with Mahmoud Abbas the day before the press conference, I was told by a top Jordanian official in Amman that Abbas was abundantly clear during the meeting that there is not and will never be an alternative to a two-state solution based on the API. Moreover, Abbas indicated that Hamas's position on a two-state solution is unequivocal, and in any case, Gaza and the West Bank must constitute a single Palestinian state.

While Netanyahu often pretended that he still believes in a two-state solution, during the many encounters he had with former Secretary of State John Kerry (including a joint meeting with Egypt's President Sisi and Jordan's King Abdullah in Aqaba in 2016) where he was presented with a comprehensive peace plan, he repeatedly changed his position.

Netanyahu habitually claimed that his extremist right-wing partners oppose the creation of a Palestinian state under any circumstances and that his government would collapse if he were to actively pursue the idea, as if he could not form a new government with the left and center parties who are committed to a two-state solution. Nevertheless, he continued to sing the song of two states for public consumption and to get the Obama administration off his back.

Regardless of what new ideas Netanyahu and Trump concocted, one thing remains certain: there is simply no other realistic solution to the Israeli-Palestinian conflict other than two independent states, Jewish and Palestinian.

The viability of this solution does not only rest on preserving Israel as a democracy with a Jewish national identity while meeting the Palestinians' aspiration for a state of their own. A careful scrutiny of other would-be alternatives floating around show that they have no basis in reality.

Jordan is not and will never become a Palestinian state (as some Israelis advocate) because the Hashemite Kingdom will resist that with all its might; a bi-national state is a kiss of death to the Zionist dream; the establishment of a Palestinian state in Gaza while incorporating much of the West Bank into Israel is a non-starter; the creation of a federation between Israel, Jordan, and Palestine is a pipe dream; and finally, confining Palestinians in the West Bank to cantons to run their internal affairs as they see fit, while Israel maintains security control, will be violently resisted by the Palestinians until the occupation comes to an end.

It is true that Arab states view Israel today as a potential ally in the face of the Iranian threat, and there may well be a historic opportunity to solve the Israeli-Palestinian conflict in the context of a comprehensive Arab-Israeli peace. This opportunity, though, can be materialized **only** in the context of the API.

The central requirement of the API is a settlement to the Israeli-Palestinian conflict based on a two-state solution, which would subsequently lead to a regional peace. Indeed, only by Israel first embracing the API will the Arab states lend their support to a two-state solution by putting pressure on the Palestinians to make the necessary concessions to reach a peace accord.

Those who claim that a two-state solution's time has passed and new and creative ideas should be explored must know that many new ideas have been considered. None of them, however, could provide a solution that meets Israeli or Palestinian requirements for independent and democratic states enjoying Jewish and Palestinian national identities, respectively.

Netanyahu has found in Trump a co-conspirator. Both have a proven record of doubletalk, misleading statements, and often-outright lies. Both are blinded by their hunger for power and are ready and willing to say anything to please their shortsighted constituencies. Neither has the vision or the courage to rise above the fray, and nothing they have uttered jointly meets the hardcore reality they choose to ignore.

What Netanyahu and Trump have demonstrated during their press conference was that both seem to revel in illusions where they find a zone of real comfort, while leaving Israelis and Palestinians to an uncertain and ominous future.

STRATEGY OF FORCE COUPLED
WITH SOUND DIPLOMACY

April 12, 2017

President Trump's unexpected attack on Syria's Shayrat airbase in response to President Assad's sarin gas attack on his own citizens changed the dynamic of Syria's civil war and potentially its eventual outcome. Trump's attack sent a clear message not only to Assad, but to Russia and Iran, which are staunch supporters of Assad, and to North Korea, which has been testing US resolve regarding its missile program. This single salvo has repaired some of the United States' global credibility, which was tarnished by the Obama administration, especially in connection with Syria. At the same time, Trump's attack imposed a new responsibility on the US to follow through with a well-thought out strategy that stands a good chance of ending Syria's horrific civil war and diminishing the North Korean threat.

Any new strategy requires a clear definition of its ultimate goal. If the goal is to end the civil war in Syria, then careful consideration must be given to the role and requirements of all the stakeholders involved in the war, without which no sustainable agreement can be achieved.

Although finding a solution to the conflict is extremely difficult, now that the US is directly involved, Trump has no option but to try. I maintain that since all the parties involved seek an end to the conflict on certain terms, the Trump administration needs to consider their needs but follow a strategy based on Theodore Roosevelt's foreign policy approach of "speak softly and carry a big stick."

First, Trump must demand that the indiscriminate killing of innocent men, women, and children stop immediately as he has already intimated. Although the heinous act of using chemical weapons must not be tolerated, the wholesale killing of civilians by barrel bombs and starvation is no less condemnable. Assad must also be warned that if he fails to comply, the US will attack new targets in Syria, particularly runways, hangars, and munition depots.

Assad's patrons Russia and Iran will take such a warning seriously because, notwithstanding their public bluster, neither wants to engage the US militarily, especially now that Trump has established his credibility to take punitive actions to stop the senseless killings and his unpredictability as to when and how he will act.

The second part of the strategy is for Trump to extend his hand to all the players who have stakes in the war and its ultimate outcome—especially Russia, Iran, Assad, and the rebels—to start serious negotiations with the purpose of ending the civil war.

Although the players seem to agree that ISIS must be liquidated and that they must cooperate to achieve this objective, the search for a solution to the civil war must not await the demise of ISIS, and the negotiations to end the war should begin immediately.

The Trump administration recognizes that Russia is the most significant player with strategic interests in Syria going back nearly five decades. Russia has a naval base in the city of Tartus and will insist on maintaining its presence and influence in Syria.

Similarly, Iran's ambition to become the region's hegemon suggests that it will not relinquish under any circumstances its strategic interests from the Gulf to the Mediterranean, where Syria serves as the linchpin.

Both Russia and Iran will continue to support Assad as long as he serves their interests. For this reason, Trump cannot vacillate; he must accept that Assad will continue to serve as president during a transitional period, perhaps for three to four years.

Trump and Putin can work together on the establishment of a representative government consisting of the main sectors of the population—the Sunnis (represented by the Free Syrian Army), the Kurds, the Alawites, and the Christians—for at least five years, during which the focus should be on rebuilding the country and restoring internal security.

During this period, a loose federation should be created whereby each of the main sectors establishes semi-autonomous rule and agrees to engage in a process of peace and reconciliation to prevent revenge and retribution and to pave the way for economic and security cooperation.

The repatriation of the refugees must also be dealt with, and the parties should agree on a program that allows the refugees to return to their homes. Given the extensive destruction of the country, all the stakeholders should embark on raising the billions of dollars necessary to rebuild infrastructure and support the rehabilitation of refugees.

Between now and the time when such an agreement is reached, a no-fly zone should be created in Syria along its borders with Turkey and Jordan to provide a safe haven for the internally displaced and refugees.

To be sure, Trump should be clear that the US is more than willing to engage diplomatically to solve the war in Syria, which by extension threatens its security and the security of its allies. Trump should also emphasize that the US is willing to use force when necessary to achieve its objectives.

Trump's order to attack a Syrian air base while having dinner with Chinese President Xi Jinping was also intended to send a loud and clear message to the North Korean regime. Moreover, dispatching a naval strike group to the Western Pacific Ocean near the Korean Peninsula sends an unambiguous message to China that it is time to rein in North Korea's provocations, because the longer the conflict persists, the more complicated it becomes.

Through his actions against Assad and toward North Korea, President Trump reasserted the United States' position on the global stage by challenging its enemies to take heed of its resolve while inviting a diplomatic solution based on the national interests of all players involved.

Russia has a special interest to resume normal relations with the US and is eager to have the sanctions lifted. Secretary of State Tillerson's visit to Moscow should pave the way for starting serious negotiations to end the conflict in Syria, as long as it ensures Russia's long-term strategic goals.

China's main interest is to maintain, and even improve, its trade relations with the US. With some American incentives, China would more than likely take whatever steps necessary to tame North Korea and prevent any confrontation between the US and North Korea that could precipitate regional upheaval that China wants to avoid at any price.

Similarly, Iran wants to prevent any military entanglement with the US, knowing full well that it would emerge humiliated from such a confrontation, which would adversely impact its national interests in Syria and leave it subject to new crippling sanctions.

The US today is in a better position than it has been in more than sixteen years to reestablish its global credibility and moral and security responsibilities.

Trump's unpredictability and his readiness to use force when necessary can be an asset, but it is no substitute for a sound and effective strategy—a strategy that offers carrots while carrying a big stick, with a clear objective always in sight.

TRUMP'S "HISTORIC" VISIT TO THE MIDDLE EAST: MUCH ADO ABOUT NOTHING

June 25, 2017

S adly, President Trump's visit to the Middle East only confirmed my skepticism about what might come out of it. Trump went to the region with nothing to offer to mitigate the Israeli-Palestinian conflict and received no commitment from either Israeli or Palestinian leaders to resume the peace negotiations in earnest, but he received lots of platitudes and empty good-will gestures.

In his meeting with the Saudi King Salman and the rest of the heads of Arab states, he heard chanting against the Iranian threat and joined the chorus without offering any specific idea as to how he might address Iran's support of violent extremists and its hegemonic ambitions.

To be sure, however, there were many photo ops. Israeli and Arab officials alike clamored to take a photo with a besieged president who was reveling in the accolades of the moment and doing his best not to think about the dark clouds awaiting him back home.

That said, there is no doubt that the US remains the most indispensable power in the Middle East, and just about every state in the region relies heavily on US political support and protection. This, however, does not suggest that the US has a magic wand that it can simply wave and change overnight the dynamics of the multiple conflicts sweeping and consuming the region. None of Trump's predecessors has had that kind of power, and Trump has even less.

During his meetings with Saudi officials, he said nothing about their gross violation of human rights and the kingdom's promotion of Islamic Wahhabi extremism. On the contrary, he was delighted to conclude an arm deal worth over $110 billion, becoming more like a merchant of death rather than a messenger of peace.

On the relationship between the Arab states and Israel, Trump offered no recipe as to how they can reach a comprehensive peace agreement. He stated that "King Salman feels very strongly and, I can tell you, would love to see peace with Israel and the Palestinians."[4]

The fact is that the Arab states want peace between Israel and the Palestinians based on a two-state solution, and conditioned normalization of relations with Israel based on that premise, which was articulated in the API introduced by the Arab League in 2002.

On the Israeli-Palestinian conflict, Trump seems to have realized that the conflict is far more intractable than when he stated before his trip "There is no reason there's not peace between Israel and the Palestinians—none whatsoever."[5] But once he listened to the Israelis and Palestinians, he stated that "I've heard it's one of the toughest deals of all."[6]

Whereas he took no initiative to advance the Israeli-Palestinian peace process, to the chagrin of Netanyahu and his cohorts, Trump backtracked on his promise to relocate the US embassy to Jerusalem and asked Netanyahu to slow down the building and expansion of settlements. To the disappointment of many in Israel, he refused to allow any Israeli officials to accompany him during his historic visit to the Western Wall.

The statements made by Prime Minister Netanyahu and President Abbas that they are ready and willing to resume negotiations are old, tired, and inconsequential. Both sides have been expressing such a sentiment for years, and nothing that Trump has said or done will change the positions of either Abbas or Netanyahu.

Netanyahu is not committed to a two-state solution, and Abbas is unable to make any concession and politically (if not physically) survive. Trump could have challenged both leaders to take some measures to demonstrate their commitment to peace and create a conducive atmosphere that would pave the way for serious negotiations, but he did not attempt to do even that.

Among other measures, Trump could have asked Netanyahu to release some Palestinian prisoners, allow for freer movement of Palestinians, and open the door for mutual tourism. Trump could have also leaned on Abbas to stop public incitements and acrimonious public narratives and end financial aid to the families of terrorists.

Although Trump wants a deal, he assigned his son-in-law Jared Kushner and former Trump Organization attorney Jason Greenblatt, two novice individuals who know even less about the complexity of the conflict than he does, to find a solution that eluded several presidents before him.

Notwithstanding their desire to end the Israeli-Palestinian conflict, the Iranian threat assumes greater urgency for both Israel and the Arab states. Both sides have long since concluded that Iran is a common enemy and poses a real danger to their national security. As they see it, although the Iran deal has delayed its pursuit of nuclear weapons, Tehran is still committed to becoming a nuclear power.

Regarding the concern over the Iranian threat, Trump said nothing that was not known before: "There is a growing realization among your [Israel] Arab neighbors that they have common cause with you in the threat posed by Iran, and it is indeed a threat, there's no question about that."[7]

It is true that Tehran is deliberately destabilizing the region by its support of terrorist organizations and by meddling in Syrian, Lebanese, and Yemeni domestic affairs to serve its hegemonic ambition. Israel and the Arab states have for several years collaborated strategically by sharing intelligence and developing clandestine security cooperation to stop Iran from realizing its regional objectives.

Other than boasting that "We are telling you right now that Iran will not have nuclear weapons," Trump offered no concrete steps as to how to deal with the Iranian menace.[8] Instead, he encouraged the Sunni Arab states to ally against Shiite Iran, which can only further heighten tensions between the two sides and further destabilize the region, which is already in turmoil.

Trump ignores the basic fact that regardless of Iran's mischiefs and transgressions, it is here to stay. Tehran has been complying with all the provisions of the nuclear deal and the country has just reelected President Rouhani, a moderate who has expressed on many occasions that he wants to improve relations with the US and the Arab states.

However, Trump's statement to the Sunni leaders was: "Until the Iranian regime is willing to be a partner for peace, all nations of conscience must work together to isolate Iran, deny it funding for terrorism, and pray for the day when the Iranian people have the just and righteous government they so richly deserve."[9]

Indeed, regardless of the intense objection of the Israelis and the Arab states to the Iran deal, Trump did not tear it up as he promised during his campaign for President, and his administration continues to fully comply with the deal's requirements by lifting the sanctions, as stipulated in the accord.

Wisdom dictates that the US should build on the Iran deal and work with Iran to help bring an end to the horrifying civil war in Syria and stop the senseless proxy wars between Iran and Saudi Arabia in Yemen and Iraq, from which neither side can emerge victorious.

Trump's visit to the region was full of opulence and symbolism, with little or no substance. There was no progress in the search for a solution to the Israeli-Palestinian conflict. The Arab states continue to refuse to normalize relations with Israel before resolving the Israeli-Palestinian conflict, and they have received no assurance that the US will deal with Iran with an iron fist.

The only thing that came out of Trump's visit is that he could get a respite from the political turmoil in which he is marred back home. Otherwise, the trip was much ado about nothing.

TRUMP'S "NEW" STRATEGY IN
AFGHANISTAN IS DOOMED TO FAIL

August 23, 2017

P resident Trump's new strategy against the Taliban in Afghanistan is doomed to fail, just like Bush's and Obama's before him. At best, the reported dispatch of an additional four thousand American troops, as recommended by his security chiefs, will prevent the total collapse of Afghanistan and thwart the Taliban from winning. Given the complex nature of the conflict, however, the status quo will not change in any significant way.

One might think that after sixteen years, the US should have learned that the Taliban will not be defeated. The only solution rests on a negotiated agreement with the Taliban while inviting the Afghan tribes to do the heavy lifting, as they are the only party who can effectively work with the Taliban to reach an enduring agreement. Together, they can fight against the various terrorist groups that have converged on Afghanistan, because they want to end foreign interventions that have done nothing but cause socio-political havoc and instability since the Soviet invasion in 1979.

The only pointed and correct statement Trump made in his "new strategy" is that the US should not undertake the practice of nation-building and certainly not dictate how the Afghan people live their lives and govern themselves. The US, with the support of the tribes, should focus on combating terrorism, especially from al-Qaeda, ISIS, and other radical extremist groups.

The Taliban should receive a clear signal that they are an important part of the new strategy to reach a peace accord, provided they demonstrate their willingness to negotiate in earnest, knowing that otherwise they will have to continue to be engaged in an intractable fight against US forces without any chance of succeeding.

It is true and necessary for the US to develop strategic partnerships, especially with India and Pakistan, to help in the fight against terrorism, and use its political, economic, and military assets to that end. However, whereas India would be willing to partner with the US, it is not a given that the besieged Pakistani government will be able to fully commit itself even if it chooses to, because a) the ongoing political turmoil in Islamabad prevents the development of a cohesive policy to combat the plethora of terrorist groups, which makes the task extremely difficult, and b) Pakistan does not want to fight the Taliban knowing that they will sooner or later be a part of the Afghan government (if not in control of it), with which they have to coexist.

For these reasons, it is naïve to think that after sixteen years of fighting, dispatching an additional military force of four thousand soldiers will change anything. In fact, at its peak over 100,000 American soldiers were unable to dramatically change the dynamic of the conflict and create a sustainable political and security structure that would allow US troops to leave.

No one in the Trump administration, including the Pentagon, is offering any convincing argument that additional forces would win the war. At best, they can arrest the continuing advances of the Taliban, which is now in control of nearly half the country.

Although Trump correctly shifted away from a time-based approach and instead linked it to progress made on the ground, this effort will succeed only if the US immediately embraces peace talks while fighting foreign terrorist groups.

To be sure, *there will not be a military solution to the Afghan war*. Trump now has the opportunity to change the dynamic of the conflict by looking at the Taliban not as the enemy, but as the partner in the search for a sustainable solution.

The sooner the US accepts this reality the better, so that the US can focus on a practical outcome that can emerge only through negotiations with moderate elements of the Taliban and with full participation of the tribal leaders.

In a conversation I had with Ajmal Khan Zazai, tribal leader and Paramount Chief of Paktia province in Afghanistan, he noted that previous American military approaches have never had a chance of succeeding, due to their "[obsession] with their version of 'democracy' and 'human rights' .... They don't believe in homegrown or Afghan local solutions led by the tribes ..." He emphasized the fact that "Afghanistan is a tribal country, the tribes are the past, present, and future."[10] I fully agree that excluding the tribes from this battle against violent extremism, including al-Qaeda and ISIS, will simply not work.

To prevent repeating past mistakes, the Trump administration must now reach out to the tribal chiefs and together develop a strategy that would allow the Taliban to fully participate in peace talks with the objective of reaching a long-term solution.

The chiefs would require US financial assistance to the tune of four to five hundred million dollars a year, over a few years (which is a fraction of what we spend today). The purpose of this would be to recruit and train their *own* militia to fight their *own* battles against the assortment of terrorists.

Under such a scenario, the Taliban will have to commit themselves to fight, alongside the Afghan military, against all extremist and terror groups, particularly al-Qaeda and ISIS. Once the Taliban becomes a part of the government, they will develop a vested interest in the stability of Afghanistan and will have every reason to prevent Pakistan and Iran, in particular, from meddling in the internal affairs of their country.

To be sure, the Taliban are Afghan nationals and will not be dislodged from their own land; likewise, the support of the tribes is essential, as they want to take matters into their hands. They know that time is on their side because no foreign power has ever been able to conquer Afghanistan, dominate the country, and change the Afghan way of life.

Every foreign power was forced to eventually leave because they could not sustain their conquest or domination. If the US wants to end this debilitating war, it must focus on local forces for a permanent solution and leave Afghanistan sooner than later with some dignity.

AN OPEN LETTER TO PRESIDENT TRUMP

"I've had it with you troublemakers."

August 30, 2017

I find it extremely hard to call you "President Trump" because sadly for America, you neither act like a president nor speak like one. You neither have the moral authority that a president needs to project, nor the courage of one. You have neither the vision of an enlightened president, nor the diplomatic savvy of one. You have neither the capacity to lead the nation as president, nor the competence. You have neither the credibility that the president must enjoy, nor the ability to get things done. You have neither the stability that the president must demonstrate, nor the consistency. You have neither the country's interest at heart like a president, nor the grasp of what America's role in world is all about. Here is why:

Your statement about the events in Charlottesville was appalling. There is no moral equivalency between white supremacists, Nazis, and the KKK, and law-abiding citizens who want to preserve America's moral values, freedom, decency, and tolerance. You callously stated that there were "some very fine people on both sides," which outraged Democrats and Republicans alike.[11] Mr. Trump, there is only one side: the one of bigots and racists.

You have made a mockery of the judiciary, rebuking judges for doing what is constitutionally required of them; you doubt the judgment and competence of judges because of their ethnic backgrounds, and you questioned the courts' legal decisions because they did not suit your desired outcome. To be sure, you want and believe you have the right to operate above the law, and find it strange that the judiciary is independent and not even the president can bend the law. Your most recent egregious contempt for our judiciary was pardoning an open racist such as former Maricopa County, Arizona, Sheriff Joe Arpaio, who was found guilty of criminal contempt for violating the constitution by using racial profiling to jail Latinos.

You have made lying an art form. Between January 21 and July 19 of this year, you have lied 113 times,[12] believing that if you repeat these lies time and again, they will eventually sink in as the truth in the public's mind. Your credibility, however, is shot, and only a fool can trust a word you say.

You constantly label any news not to your liking as "fake news," but you thrive on press coverage to satisfy your insatiable lust for self-aggrandizement. Your relentless charges against the media, accusing them of spreading fake news, open the door for violence against reporters while you try to obscure your own false public statements.

You are a dictator in soul and spirit. No wonder you embrace despots like Russia's Putin, Turkey's Erdogan, and the Philippines' Duterte. You envy them because they can purge and rampage their country with impunity, and you can't. When things do not go your way, you become enraged, vindictive, and mean.

Your efforts to limit immigration to the US defy the aspirations of millions who want to realize the American dream. This is the land of immigrants, the melting pot that makes America unique. It is the riches of the newcomers, their cultural diversity, scientific achievements, experiences, and collective ingenuity that made America second to none. America is already great, and you have nothing to offer that can make it greater.

You systematically undermine the intelligence community that has performed admirably over the years, only because they concluded that Russia meddled in the 2016 election on your behalf. You have and continue to demoralize the most loyal men and women who dedicate their lives to serve the nation and on whom our national security depends.

Whereas you praise American soldiers fighting to protect our country and preserve our freedom and democracy, you arbitrarily ban transgender soldiers who have sacrificed no less than any other solider—possibly even more so due to the difficulties they face.

Contrary to your promises to aid the poor, the sick, and the despondent, you shamefully proposed a budget that would cut over the next decade more than $800 billion from Medicaid, $192 billion from nutritional assistance (including Meals on Wheels), and $272 billion overall from welfare programs, not to speak of your reprehensible proposal to cut more than $72 billion from the disability benefit upon which millions of Americans rely[13]—yet you demand billions to build a useless wall along the Mexican border.

You are narcissistic, self-absorbed, and selfish, constantly seeking glamor and adulation; you will go to any length to show off your riches but are afraid to release your tax returns, fearful of what they may reveal about your shady business deals. You do not want the nation to discover the little or no taxes you have paid, how illegitimate many of your business transactions were, and what is in fact your true wealth.

After eight months in office you have failed to pass any significant legislation, blaming everyone but yourself for your inability to realize any of your campaign promises, including an infrastructure bill, tax reform, and even repealing and replacing Obama's healthcare program, which you made a top priority.

You demand loyalty from everyone around you, but you are loyal to no one. You hired questionable personalities and fire anyone who questions your dictates. You treat government agencies as if they were your private businesses, thinking that the government works for you alone. You still do not understand that there is something called checks and balances, and no one, including you, is above the law.

You dishonorably use the office of the presidency for self-enrichment, and unabashedly use the power of your office to promote your resorts and hotels, including the Trump National Golf Club in New Jersey, Mar-a-Lago in Florida, and the Trump International Hotel in DC. Never before has any president tainted the prestige of the office of the presidency to satisfy his greed forevermore.

While you occasionally call for unity, you are the most divisive figure that has ever held the high office of President of the United States. You sow discord and disunity among the American people while catering to your shrinking base and cultivating a cult mentality, splitting the country into "us versus them."

You demean women as if they are simply objects to play with for personal pleasure. You enjoy insulting women that you do not like, using vulgar language to describe their faces and looks, and never shy away from being rude and abusive to any woman who dares challenge your abrasive and loathsome behavior.

You systematically alienate America's friends and allies, championing the slogan of "America First," which raises serious doubts about America's commitment to uphold security treaties and international trade agreements. Does it ever occur to you that America's national interest is best served by maintaining close, collaborative, and mutually supportive relations with traditional alliances such as NATO, as well as with new friends and allies?

You are quick to take credit for our sustained economic growth, even though it is the continuation of your predecessor's sound economic policy. Since you came to office, you have done nothing to spur further economic development. In fact, your erratic behavior is creating increased financial anxiety in the market, which does not augur well for making major American or foreign investments in various sectors of the economy.

At a time when effective and sound diplomacy is needed more than any time before to deal with manifold crises around the world that directly affect America's national security, you proposed to cut the State Department's budget from nearly $55 billion for fiscal year 2017 to $37.6 billion for 2018.[14] Meanwhile, hundreds of vacancies of high-level positions at the State Department and Ambassadorships around the world, needed to conduct effective foreign policy, remain unfilled.

Whereas the whole world came together and recognized that there is serious climate change supported by overwhelming scientific evidence and reached an agreement in Paris to dramatically reduce carbon emissions, you chose to withdraw the US, which is the second-largest polluter after China, from the Paris Agreement. Only recently, thirteen different federal agencies (spearheaded by the US Global Research Program) concluded that climate change is already occurring,[15] which you ignored only to appease your so-called base to the detriment of future generations.

Your reckless statements lashing out against America's enemies, using phrases such as "fire and fury like the world has never seen" in response to North Korea's threats,[16] pose catastrophic danger to America's national security, especially because of your impulsiveness and lack of strategic thinking. Former Director of National Intelligence James Clapper openly questioned your fitness to be Commander-in-Chief of the US Armed Forces,[17] with your finger on the nuclear button.

As president, you have never understood that with holding the most powerful office in the world, every word you utter, every signal or gesture you make, and every move or measure you take matters greatly and has global implications. Having a loose tongue and failing to understand the gravity of your words can send the wrong signal, which could provoke major unintended conflagrations with some of America's sworn enemies.

You do well when you read speeches written for you from a teleprompter, but when left to your own devices and speak extemporaneously, you show who you really are and what you stand for. It becomes demonstrably clear that you suffer from a moral, intellectual, and ethical void and you try to cover your shortcoming by ridiculing and scorning everybody but those who cater to your ego.

To be sure, Mr. Trump, it is time for you to plan where you will go from here. The prospect that you will remain in office to the end of your term is becoming increasingly unlikely. Your public approval rate at this juncture of your presidency is lower than any of your predecessors. A growing number of leading Republicans who want to save the party are now convinced that you do not have the temperament, knowledge, stability, or diplomatic savvy, not to speak of the moral authority, to lead the country.

I believe that you will be left with two choices: continue to defy the wishes of the majority of the American people and refuse to resign, or wait for impeachment from the House and the Senate. It is only a question of time, and time is running out for you.

If, as you claim, you are an American patriot who loves his country and cares about its future as a global power and its indispensable moral leadership role to make the world a better and safer place, resign now and do so with dignity for the sake of the country.

At a minimum, you will be remembered as the president who finally made the right decision by putting the country's fate and future wellbeing before his own.

THE US HAS TO ACCEPT NORTH KOREA AS A NUCLEAR POWER

September 7, 2017

Although President Trump is not responsible for the complete failure of the US to stop North Korea from becoming a nuclear power, his bellicose threats against North Korea and the acceleration of Pyongyang's missile and nuclear program have dangerously increased regional tension. The conflicting messages emerging from the White House, the lack of coordination with the Department of Defense, and the absence of effective diplomacy point to a total lack of a coherent strategy to deal with North Korea. It is time for the US to accept the reality that North Korea is a nuclear power. Short of a massive military attack on its nuclear facilities, which is unthinkable, no diplomatic efforts or incentives will compel Pyongyang to give up its nuclear arsenal, as the history of the conflict has demonstrated.

Instead, the US must now focus on diplomatic means to prevent North Korea from completing the development of a deliverable miniaturized nuclear warhead on an ICBM that would put the US and its allies at an unacceptable risk. This must be the red line that the regime should not be permitted to cross, and it may well be the only concession that North Korean leaders will be willing to make in return for several concessions—especially the retention of their nuclear weapons.

The lack of a comprehensive strategy to deal with the North Korean threat was sadly demonstrated by Trump's off-the-cuff bellicose statement, "North Korea best not make any more threats to the United States. They will be met with fire and fury like the world has never seen,"[18] or his tweet that followed, suggesting that "Military solutions are now fully in place, locked and loaded, should North Korea act unwisely. Hopefully Kim Jong Un will find another path!"[19]

Defense Secretary Mattis added fuel to the fire when he stated that "Any [North Korean] threat to the United States or its territories—including Guam—or our allies *will be met with a massive military response*—a response both effective and overwhelming [emphasis added]."[20] None of these threats deterred North Korea. On the contrary, it responded by firing an ICBM that could theoretically reach the US followed by exploding what is believed to be a hydrogen bomb hundreds of times more powerful than the nuclear bomb dropped on Hiroshima, Japan.[21]

For the following reasons, Pyongyang has concluded that the US will not go to war over its nuclear program because of its dire implications, which was also echoed by several senior US officials.

The administration's concerns are not limited to the horrifying devastation that such a war will inflict on US allies, especially South Korea and Japan, but includes the ominous destabilization of Southeast Asia that would put China and the US on a collision course, among other horrendous developments.

The US chose not to deploy additional naval and air assets to current forces stationed in the area, which raised serious doubts in the mind of Pyongyang about US likelihood to use force. Instead, the Trump administration pushed for additional sanctions, which North Korean leaders anticipated and have managed to live with for decades.

Despite US pressure, China was and still is unwilling to force North Korea to abandon its nuclear program. China can live with a nuclear North Korea; it does not want to see the collapse of the North Korean regime fearing waves of refugees, and it does not want an increased American military presence in its hemisphere.

Moreover, contrary to US belief, China's influence on Pyongyang is limited, knowing that North Korean leaders will adhere to their wishes only up to a point. They will, however, stand fast to protect their nuclear weapons because they believe their very survival rests on the possession of such weapons—*and they will never put them on the negotiating table.*

North Korea also knows that South Korea does not want any military conflagration because it has the most to lose. The South Korean regime has time and again indicated its willingness to negotiate even in the midst of the boisterous exchange of threats between Washington and Pyongyang, to the chagrin of Trump.

Contrary to the view expressed by US Ambassador to the UN Nikki Haley that Kim Jong Un is "begging for war,"[22] he is not. He knows that the US will not rush into a war unless he attacks the US or any of its allies' territories, which he will not even contemplate knowing that his country could potentially be wiped out by massive US retaliatory strikes.

Finally, Trump's warning that "The United States is considering, in addition to other options, stopping all trade with any country doing business with North Korea"[23] would be impossible to implement, especially with China, whose trade with the US runs into the hundreds of billions of dollars. In any event, it will be counterproductive, as the US needs China's support in dealing with North Korea.

To prevent further escalation of the conflict, the US needs to eventually accept the new reality of a nuclear North Korea just as it had come to terms with both India and Pakistan as nuclear powers, which created mutual deterrence and brought an end to the conventional wars between the two countries.

Indeed, the real threat to the US and its allies does not emanate from North Korea's possession of a nuclear arsenal, but from the development and deployment of ICBMs mounted with miniaturized nuclear warheads that could reach not only US allies, but also the US mainland itself. To remove this threat, the US *should negotiate directly* with North Korea and reach an agreement that would freeze further development of such technology, which China would certainly support.

North Korea may well accede through negotiations to this demand, as they can still claim to be a nuclear power and receive the recognition and respect of the international community that they desperately crave.

In return, North Korea will require the US to end its belligerent policy that has been in place since the end of the Korean War; to commit to not seeking regime change, which was and still is the main motivator behind their pursuit of a nuclear shield; and to end its war games with South Korea and gradually remove sanctions.

The lifting of the sanctions is extraordinarily important for mitigating the humanitarian crisis that has been inflicted on twenty-five million North Koreans, especially women and children, for nearly seven decades. Although humanitarian aid is exempt from diplomatic sanctions, more than ten million citizens are undernourished and suffer from chronic food insecurity, which is tragically ignored or forgotten by the rest of the international community.

Based on the above terms, North Korea will have to fully comply with every provision of the accord, rejoin the Non-Proliferation Treaty, and adhere to the rules and requirements of the International Atomic Energy Agency, especially on the stationing of monitors and stringent inspections to ensure full compliance.

Given the experience of previous successive American administrations with North Korea, which have tried every conceivable approach to end the North Korean nuclear program, including sanctions, negotiations, military threats, and isolation, none have worked because Pyongyang was determined not to surrender its nuclear weapons and be vulnerable to regime change.

We must now accept the fact that North Korea is a nuclear power, and rely on nuclear deterrence while normalizing relations in the process. Anything else is wishful thinking, and Kim Jong Un knows that only too well.

IS AMERICA STILL A BEACON OF
LIGHT TO OTHER NATIONS?

September 13, 2017

We do not need President Trump to tell us that he can make America great again. America is already great. The problem is that we are squandering our greatness by pursuing foreign and domestic policies that debase our moral authority and the values that made America great in the first place. We must change course, but for that we need leaders with vision, courage, and determination, which is sorely lacking. The best and the brightest who could in fact chart a new path have become disillusioned with politics, making the prospect of renewal increasingly difficult. It is time for every American patriot to raise their voice and remind one another of what makes America a great nation and what it stands for.

The US Constitution is the backbone of America's greatness, and the preamble of the Constitution says it all. It declares that: "We the People of the United States, in Order to form a more perfect Union, establish Justice, insure domestic Tranquility, provide for the common defense, promote the general Welfare, and secure the Blessing of Liberty to ourselves and our Posterity."

For me, as an immigrant to this country, America is and will always be my most cherished home. In Baghdad, where I was born, my Arab neighbors called me a "dirty Jew." When my family emigrated to Israel, my status was somewhat improved—I became a "black Jew," discriminated against because of my Sephardic heritage. In Britain, where I was educated, I was always treated as a foreigner. But in the United States, no one was concerned about my religion, ethnicity, or sect. I am accepted for who I am today, and what I believe in and stand for.

This is the America I know—"the land of the free"—because for me the values that are enshrined in our Constitution are what make America great. We must relentlessly protect these values to make America even greater, but we must first realize, however, what went wrong. Below, I present the ten most critical issues that America faces today; none are too difficult to overcome if we only will it.

The events in Charlottesville were a deeply troubling manifestation of **bigotry and hate** that became more pronounced with the election of President Trump. For a president to draw a moral equivalence between white supremacists, Nazis, and antisemites on the one hand and ordinary law-abiding citizens on the other is beyond contempt. No, there are not good people among racists who abuse their right to free speech to malign and threaten others only because of their different origin, sect, belief, or color.

America is "the land of the free," and to preserve that we must not tolerate those who want to cleanse America of what made America a great nation—the ingathering of people from all corners of the world with their diverse cultural riches, resourcefulness, and creativity. They were embraced with open arms. This is the America I know: the land of the dreamers whose dreams often come true. We must allow no one to take that away from us.

Successive American presidents have promised, especially during their political campaigns, to fight **against poverty,** but they all failed. The divide between the rich and the poor is greater today than at any time in the past. The number of children living in poverty in 2015 was 14,500,000 and sadly continues to grow.[24] Millions suffer from malnutrition; perform poorly in schools; are exposed to drugs and violent crimes; and grow up angry, confused, and lost.

Instead of becoming constructive professional individuals that contribute to their community and the state, they become hopeless, jobless, and destitute—a liability rather than an asset. No, this is not the American dream. We must commit to lifting all from poverty because we can and have the resources to do it. No one should doubt American resolve—we have withstood the test of time, and we will continue to do so.

Thousands of little towns and villages far from urban centers are crumbling—successive administrations spoke ad nauseam about **renewal,** but renewal never came. Homes are dilapidated and crowded; the young and the old wander the streets aimlessly. The old resign themselves to a meaningless life, passing time as time cruelly passes them. The young are despondent as they live a life of despair and desolation. Why can't the wealthiest nation on Earth appropriate the necessary funding to restore such disintegrating places?

Why not allow the communities themselves to choose their own sustainable development projects that they can execute with outside expertise and government aid? The involvement of locals provides them with job opportunities, allows them to develop vested interests in their community, and makes them feel empowered as human beings who can make a difference. This is a task that we must never abandon or neglect.

The healthcare system in America is broken because detached politicians never understood that **healthcare is a human right**. Every American, as former presidential contender Bernie Sanders eloquently articulated, has the *inherent right* to receive the medical care they need—and the government has the obligation to provide it. Whether it is done through the federal government or the state, no American should die because of inaccessibility to healthcare, go bankrupt as a result of high medical costs, or suffer from a curable disease.

Millions of Americans have no health insurance because they cannot afford it. We have and still are squandering hundreds of billions on foreign adventures, and much more is wasted on an inflated bureaucracy and the self-interest of officials who fight for their pet projects. There are many, like Sanders and his cohort, who look out to ensure a healthier America because this is and must be the American way.

We have become accustomed to **legislative paralysis** as if it were normal. Democrat and Republican leaders alike seem to view the other as rivals committed singularly to the presumed interest of their respective parties. They must be reminded that they represent all the people and are duty bound to cooperate and agree on any legislation that serves the American public. Years of deadlock in Congress point only to the ineptitude of so many Congressmembers whose blind ideological tenets are making them oblivious to what is good for America.

Collaboration between the parties produces better and consensual legislation that benefits all Americans. How else can we form "a more perfect union" when the zero-sum approach to politics and divisiveness reigns? America's continuing greatness rests on leaders who put the nation's and not their personal or party interests first—leaders befitting what America champions at home and abroad, discharging their responsibility with conviction and living up to the premise they were elected for.

Just the thought that **America is the world's leader** in incarceration with more than 2.2 million currently in prison (which represents an increase of

500 percent over the last forty years)[25] is simply unfathomable and unacceptable. The dramatic increase of the prison population is not related to proportionate increases in crime, but is instead mostly related to changes in sentencing laws that require mandatory incarceration even for petty crimes. As a result, prisons are overcrowded, becoming incubators of extremism and crime.

Nearly half of prisoners have not committed violent crimes. More than 470,000 are in jail for drug possession or abuse, and 12 percent for committing public disorder.[26] Billions are spent on maintaining this prison system when nearly half of the prisoners could be discharged. We must invest much of the money saved in rehabilitation programs, while providing formerly incarcerated persons the opportunity to acquire a new profession, join the work force, and become an asset to their communities.

It is not a new phenomenon to constantly and consistently **blame the media** for spreading "fake news" as many officials, including the president, do, often to cover for their own shortcomings. But using the media as a scapegoat not only undermines the freedom of the press, but also subjects journalists and reporters to violent attacks by those who blindly follow their leaders. It is true that the revolution in social media made the reporting of deliberate fake news easier and more pervasive. This, however, does not suggest that all media outlets are engaged in the dissemination of fake news.

There are scores of responsible, credible, and public service-oriented media outlets that report the unfiltered truth regardless of where such reporting may lead. This is the heart of the First Amendment. No one, including the holder of the highest office, can or should be allowed to violate this sacred right with impunity. The media's scrutiny of public officials is essential to a functioning democracy, and America must guard and respect this "fourth estate" to perform their duty for the sake of all Americans.

Climate change is not fiction—it is happening in front of our eyes, and much has been said about the indisputable scientific evidence that supports it. However, given that the US is the second biggest polluter after China, it must take the lead and work hand-in-hand with the rest of the international community to combat climate change.

Just witness what happened during the last week alone: three huge hurricanes, a powerful earthquake, and wildfires and floods occurring simultaneously, inflicting damage at an unprecedented scale. To politicize climate change at the expense of the welfare and wellbeing of future generation is *a crime*—a crime against humanity. To withdraw from the Paris Agreement on climate change is reckless, narrow-minded, and sinister. Even in doubt, America must be at the forefront of tackling the reality of global warming with its ominous implications for generations to come.

We have yet to learn a lesson from the Vietnam War, and it seems as if **waging wars of choice** has become the American way. We invaded Iraq under false pretenses. There was no nuclear program or any nuclear facilities in Iraq. We toppled the government of Saddam Hussein; dismantled the army, internal security, and bureaucracy; and planted the seeds of civil war between the Sunnis and the Shiites that continues to rage fourteen years later, giving rise to ISIS while destabilizing the entire region.

Nearly two trillion dollars were spent and 4,500 American soldiers sacrificed their lives for an elusive goal, along with 1,340,000 Iraqi civilians.[27] Syria was abandoned to the criminal whims of Iran and Russia while the world witnessed the slaughter of countless innocent civilians with equanimity. The longest war in Afghanistan continues unabated, and there is no end in sight. We toppled the Qaddafi government in Libya and forced Egypt's President Mubarak out of power with the absurd notion of introducing democracy, disregarding the nature of their societies, cultures, and their political orientations. America cannot lead when it leaves chaos and instability in its wake.

Our **foreign policy**, which presumably is guided by our values and national interest, seems to be inconsistent and is often counterproductive. Whereas we make supreme efforts to export our political system of democracy as if it were a panacea to cure all political ailments around the world, we cater to dictators—ruthless and brutal head of states who govern with an iron fist—and ally ourselves with corrupt regimes in the name of "national interest."

Diplomacy and common sense seem to give way to bombastic militaristic rhetoric, leaving our friends and foes bewildered. Whatever happened to America's leadership that much of the world needs? We simply cannot relinquish that role; we cannot abandon our moral responsibility, and we must never succumb to the caprices of anyone, including the president. America has carved a special role in the world and it must now live up to it, because there is no other power that can replace America.

The greatest danger America faces today is not being attacked by North Korea or any other enemy who wishes ill for America. The danger is from within: Republicans vs. Democrats, rich vs. poor, the bigot vs. the law-abiding citizen, rampant discrimination, common human rights abuses (especially against minority groups), widening social inequality, and our leaders' failure to do their duty as they became increasingly self-absorbed and indifferent to America's future.

The embedded political, economic, cultural, military, and technological achievements of America remained unmatched. We must now rebuild on this strength and fight for America's soul. This is what the American people want, and what the world expects from us.

CONGRESS: DON'T TAMPER WITH
THE IRAN DEAL, BUILD ON IT

October 19, 2017

The Trump administration's approach to the Iran deal is problematic, as it is taken out of the context of the multiple conflicts raging throughout the Middle East, the extent to which Iran is involved, and the role it can play in resolving them, including the conflicts in Syria, Yemen, Iraq, and Lebanon. The question is, will Tehran be more cooperative in the search for solutions to these conflicts if the signatories to the Iran deal, especially the US, fully adhere to it, or will Iran add fuel to the regional fires if the deal is terminated by Trump, if Congress fails to reach a drastically different accord?

By all accounts, Iran continues to fully adhere to all the provisions of the deal. The irony is that when the US finally makes a deal after years of mutually intense enmity following the 1979 Iranian Revolution, it reneges on it, which only reinforces the Iranians' belief that the US cannot be trusted and is still committed to regime change.

Although the deal was limited to Iran's pursuit of a weaponized nuclear program, it offers opportunities to build on it in the search for solutions to the regional conflicts, especially Iran's continuing transgressions. Trump's reckless decision will take away any incentive that could entice Iran to be a positive regional player.

I am not condoning Iran's reprehensible behavior. I condemn in the strongest terms its support of violent extremists and terrorist organizations; I condemn it for being one of the most vicious culprits behind Syria's tragic civil war, and its ruthless support of the Houthis in Yemen, the Shiite insurgents in Iraq, and Hezbollah in Lebanon. That said, Iran cannot simply be dismissed as if it were irrelevant to the unfolding tragic events in the region, which cannot be resolved without Iran's full participation.

Those who deal with Iran will do well to remember that there is a psychological dimension to Iran's behavior. Iran is a major Middle Eastern power; it is a proud nation with a rich, millennia-long history and huge human and natural resources, enjoying a critical geostrategic position and importance unmatched by any other country in the region.

This of course does not excuse Iran's behavior, but given its deeply rooted national pride, it does not respond well to intimidation and threats. Now that Iran is in full compliance with the deal that was negotiated in good faith by the Obama administration, Tehran enhanced its credibility and stature in the eyes of the international community. Sadly, the same cannot be said about the Trump administration.

Why should Tehran agree to renegotiate the deal when the EU, Russia, and China remain committed to it as it stands? Last Monday the European Union backed the accord, saying that "The EU is committed to the continued full and effective implementation of all parts of the JCPOA" because it is working and is a key part of nuclear non-proliferation efforts.[28] Risking the Iran deal will isolate the US rather than Iran, because the US is the party who is violating the spirit and letter of the agreement.

The likelihood that Congress will modify the agreement to make it palatable to Trump is extremely slim; it would open the door for Iran to back out of the deal and resume its development of its nuclear program, which would inevitably lead to the proliferation of nuclear weapons.

If Trump is true to his word and terminates the deal completely, it will trigger the re-imposition of sanctions against the will of our European allies, which will only widen the rift with the US, as they are determined not to follow Trump's misguided and incongruous policy.

The fact that a president who is naïve about foreign relations and the implications of terminating the deal is refusing to listen to the advice of his national security team (including Defense Secretary Mattis) that the deal serves US national security interests is astonishing.

Instead, Trump is listening to Israel's Prime Minister Netanyahu, who is ignoring the fact that once the deal is terminated, Iran will be free to resume its nuclear program, which could potentially pose a serious threat to Israel's national security (a situation he wants to prevent). Moreover, he looks at Iran through the narrowest of lenses, as if Tehran responds only to the language of force and sanctions, which is beyond the pale.

Even if Iran is determined to acquire nuclear weapons somewhere down the line, which should not be overruled, to suggest that its intent is to destroy Israel or any other US ally in the region is absurd. Tehran is deliberate, careful, and rational; it knows that once it embarks on developing nuclear weapons, Israel, the US, or both will use any means (including military force) to prevent it from achieving its goal. Indeed, however hardline Iran might be, the regime is not suicidal.

Any modification to the deal should first be attempted through diplomatic channels. That is, if the purpose is to prevent Iran from pursuing a weaponized nuclear program once the current deal expires, then why not engage Iran now in quiet diplomacy (notwithstanding its vocal public opposition) and gauge where it really stands and what sort of quid pro quo Tehran would seek to modify the agreement.

To be sure, in the search for a solution to the conflict with Tehran, the US must seek areas where there are mutual interests that serve both sides well. The raging conflicts in the Middle East provide opportunities to work with Iran to bring an end to the civil war in Syria, mitigate the conflict in Yemen, and even cooperate on addressing violent extremism and radicalization. Yes, Iran seeks regional hegemony, but as long as it is treated with respect and feels assured that the US is not seeking regime change now or at any time in the future, it will tamper its ambitions.

Trump's thoughtless and damaging campaign promise to tear up the Iran deal on his first day in office did nothing but embarrass the US, rather than demonstrate what he foolishly keeps claiming—that the deal itself was the worst deal the US has ever made.

If Republican Senators and Representatives have any spine left, they should stop behaving like a cult that blindly follows a blind leader and pass a bill that would prevent Trump from terminating the deal, similar to the one they passed that usurped from Trump the power to lift the sanctions on Russia by executive order.

Congress may be able to modify the deal, but losing the support of our allies—who are determined to keep the deal in place and refuse to re-impose sanctions on Iran—would be the greatest embarrassment to what's left of America's leadership.

CHILD POVERTY IN AMERICA IS INDEFENSIBLE

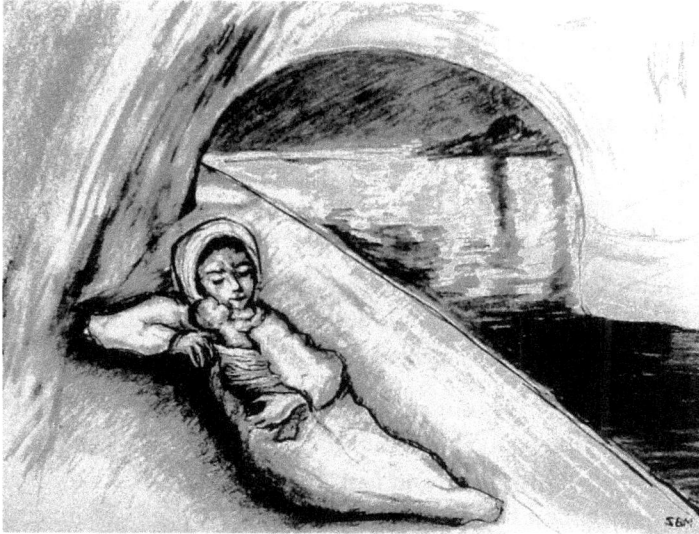

October 25, 2017

The Trump administration's proposals on the annual budget, efforts to repeal and replace the Affordable Care Act (ACA, colloquially known as Obamacare), and restructuring of the tax system all point to a sad and even tragic conclusion. The poor will be poorer, dilapidated towns will continue to crumble, and crime will rise; worst of all, our underprivileged children will be weaker and suffer from a lack of medical care and malnutrition with little or no prospect for better and brighter tomorrows.

The state of poverty in the United States, particularly among children, is abhorrent and scandalous, putting America, the richest and most powerful country in the world, in a shameful light. Successive American administrations are guilty of outrageous negligence toward poor children and have inflicted incalculable damage to millions who continue to suffer, causing a tremendous loss of human resources and productivity to the country.

The following heart-wrenching statistics demonstrate the magnitude of the problem. One in eleven children, approximately 6.5 million nationwide, live in extreme poverty (an average of $12,129 per month for a family of four). One in five infants-to-preschool-aged children (4.2 million) live in conditions of foreboding poverty, compounded by the fact that this age is a time of rapid brain development. Black and Hispanic children disproportionately suffer from poverty—one in three and one in four respectively—compared to one in eight for their white counterparts.[29] If this is not the result of a colossal failure in the US economic system and its defunct policies, then it is difficult to think what would be.

There is no part of the country that does not experience intense poverty from which children suffer the most. Here are some samplings: in Boston, MA, the child poverty rate is 26.9 percent. In Marion County, IN, 31 percent of children under eighteen live in poverty. In Doña Ana County, NM, the child poverty rate is 39 percent; and in Cameron County, TX, the child poverty rate is a shameful 47 percent.[30]

A more explicit case in point provides a most gloomy picture about the plight of poor children in this wealthy country. The state of Kentucky is such an example of the cyclic and greatly threatening effects of childhood economic deprivation to our general society. With 25% of its child population in poverty,[31] it is common to hear that right down the road from an economically stable community is an area of deep impoverishment and scarcity. These Americans are unable to rely on the support of any community, as they are often stigmatized by those more privileged and must hide what little they *do* have from others who are equally desperate and hungry.

The children of these families suffer from developmental issues resulting not only from malnutrition, but also from broken homes, lack of education, and the absence of any stable emotional base. The most saddening truth of the situation is that these children were *born* into a mentally, emotionally, and physically oppressive system. A report by a *USA Today* affiliate, *The Courier Journal*, found that these children of poverty could be aided by an Earned Income Tax Credit for their families—one of the very programs hit with funding cuts in Trump's proposed budget.[32]

In his inaugural address, Trump stated that "The forgotten men and women of our country will be forgotten no longer .... Mothers and children trapped in poverty in our inner cities ... students deprived of knowledge ... their success will be our success." If this was his pledge, why is he cutting support from the very programs that sustain these ends?

By now of course we have become used to Trump's hypocrisy and his disdainful policies that set the country backward while subjecting a substantial segment of another generation of youth to hopelessness and deprivation. Instead of giving these millions of destitute children every opportunity to flourish in an open society and contribute to the well-being of their communities, he stifles their growth and makes them permanently dependent on government aid as they continue to struggle in silent desperation.

Many of these children do not finish high school; they wander the streets, jobless and adrift, and end up turning to crime. Tens of thousands are incarcerated for petty theft or other minor misdemeanors. When they leave the prisons, many commit more serious crimes. Their prospect of becoming positive and productive citizens further dissipates. For them, the American dream is a living nightmare that is heightened by Trump's ill-conceived budget that the Republican-dominated Senate brazenly passed a week ago.

Here is the glaring cruelty of Trump's budget cuts. Over the next ten years, **$190 billion** will be cut from the Supplemental Nutrition Assistance Program (food stamps), and **$616 billion** will be cut from Medicaid and the Children's Health Insurance Program (CHIP). In addition, the cut from Temporary Assistance for Needy Families (welfare) will be **$21.6 billion**. There is a proposed **cut of $40.4 billion** from earned-income tax credits and child tax credits.[33]

The Brookings Institution's analysis of the Graham-Cassidy Bill (which would effectively terminate the ACA) found that around twenty-one million people would lose health coverage through 2026.[34] It is predicted that his plan to end subsidies for the ACA—received by nearly six million people (over half of all people who buy insurance through exchanges) in 2017—will cause premiums to rise for all customers and foist unbearable out-of-pocket costs onto low-income Americans.[35]

Under the pretext of correcting fraudulence in such social welfare programs, Trump's plan will eliminate significant funding from children whose lives depend on it.

Even further, his tax plan would greatly benefit the wealthiest Americans, only benefit the middle class modestly, and have no direct impact on the bottom third of the population other than to keep the poor poor and create even more poverty.

These notions not only contradict his promises to lift the downtrodden from their daily misery, but also reaffirm his indifference to the plight of deprived children and his bigoted attitude toward the Hispanic and Black children among them, who constitute a majority. What most people are unaware of is that according to Organization for Economic Co-operation and Development rankings of child income poverty rates, the United States disgracefully falls in between Mexico and Lithuania.[36]

Meanwhile, Trump insists on appropriating $1.5 billion to build a shameful wall along the Mexican border, defying the premise that the country's greatness was made possible because generations of new immigrants contributed so much to the creative and moral fabric of our society.

Even though the final budget and healthcare bill may somewhat be modified by the House, the fact that Trump proposed such deep cuts speaks volumes about his disregard of the most critical segment of the population. Millions of poor children live in families that have little or no means to improve their lot, which has a significant impact on their growth and character. Here is where the billions of dollars should be invested, which could make a real difference in the lives of our precious children instead of being wasted on useless projects such as the Wall.

It is a choice that Trump and his Republican party, which is in disarray, must come to grips with. No American child should be left behind. That is something that bipartisan representatives of the American people fought for in 2011, and that is the humane principle that we must defend today.

TRUMP'S RECOGNITION OF JERUSALEM
AS ISRAEL'S CAPITAL AND THE PROSPECT
OF A TWO-STATE SOLUTION

December 12, 2017

I was in Israel when Trump made his announcement recognizing Jerusalem as Israel's capital. Initially, I thought Israelis would pour out into the streets celebrating this "historic" moment, but other than small chatter here and there, and some expressions of jubilation, not much else gripped the nation. On the Palestinian side, relatively small demonstrations broke out in the West Bank and Gaza, which continued in the following days with limited violence, and condemnation of the US declaration was heard from most Arab and Muslim capitals. This is pretty much where things stand today.

Perhaps it is too early to draw a definitive conclusion, but based on everything I have seen and heard while in the area and since then, not much more is likely to happen. The question that many people are asking is why, and could anything positive come out of this declaration?

About a year ago, when Trump initially stated his intention to relocate the American Embassy from Tel Aviv to Jerusalem, I predicted that the move would have major consequences and may well destroy the prospect of a negotiated peace agreement between Israel and the Palestinians based on a two-state solution.

Yes, this would have been the case had Trump's declaration been phrased in a manner that included East Jerusalem directly or indirectly as part of Israel's capital, and ignored the need for a two-state solution. But this is not what happened. In fact, what he stated clearly implied that East Jerusalem was not part of the equation.

Regardless of how strongly I disagree with Trump's overall foreign policy, he was correct to state that "The record is in. After more than two decades of waivers [to relocate the US embassy to Jerusalem], we are no closer to a lasting peace between Israel and the Palestinians."[37] Indeed, the final status of Jerusalem never constituted a make-or-break issue in any previous negotiations. Thus, there is no reason to assume that declaring Jerusalem as

Israel's capital affects East Jerusalem, when in fact everything else he stated—implicitly if not explicitly—was limited to West Jerusalem.

"Jerusalem," he said, "is the home of the Israeli Parliament, the Knesset, as well as the Israeli Supreme Court. It is the location of the official residence of the Prime Minister and the President. It is the headquarters of many government ministries." All of these institutions are located in West Jerusalem, and none are likely to be relocated to East Jerusalem. The Trump administration made it clear to the Israelis that any such move will not be tolerated, as it would cause undue turmoil that would completely undermine US efforts to advance the peace process.

Trump further noted in his declaration that "Jerusalem is today, and must remain, a place where Jews pray at the Western Wall, where Christians walk the Stations of the Cross, and where Muslims worship at Al-Aqsa Mosque." This in no way is any different from what has been on the negotiating table in every set of peace talk since the 1993–1995 Oslo Accords. In fact, during the Olmert-Abbas negotiations in 2008, a basic agreement was reached on the future of Jerusalem along these lines to preserve the unity of the city.

Moreover, it is important to emphasize the fact that nearly thirty years ago the US leased land in **West Jerusalem** on which to build the future American embassy. It was not contemplated then, and it is not expected now, that the US embassy should or would be built in East Jerusalem.

No Israeli government, including the current one led by Netanyahu, has requested to build the American embassy on the East side of the city. Thus, the future building of the US embassy in West Jerusalem does not constitute recognition of Israel's sovereignty over East Jerusalem.

From the Trump administration's perspective, there was nothing in his statement that is contrary to the premise that Jerusalem will still end up the capital of both Israeli and Palestinian states. In fact, it may engender a new momentum toward the resumption of peace negotiations, as the Palestinians now realize the longer they wait, the more ground they are likely to lose. "I've judged this course of action," Trump said, "to be in the best interests of the United States of America *and the pursuit of peace between Israel and the Palestinians.* This is a long-overdue step to advance the peace process and to work toward a lasting agreement" [emphasis added].

Further in Trump's statement, he said: "*We are not taking a position of any final status issue, including the specific boundaries of Israeli sovereignty in Jerusalem, or the resolution of contested borders. Those questions are up to the parties involved*" [emphasis added]. He further stated that "The United States would support a two-state solution if agreed to by both sides." Neither of these assertions contradict in any way similar statements made by previous American administrations. Trump knows that a two-state solution remains the only practical option.

Even though President Abbas criticized Trump for his declaration and pronounced the US as biased and no longer an honest broker, the US (especially Congress and most previous administrations) has in fact always been biased in favor of the Israelis. That said, Abbas and all other heads of Arab states know that only the US can exert the kind of pressure on Israel necessary to exact compromises central to reaching an agreement.

In return for Trump's announcement, Netanyahu quietly conceded to not expanding the settlements outside the three blocks along the 1967 borders and also agreed to engage in confidence-building measures, especially joint economic development projects with the Palestinians.

Abbas may now be dismissive of the United States' critical role in negotiations with Israel, but neither he nor his successors can afford to ignore its role in future negotiations and expect a peace agreement with Israel that meets the Palestinians' basic requirements.

Most Arab states' criticism of Trump's declaration, led by Saudi Arabia, was largely muted, not only because they are preoccupied with domestic and regional tensions, but because they understand the real implications of the declaration, which has little or no effect on the reality on the ground and the ultimate framework of a peace accord.

Notwithstanding the aforementioned, the EU now has an enhanced opportunity to play a significant role in guarding the principle of a two-state solution by undertaking significant people-to-people confidence-building measures between Israelis and Palestinians. The EU can, and in fact should, use its financial aid for the Palestinians and its extensive trade with Israel as levers to effect significant change in the Israeli-Palestinian political climate, which is a prerequisite to substantive and successful peace negotiations.

To be sure, from my perspective, nothing in Trump's declaration fundamentally changes the principle of a two-state solution as a prerequisite to peaceful and enduring coexistence between Israel and the Palestinians. Those who claim that a two-state solution has all but vanished because of Trump's recognition of Israel seem to be engaged in illusions.

They have forgotten what the Zionist dream was all about—the creation of a Jewish state imbued with its long historic experiences, culture, religion, and identity that can be secure and enduring only if it remains a *Jewish and democratic state* that offers a home with security to any Jew, and remains as such to eternity.

The one-state option defies every principle of the Zionist dream, and no Israeli government, regardless of its political orientation, will settle on anything less than a Jewish state with a sustainable Jewish majority to ensure the national identity of the state. To be sure, the current status quo is simply unsustainable.

Trump's declaration does not in any way foreclose the Palestinians' aspiration of establishing their own capital in East Jerusalem while maintaining the unity of Jerusalem as a single city and as a microcosm of Israeli-Palestinian peaceful coexistence.

Notes

1   Tamar Pileggi, "Bennett Vows to Pursue Ma'ale Adumim Annexation this Month," *Times of Israel*, Jan. 1, 2017, https://www.timesofisrael.com/bennett-vows-to-pursue-maale-adumim-annexation-in-january/.

2   Peter Baker, "'Trump Effect' is Already Shaping Events around the World," *New York Times*, Nov. 28, 2016, https://www.nytimes.com/2016/11/28/world/middleeast/trump-effect-is-already-shaping-events-around-the-world.html?_r=0.

3   Emily Tamkin, "One-State Solution, or Two? Trump's 'Happy with the One that Both Parties Like,'" *Foreign Policy*, Feb. 15, 2017, https://foreignpolicy.com/2017/02/15/903972-bibi-israel-palestinians-netanyahu/.

4   Peter Baker and Ian Fisher, "Trump Comes to Israel Citing a Palestinian Deal as Crucial," *New York Times*, May 22, 2017, https://www.nytimes.com/2017/05/22/world/middleeast/trump-israel-visit.html?_r=0.

5   Stephen J. Adler, Jeff Mason and Steve Holland, "Exclusive: Trump Complains Sau-

dis Not Paying Fair Share for U.S. Defense," *Reuters*, Apr. 27, 2017, https://www.reuters.com/article/us-usa-trump-mideast-exclusive-idUSKBN17U08A.

6   Baker and Fisher, "Trump Comes to Israel."

7   Ibid.

8   Emily Tillett, "Trump Reaffirms Commitment to Israel, Achieving Peace in Middle East," *CBS News*, May 23, 2017, https://www.cbsnews.com/news/trump-reaffirms-commitment-to-israel-achieving-peace-in-middle-east/.

9   David A. Andelman, "Trump's Anti-Iran Aggression couldn't Come at a Worse Time," *CNN*, Jun. 28, 2017, https://www.cnn.com/2017/05/22/opinions/trump-iran-middle-east-andleman-opinion/.

10   Ajmal Khan Zazai in conversation with the author, July 2017.

11   Rosie Gray, "Trump Defends White-Nationalist Protesters: 'Some Very Fine People on Both Sides,'" *The Atlantic*, Aug. 15, 2017, https://www.theatlantic.com/politics/archive/2017/08/trump-defends-white-nationalist-protesters-some-very-fine-people-on-both-sides/537012/.

12   David Leonhardt and Stuart A. Thompson, "Trump's Lies," *New York Times*, June 23, 2017, https://www.nytimes.com/interactive/2017/06/23/opinion/trumps-lies.html.

13   Julie Hirschfeld Davis, "Trump's Budget Cuts Deeply into Medicaid and Anti-Poverty Efforts," *New York Times*, May 22, 2017, https://www.nytimes.com/2017/05/22/us/politics/trump-budget-cuts.html?_r=0.

14   John Rogin, "Lindsey Graham: Trump's State Department Budget could Cause 'a Lot of Benghazis,'" *Washington Post*, May 23, 2017, https://www.washingtonpost.com/news/josh-rogin/wp/2017/05/23/lindsey-graham-trumps-state-department-budget-could-cause-a-lot-of-benghazis/.

15   Lisa Friedman, "Scientists Fear Trump will Dismiss Blunt Climate Report," *New York Times*, Aug. 7, 2017, https://www.nytimes.com/2017/08/07/climate/climate-change-drastic-warming-trump.html?smid=tw-nytimes&smtyp=cur.

16   Peter Baker and Choe Sang-Hun, "Trump Threatens 'Fire and Fury' against North Korea if It Endangers US," *New York Times*, Aug. 8, 2017, https://www.nytimes.com/2017/08/08/world/asia/north-korea-un-sanctions-nuclear-missile-united-nations.html.

17   Leinz Vales, "James Clapper Calls Trump Speech 'Downright Scary and Disturbing,'" *CNN*, Aug. 24, 2017, https://www.cnn.com/2017/08/23/politics/james-clapper-trump-phoenix-rally-don-lemon-cnntv/index.html.

18   Baker and Choe, "Trump Threatens 'Fire and Fury.'"

19   Donald J. Trump, Twitter post, August 11, 2017, 7:29a.m., https://twitter.com/realDonaldTrump/.

20   "Secretary Mattis Statement at the White House," *US Department of Defense,* Sep. 3, 2017, https://www.defense.gov/Newsroom/Transcripts/Transcript/Article/1298860/secretary-mattis-statement-at-the-white-house/.

21   Geoff Brumfiel, "Here are the Facts about North Korea's Nuclear Test," *CNN,* Sep. 3, 2017, https://www.npr.org/sections/thetwo-way/2017/09/03/548262043/here-are-the-facts-about-north-koreas-nuclear-test.

22   David E. Sanger and Choe Sang-Hun, "U.S. Urges Fuel Cutoff for North Korea, Saying It's 'Begging for War,'" *New York Times,* Sep. 4, 2017, https://www.nytimes.com/2017/09/04/world/asia/north-korea-missile-test.html?_r=0.

23   Donald J. Trump, Twitter post, September 3, 2017, 12:14p.m., https://twitter.com/realDonaldTrump/.

24   "Child Poverty in America 2015: National Analysis," *Children's Defense Fund,* Sep. 13, 2016, https://www.childrensdefense.org/wp-content/uploads/2018/08/child-poverty-in-america-2015.pdf.

25   "Fact Sheet: Trends in U.S. Corrections," *The Sentencing Project,* accessed Sep. 10, 2017, https://sentencingproject.org/wp-content/uploads/2016/01/Trends-in-US-Corrections.pdf.

26   Peter Wagner and Bernadette Rabuy, "Mass Incarceration: The Whole Pie 2017," *Prison Policy Initiative,* Mar. 14, 2017, https://www.prisonpolicy.org/reports/pie2017.html.

27   Daniel Trotta, "Iraq War Costs U.S. More than $2 Trillion: Study," *Reuters,* Mar. 14, 2013, https://www.reuters.com/article/us-iraq-war-anniversary/iraq-war-costs-u-s-more-than-2-trillion-study-idUSBRE92D0PG20130314.

28   "Iran Nuclear Deal: EU Statement on the Joint Comprehensive Plan of Action," *Council of the European Union,* Oct. 16, 2017, https://www.consilium.europa.eu/en/press/press-releases/2017/10/16/iran-nuclear-deal-eu-jcpoa/.

29   "Child Poverty in America 2015: National Analysis."

30   Alvaro Lima et al., "Poverty in Boston," *Boston Planning and Development Agency, Boston Redevelopment Authority Research Division,* Mar. 2014, http://www.bostonplans.org/getattachment/01cef762-956d-4343-a49a-b41c280168ae/; "Marion County, Indiana," STATS Indiana, accessed Oct. 22, 2017, http://www.stats.indiana.edu/profiles/profiles.asp?scope_choice=a&county_changer=18097; "Kids Count in New Mexico: 2016 Data Book," New Mexico Voices for Children, accessed Oct. 22, 2017, https://www.nmvoices.org/wp-content/uploads/2017/01/NMVC-DataBook2016-Web.pdf; Alexa Ura, "Latest Census Data Shows Poverty Rate Highest at Border, Lowest in Suburbs," *The Texas Tribune,* Jan. 19, 2016, https://

www.texastribune.org/2016/01/19/poverty-prevalent-on-texas-border-low-in-suburbs/.

31 Taylor Inman, "New Census Data Reveals that 25% of Kentucky Children Still Live in Poverty," *WKMS*, Sep. 18, 2017, https://www.wkms.org/post/new-census-data-reveals-25-kentucky-children-still-live-poverty#stream/0.

32 Miranda Klein, "One in Four Louisiana Kids Live in Poverty," *Courier Journal*, Jun. 13, 2017, https://www.courier-journal.com/story/news/2017/06/13/one-four-louisiana-kids-live-poverty/390506001/.

33 "Budget of the U.S. Government: A New Foundation For American Greatness Fiscal Year 2018," *The White House, Office of Management and Budget,* accessed October 23, 2017, https://www.whitehouse.gov/sites/whitehouse.gov/files/omb/budget/fy2018/budget.pdf.

34 Matthew Fiedler and Loren Adler, "How will the Graham-Cassidy Proposal Affect the Number of People with Health Insurance Coverage?" *Brookings,* Sep. 22, 2017, https://www.brookings.edu/research/how-will-the-graham-cassidy-proposal-affect-the-number-of-people-with-health-insurance-coverage/.

35 Kevin Liptak, Tami Luhby and Phil Mattingly, "Trump will End Health Care Cost-Sharing Subsidies," *CNN*, Oct. 12, 2017, https://www.cnn.com/2017/10/12/politics/obamacare-subsidies/index.html.

36 "CO2.2: Child Poverty," *OECD, OECD Social Policy Division - Directorate of Employment, Labour and Social Affairs,* accessed Oct. 22, 2017, http://www.oecd.org/els/CO_2_2_Child_Poverty.pdf.

37 Donald J. Trump, "Statement by President Trump on Jerusalem," *The White House,* Dec. 6, 2017, https://www.whitehouse.gov/briefings-statements/statement-president-trump-jerusalem/.

2018

A PARTY THAT HAS LOST ITS SOUL

January 10, 2018

A s the midterm political campaigns begin, perhaps we should pause and think about where this country is headed under the leadership of Trump, with the House and Senate in control of the Republican Party—a party that has lost its soul and its way, failing to safeguard America's national interests. This is a party that not only strives to cling to power—which is not itself unusual—but seeks it at all costs with no scruples and no moral compass. It seems that the Republican establishment will do whatever it takes to promote their narrow conservative agenda, which caters to the rich and powerful, while supporting a president who has nothing to offer the country but disgrace.

The Republicans, who are deeply engrossed in partisan politics, have enabled Trump in order to further their own political objectives, while ignoring the fact that they were elected to protect America's global and national security interests and the wellbeing of the American people. The Republican Party will be held responsible for what may well be irreparable damage to America's global leadership and moral standing.

It appears as though Trump and the Republican leadership are dancing to each other's tune. Occasionally, some Republican Senators, including Corker and Flake, criticize Trump for his repeated false statements and lack of political savvy and instability. Generally, however, party members revel in the fact that they now have a president who will sign anything they put on his desk.

The Republican establishment is determined to shove down the throats of the American people what they failed to do during Obama's tenure: enacting policies that are harmful to the majority of the American public.

Known for their hunger to cut taxes, the Republican House and Senate raced to pass major legislation overhauling the tax code with the slimmest majority in Congress. They consider the tax bill a major triumph, when in fact it is nothing but a travesty. The bill will certainly make the rich richer, while the poor and the unemployed, particularly unskilled workers, will have to wait for handouts with little or no prospect for a dignified existence.

The Republicans are bent on dismantling everything that President Obama was able to achieve, particularly the Iran deal, which could potentially plunge the Middle East into nuclear proliferation if nullified. They doggedly worked to repeal Obama's Affordable Care Act (ACA), which would deprive millions of people of healthcare. They applauded the United States' withdrawal from the Paris Agreement on climate change to the dismay of the entire international community, ignoring all scientific evidence that climate change is in fact already upon us. Beyond that, they rolled back countless environmental protections, effectively dismantling the EPA.

No, this is not what the vast majority of the American people aspire for. We envision:

An America that shares the world's concerns about climate change and leads other nations by example to combat global warming and save the planet from the dire consequences that it will inevitably pose.

An America that protects its national security interests and achieves that not by dismissing the **genuine** national security concerns of other nations, but by working to reduce tensions and build mutual trust.

An America that does not tolerate the gross violation of human rights by ruthless despots simply because our national interest assumes precedence over such abuses. On the contrary, our national interest is best served when we stand fast in protecting human rights everywhere.

An America that embraces other cultures, thereby enriching our own, and fosters greater affinity and closer relationships with other nations, including our adversaries, through continuing cultural exchanges.

An America that projects moral leadership and stands ready to act to avert hunger and disease, especially among children in conflict-ridden countries, by providing aid while assuming a leading role in resolving such conflicts.

An America that maintains an open-door policy—the tradition of being a nation of immigrants—by welcoming those, regardless of their creed, race, or color, to our shores who want to realize the American dream and do their share to contribute to America's economic, cultural, and scientific riches.

An America that mitigates conflict with its adversaries and deepens its ties with allies and friends, respects international treaties, and lives up to any commitment made, not only to maintain our credibility, but also to make the world a safer and more peaceful place.

Yes, America can be all of that and more, because these values are embedded in our cultural and moral fabric. Only the American people can make America what it is destined to be. Any political party or president that does not lead the country in this direction is not fit to be in power.

Republican congressmembers must now demonstrate where their loyalty lies—to the country or to a corrupt party establishment and a president who has never been able to articulate any coherent policy and leaves it to the party leadership to spoon-feed him whatever rubbish they deem necessary to serve their corrupt political agenda.

If the Republicans continue on their current path and keep swallowing everything that Trump spits out, come November they will pay the price—and deservedly so—for selling their souls while riding on the backs of the poor and the despairing.

THE DANGEROUS EROSION OF
US GLOBAL LEADERSHIP

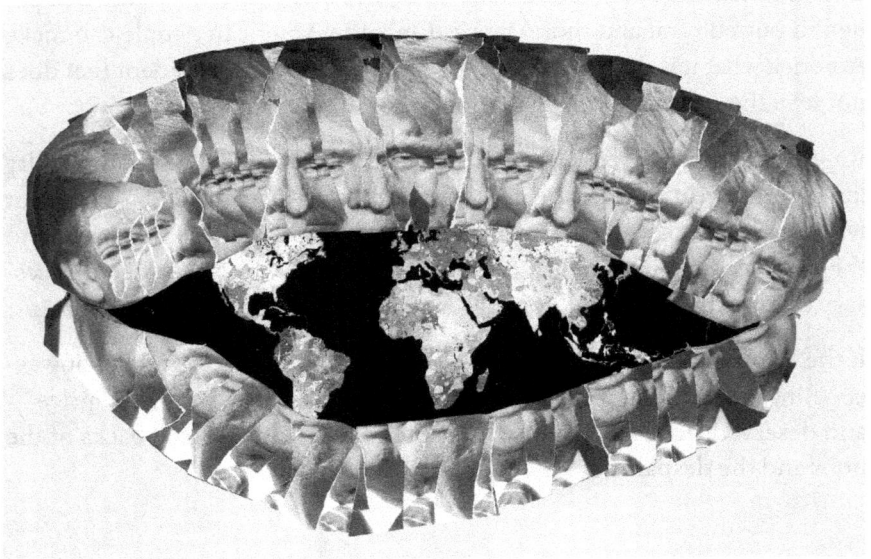

January 24, 2018

Only one year after Trump was inaugurated, the US has already suffered an alarming setback to its global leadership role and badly damaged its image. In short order, Trump managed to bewilder our friends and allies, intensify the enmity between us and our foes, and evoke fear, concerns, and unpredictability to the dismay of the international community. I cannot imagine how much further America's reputation will decline as an increasing number of countries, including our allies, resign themselves to the lack of American leadership under Trump's watch, which will have major adverse repercussions on our national interest and influence the world over.

Trump's "America First" notion, abandonment of our soft power, and reckless utterances have deeply troubled countries with strong ties to the US, enraged those who have been maligned by his reprehensible rhetoric, and delighted our adversaries, while leaving America increasingly isolated.

On the issue of North Korea's nuclear weapons and anti-ballistic missiles, instead of engaging Pyongyang in quiet diplomacy to resolve the conflict, he resorted to bellicose rhetoric and threats that only heightened tensions and brought the US and North Korea ever closer to the unthinkable—nuclear war.

On the Iran deal, rather than trying to peacefully negotiate any changes, especially to the sunset provisions, Trump decertified the deal and threatened to resume old and impose new sanctions, which would torpedo it completely. He demanded that Congress modify the deal, even though the other five signatories to the accord vehemently reject any tampering of the deal because of Iran's continued full adherence. Tehran rejects any changes and threatened to withdraw from the deal and resume its nuclear program, which could lead to the proliferation of nuclear weapons and subject the region's inhabitants to living in the shadows of nuclear conflagration.

On immigration, Trump's racist attitude toward Muslims and people of color has severely undermined America's unique image as a country of immigrants, which made America great in the first place. His reference to Africa, Haiti, and El Salvador as "shithole" countries provoked unprecedented international outrage.

Scores of American ambassadors around the world were summoned to explain the inexplicable, which the ambassadors themselves could not fathom. Why would a sitting US president utter such filth, in the White House no less? Former Massachusetts Governor Mitt Romney put it succinctly when he said: "What he [Trump] communicated caused racists to rejoice, minorities to weep, and the vast heart of America to mourn."[1]

As for international treaties and accords, Trump has completely disregarded our commitment to live up to such agreements. He insists on renegotiating the terms of NAFTA, and effectively withdrew from the Trans-Pacific Partnership (connecting the Americas with Asia and Australia). He pulled the US out of the Paris Agreement on climate change and withdrew from the United Nations Educational, Scientific and Cultural Organization (UNESCO), accusing it of anti-Israel bias.

As a result, he acutely damaged America's credibility, making many countries wary of entering into bilateral agreements with the US, as they can no longer trust his administration to live up to its commitments. This leaves a wide opening for our adversaries to fill the vacuum he created.

Trump has further shocked all democracies around the world with his incessant assault on the press. Although a few of his predecessors have occasionally ostracized the press, none has mounted such vile criticism. He accuses all media outlets (except for FOX News) of being the enemy of the people, claiming they are biased and spreading "Fake News" to purposefully malign him and deride his policy initiatives.

Sadly, whereas America was seen as the beacon of freedom and democracy to be emulated, Trump is consciously undermining one of our central constitutional pillars—the free press—to the utter consternation of democracies around the world.

On the question of the United States' reliability, many countries that depend on America for their national security are worried about Trump's real commitment to safeguarding their security. His criticism of NATO, which is the core of West European security, and his appeasement of Russia, which is viewed as the West's staunchest enemy, raises questions as to where he would stand if they were threatened.

This concern is expressed by our allies in the Middle East and Europe, further diminishing America's role. Germany's Chancellor Merkel expressed her misgivings, stating that: "The times in which we could completely depend on others are, to a certain extent, over ... we Europeans truly have to take our fate into our own hands .... We have to know that we must fight for our future on our own, for our destiny as Europeans."[2]

The fact that Trump lies as often as he breathes deeply troubles countries around the world because they can no longer take his word for granted on issues of major importance to them.

 Trump seems to be totally oblivious to the reality that without American global leadership, which has spanned over seven decades, the world will be even more chaotic than today. Trump has no end-strategy for Syria, Iraq, and Afghanistan, nor the focus or interest in stemming widespread, destabilizing violent conflicts and human rights abuses around the world.

It is sad that in the most recent Gallup poll "Rating World Leaders," the US is ranked third, behind Germany and China (and just ahead of Russia).[3] The damage that Trump has caused to American credibility and moral global leadership will not be readily repaired after electing a new president. It will take time and a president who is stable, politically skilled, and intellectually competent, with vision and an understanding of America's pivotal role in the international arena, before America's global leadership can be restored.

The Republican Party has become complicit in Trump's mischief and misguided policies. It is now up to the Democrats to get their act together, regain control of the House and Senate, and shackle Trump before he causes irreparable damage to America's global role and responsibility.

MURDER BY CONGRESS

February 16, 2018

O nce again, we are faced with another mass shooting. This time the cold-blooded killings took place at Marjory Stoneman Douglas High School in Florida, killing fourteen innocent students and three adults. This horrific mass murder of young and old attests to the criminal negligence of our lawmakers and president, who dispense with their responsibility by offering to the bereaved families hollow condolences and fake prayers.

No parent can draw comfort from these empty expressions. Nothing can assuage the agony and unbearable pain that parents feel when their child is lost to an outrageous and utterly senseless attack that could have been prevented.

When will lawmakers face the bitter truth that America is at war with itself? A *de facto* civil war is consuming us from within. Firearms are mercilessly robbing the lives of nearly forty thousand each year—nearly five times more than American soldiers killed in the Iraq and Afghanistan wars combined (which number 4,530 and 2,408, respectively).[4] On average, ninety-three people are killed from gun violence every day, and at least 239 school shootings have occurred across the United States since 2012; a majority of the over four hundred casualties are children under the age of nineteen.[5]

And yet, after every such unconscionable carnage, you hear our derelict political leaders suggesting that it is not the right time to talk about gun control laws when the families and friends of the victims are agonizing about the loss of their loved ones.

When will the right time come? How much more pain and suffering must our own fellow citizens endure before we act?

Shame on every single House and Senate member who each year takes millions in blood money as a political contribution from the National Rifle Association (NRA) to ensure their reelection. Perhaps only when some of these lawmakers lose a child of their own will they begin to grasp the excruciating pain that parents bear when their telephones ring, only to be told that their child was just gunned down at school by a random shooter. Yes, every lawmaker should stop and think how it really feels. But then again, are they even capable of feeling?

The Book of James (2:26 NKJV) says it best: "Faith without works is dead." Without action, "thoughts and prayers" cannot be counted on to stop random mass killings; this has been proven by history time and again. The occasion for condolences and prayers expired a long while ago.

How regressive and totally ignorant can our congressmembers be when they defend the Second Amendment of the Constitution: "A well-regulated Militia, being necessary to the security of a free State, the right of the people to keep and bear Arms, shall not be infringed"? This amendment was written over two hundred years ago, when firearms were essential for self-defense against foreign militaries and tyranny.

Wake up, you so-called legislators. Time has changed. There is no Gold Rush and no Wild West. Every congressmember, and Trump in particular, who opposes the passage of effective gun control, has the blood of innocent men, women, and children on their hands. Every single one.

Those hypocrites who oppose gun control keep telling us that guns don't kill people, people kill people. What a revelation! Does it take a genius to realize that if guns were not readily available, a would-be killer could not possibly execute dozens of people with a knife or a club before getting killed or captured? Here is the absurdity of their argument in real numbers, as demonstrated by only a handful of examples of mass shootings that unequivocally make the point:

In the Las Vegas shooting: 851 injured, fifty-eight killed—in Orlando's Pulse Nightclub: forty-nine killed—at Virginia Tech: thirty-two killed—at Sandy Hook Elementary: twenty-seven killed—at Marjory Stoneman Douglas High School: seventeen killed.[6] How many of those victims would have been killed if the perpetrator did not possess a gun?

Take a look at some countries with strict gun laws; their **annual** death by firearms speaks for itself: in the United Kingdom, with a population of 56 million, on average fifty to sixty are killed; in Germany with a population of 82.29 million, an average of 165; and in Japan with a population of 129 million, thirteen or (often) fewer are killed by guns.[7]

In Australia, before enacting strict gun control laws in 1996 following the deadliest mass shooting in Australian history, there were thirteen mass shootings in eighteen years. In the same time period following the legislation, there were zero.[8]

Every one of us must confront the truth. Just imagine, if we were engaged in another foreign war and suffered nearly three thousand casualties—the average number of Americans killed each month by firearms—how would we react? Why are we not hearing the outcry of every American who is sickened by these horrifying occurrences?

Yes, we can and indeed must blame every member of Congress for their criminal neglect. But we the American people must not remain silent in the face of this non-stop unfolding horror.

Where are the tens of millions of Americans who seek gun control? Why aren't we demonstrating in the streets day-in and day-out, demanding action? We have the power to end this national travesty by not giving our vote to any elected official who does not commit to enact gun control laws and hold them accountable.

Every legislator who does not act on gun control is complicit in all murders and atrocities committed by the barrel of a gun. They are responsible for all past and future killings of every man, woman, and child who dies in vain by firearms. This will be the badge of shame that they will wear for as long as they live.

TRUMP AND KIM JONG UN—SAILING ON UNCHARTED WATERS

March 28, 2018

The prospective meeting between President Trump and North Korea's Chairman Kim Jong Un would be historic, and regardless of the outcome, it will have major implications for years to come. The conflict over North Korea's nuclear arsenals and ballistic missiles is complex. It is driven by a mindset seething with mutual suspicions and profound distrust between the US and North Korea, which dates back nearly seven decades and has profoundly prejudiced their ultimate intentions. North Korea has violated several agreements with successive US administrations to end its nuclear program, while the US has maintained open hostility and made no secret of its desire to effect regime change. What has dramatically changed the dynamic of the conflict, however, is the convergence of four major developments that made it possible for Kim to invite Trump to negotiate an end to the conflict.

First, North Korea has succeeded in becoming a nuclear power, with a stockpile of weapons large enough to deter any enemy, including the US, from using force to depose the North Korean dynasty with impunity. It has mastered the technology of intercontinental missiles, which provides it with a delivery system for nuclear warheads, and has concluded that it can no longer improve its position by prolonging the conflict. Having reached such a milestone, North Korea has changed the dynamic of the conflict, making it possible for Kim to negotiate from a position of strength.

Second, although sanctions and international isolation have certainly played a role, they were not as decisive as the Trump administration is trying to project. Indeed, North Korea has suffered from the sanctions for many years, but has come to the negotiating table in the past for **tactical reasons,** seeking temporary relief from the sanctions only to resume the development of its nuclear and missile technology. Now, however, having become a recognized nuclear power, Kim is **seeking a strategic change** that would permanently lift sanctions to alleviate the economic hardship on his people and provide them with their basic and urgent needs, while demonstrating that the regime is delivering on its promises.

Third, by meeting President Trump for face-to-face talks, Kim would also be **accorded the legitimacy** he has been craving, while ensuring that North Korea is treated with respect as an independent state among the community of nations. North Korea's participation in the Winter Olympics provided the initial thaw between North and South Korea and created the opportunity for South Korea's President Moon Jae-in (whose country would be most affected under the conditions of war or peace) to broker a face-to-face meeting between Trump and Kim, to which the latter was already disposed to accept. Although the North Korean delegation (led by Kim, which is most unusual) traveled to China to keep Beijing abreast of developments regarding the pending summit and to ensure its support, it is also indicative **of Kim's seriousness about reaching an agreement** with the Trump administration.

Finally, as odd as it may seem, in the mutual public acrimony between Trump and Kim—the name-calling, the insults, the threats and counter-threats, coupled with their crude audacity and bluster—the two have found their match. Defiant, daring, and detested by the international community with overblown egos, both wanted to demonstrate that they can go against the political current and diplomatic niceties to achieve what their predecessors have failed to realize.

Pyongyang, however, will come to the negotiating table with a set of demands, including the assurance that the US will recognize the North Korean regime as the legitimate government and not seek regime change, lift all sanctions without linking them to human rights, end military exercises with South Korea, substantially reduce and ultimately remove its military forces in South Korea, and sign a peace treaty once a comprehensive agreement is reached.

The main demands of the US are the denuclearization of the Korean Peninsula, which the Trump administration views as central to any agreement; that North Korea freezes further testing of ballistic missiles; that it immediately ends the development of miniaturized nuclear warheads that could be mounted on intercontinental missiles; and finally, that it rejoins the Non-Proliferation Treaty (NPT) and accepts the most unfettered monitoring regime by the International Atomic Energy Agency (IAEA).

Regardless of how well-intentioned both leaders may be to end the conflict, given the time constraints and the inability of either leader to deal with technological intricacies coupled with an environment completely lacking in trust, the prospective summit cannot and will not resolve these complex issues. Thus, neither side should have any high expectations to reach an agreement in short order. For North Korea and the US, the stakes are high, and the premature collapse of the negotiations could make matters worse, which both sides must avoid. At best, they can pave the way for substantive negotiations that would follow.

Secretary of State Designate and former CIA Director Mike Pompeo is certainly knowledgeable of Kim's position and the nature of relations he wants to forge with South Korea and other states in the area. Although Pompeo is a hardliner and extremely suspicious of the North Korean leader, he must seize this historic opportunity to forge a lasting agreement.

The wild card here is the appointment of John Bolton as National Security Advisor, who is known for his extreme views. He has advocated the abrogation of the Iran deal and the bombing of North Korea to destroy its nuclear arsenals, which could precipitate a horrific war and cause the death of hundreds of thousands of North and South Koreans, Japanese, and Americans, and potentially lead to a much wider regional war.

Pompeo, with the support of Secretary of Defense Mattis, who deeply believes in a diplomatic solution and enjoys Trump's confidence, must disabuse Bolton of his ideas and persuade Trump that **force against North Korea will invite disaster.** Pompeo must, however, be realistic about what can initially be achieved and build on it to reach a lasting agreement. For this reason, he must come to the negotiating table with the understanding that a transitional period of five to seven years will be necessary, during which both sides will have to undertake confidence-building measures to nurture trust and reach interim agreements that deal with various aspects of the conflict, which will eventually lead to denuclearization.

Any initial agreement must meet both sides' initial demands: for North Korea, the lifting of sanctions, albeit gradually, is a central issue, without which it will have no reason to enter any negotiation. For the US, the immediate cessation of any nuclear testing and the freezing of further development of North Korea's intercontinental missiles is the prerequisite to the continuation of the negotiating process.

The talk of war against North Korea, as Bolton has been advocating, must be removed from the lexicon because it is beyond insanity. The solution lies with diplomacy and diplomacy alone, which must be pursued especially now that the conditions to reach an agreement are more favorable than any time before.

The changing dynamic of the conflict in favor of Kim and Trump's aspiration to reach an agreement that his predecessor failed to achieve offer a historic opportunity to end a seventy-year-old conflict that neither leader can afford to squander.

THE DYING IN SYRIA RESTS ON THE
CONSCIENCE OF THE WEST

April 25, 2018

Pesident Trump's characterization of the US attack on specific Syrian chemical storage and research facilities as "mission accomplished" is technically accurate, as the intended targets were in fact destroyed. But declaring mission accomplished in the context of the continuing unfolding tragedy being inflicted on the Syrian people is cynical and disheartening at best. Such an isolated attack does not in any way exempt the US from its moral responsibility to bring an end to a war in which the Syrian people have fallen victim to foreign powers and a deeply corrupt regime. The death and destruction sweeping Syria is incomparable to any other violent conflict since World War II, and America cannot afford to remain silent in the face of these unprecedented atrocities.

The lessons from the disastrous war of choice in Iraq and the prolongation of the war in Afghanistan should not paralyze the US, as was the case under the Obama administration. The US can no longer turn its back on the Syrian people. It must carefully consider the repercussions that America's allies in the region will sustain should Syria be left completely to the whims of Russia, Iran, and Turkey, who met twice in Ankara and are working in unison against the US and its allies' strategic interests in the region.

Given the regional turmoil, the US role is more critical now than it has ever been since the 1970s. Although Russia plays a pivotal role in Syria and its full cooperation is critical in the search for a solution, the US cannot cede Syria completely to Putin's caprices.

The US must now develop a multi-pronged policy that would allow it to assume a more decisive role in the search for a solution to Syria's civil war. Each component of the new policy stands alone, but together they form a comprehensive strategy that must be implemented, however problematic its individual components might be and regardless of how doubtful it is that Trump will in fact act. The risk of doing nothing could plunge the Middle East into a war that will inevitably drag the US into a fight not of its own choosing and under the least favorable circumstances.

First, instead of withdrawing US troops from Syria, Trump must triple the number of US military personnel to achieve three distinct objectives: 1) send a clear message to Russia, Iran, Turkey, and Assad that the US is here to stay and intends to play a significant role in the search for a solution; 2) warn Assad that any further mass attacks on civilians by either conventional or chemical weapons will invite swift American retaliation against many of his military assets, including air fields, hangars, weapons depots, and air defense systems, at a time and place of its own choosing; and 3) prevent the resurgence of ISIS and restore US credibility so that no party will be mistaken about the United States' seriousness.

Second, the US must warn Iran not to seek the establishment of any military bases in Syria, and enlist Russia to exert pressure on Tehran to prevent an Israeli-Iranian conflagration, which can only undermine Russia's influence in Syria. Putin more than likely will be supportive, as he does not want to share the spoils from the civil war in Syria with Iran and Turkey. That said, the US must warn Russia that mass murder by the Syrian government will not be tolerated and that inaction by Russia to rein in Assad will compel the US and its allies to punish Assad, which Russia wants to avoid. Moreover, the US should also make it clear to Russia that should it decide to supply Assad with the S-300 air defense system, as

Russia's Foreign Minister Sergey Lavrov suggested, it will only aggravate the situation, as Israel will not hesitate to attack such a system if it feels threatened by it.

Third, irrespective of the growing strains in relations with Turkey, the US must insist that Turkey's President Erdogan cease any attacks against the Syrian Kurds and withdraw his forces from Syria. The US must stop Turkey from overrunning the Kurds in Syria, and warn Erdogan that fighting the People's Protection Units (YPG, the military arm of the Syrian Kurds) under the pretext of fighting the Kurdistan Workers' Party (PKK) will not be tolerated any longer. The Syrian Kurds have been a most loyal and reliable fighting force against ISIS, and the US has a moral obligation to protect them from Erdogan—a ruthless dictator who seeks to maintain a permanent presence in Syria. This is a part of his larger political Islamization agenda to spread Turkey's influence throughout the region.

Fourth, the US should prevent Assad from regaining full control in Syria unless a transitional government representing all major sects in the country is established, which should be in place for at least five years. Such a government will have to initially be led by Assad, because Russia and Iran need Assad to maintain their "legitimate" presence in the country, and Assad needs them to stay in power, two things about which the US can do little. That said, however, a new leader (who could still be an Alawite) should be elected, as long as the majority Sunni population and the Kurds are adequately represented.

Fifth, the US should now revisit the idea of establishing a no-fly zone east of the Euphrates, and another along the Syrian-Jordanian border. Such protected areas would allow many Syrian refugees to return safely. A no-fly zone enforced by the US and its allies will prevent Assad from attacking areas still held by the rebels and help wind down the daily bloodshed. The point here is that as long as Assad's position is not threatened, he will opt to cooperate, which will also reduce Russian resistance to the establishment of a no-fly zone. It should be noted that Russia is now experiencing war fatigue and may welcome US involvement, which could also improve bilateral relations with Washington, a situation both Putin and Trump seek.

Sixth, Trump must not under any circumstances decertify the Iran deal and instead should seek to renegotiate (with our allies Britain, France, and Germany) some of the provisions related particularly to the sunset clause and present it to Russia and China to gain their support. Otherwise, the decertification of the Iran deal, coupled with the withdrawal of American troops currently in Syria, will be a recipe for a disaster. Such moves will allow Iran to resume its nuclear weapons program, dig in its heels in Syria, and put pressure on other states in the area to pursue their own nuclear weapons programs. This certainly runs contrary to American and particularly Israeli national security interests. Trump must listen to France's President Macron to improve the current deal, and not to the fear-monger Netanyahu, who is too self-absorbed to grasp the dire regional implications of decertifying the deal.

Moreover, decertifying the Iran deal only a few weeks before the planned summit between Trump and North Korea's Chairman Kim Jong Un will severely undermine US credibility. It would send a clear message to the North Korean leader that the US cannot be trusted and may well torpedo any prospective deal between the two sides.

Seventh, for the US to become an active and forceful player in Syria, it must show some compassion toward Syrian refugees. Even though it is difficult for Trump to comprehend that Muslims are not inherently violent or outright terrorists, the US cannot relinquish its moral obligation and behave like a pariah state. Trump must admit to the US a sizeable number of Syrian refugees and restore America's traditional humanitarian stance in providing assistance wherever and whenever it is needed.

In the wake of the horror of World War II, the phrase "Never Again" was coined to suggest that the international community will never allow any country anywhere and at any time **to commit human atrocities with impunity.**

President Obama and now Trump have put America to shame for failing to live up to its moral responsibility as the global leader, by abandoning the Syrian people to a despot and his brutal allies, Russia and Iran.

DECERTIFYING THE IRAN DEAL IS DANGEROUSLY RECKLESS

May 8, 2018

The decertification of the Joint Comprehensive Plan of Action (JCPOA) by Trump is most unfortunate. It seems that Trump was not swayed by either France's President Macron or Germany's Chancellor Merkel to preserve the deal. Instead, he appears to have taken Israeli Prime Minister Netanyahu's advice to decertify it, even though Iran continues to fully adhere to all of its provisions. It is dangerous that neither Trump nor Netanyahu appears to fully grasp the dire regional and international implications of the unilateral decertification of the deal by the US.

In January, Trump gave Britain, France, and Germany an unrealistic deadline—May 12—to fix what he considers the deal's defects, including the sunset clauses under which some of the terms expire, Iran's ballistic missiles program (which was not part of the deal), and the monitoring of suspected Iranian nuclear sites. This was mission impossible without the support of Russia and China, not to speak of the short time frame.

Netanyahu's public stunt, displaying thousands of documents to provide further proof that Iran has been conducting a secret nuclear weapons program, is not new. His claim that the Iran deal was based on information that was not known before does not justify the decertification of the deal, especially because Iran has been fully adhering to all provisions of the deal.

The fact that Iran was pursuing a nuclear weapons program was the main reason behind President Obama's effort to strike the deal. As EU foreign policy chief Federica Mogherini said in Brussels, "the deal was put in place exactly because there was no trust between the parties."[9] Secretary of Defense Mattis echoed precisely the same sentiment, adding that "the verification [procedure] ... is actually pretty robust as far as our intrusive ability to get in."[10]

The deal is certainly far from perfect, but withdrawing from it and starting from scratch may be impossible, especially in light of Iran's vehement refusal to modify the deal, as was expressed by Foreign Minister Zarif: "we will neither outsource our security nor will we renegotiate or add onto a deal we have already implemented in good faith."[11]

The decertification of the deal will force Iran to choose one of two options. The first is to exploit the division between the US and the other signatories. In this case, Tehran could continue to adhere to the provisions of the deal, even though Iran will still suffer from unilateral (but not as severe) American sanctions. Under US law, Trump must wait at least 180 days before imposing their most severe consequences, which includes targeting banks of countries that fail to appreciably cut their oil purchases from Iran.

The second option for Iran is to withdraw from the deal altogether, restart its nuclear weapons program, and potentially even withdraw from the NPT to prevent the monitoring of its nuclear program by the IAEA, which is the worst thing for Israel and other American allies in the region.

The severe disadvantages of decertification

First, most observers agree that Iran would resume its nuclear weapons program, which could quickly lead to the proliferation of nuclear weapons in the Middle East. This would also increase regional tension and a growing sense of insecurity by other countries in the area, which is a recipe for sparking new and further intensifying current violent conflicts.

Second, given the intense enmity between Israel and Iran, the Israeli government might well decide to preemptively attack Iran's nuclear facilities before Tehran reaches the breakout point. This would more than likely lead to an Iranian-Israeli war and pull other countries, including the US, into the fray, which could have dreadful consequences throughout the Middle East.

Third, such development would also deepen Iran's resolve to further entrench itself in Syria, which is precisely what Israel wants to avoid. This too will prompt Israel, as it has done in the past, to attack Iranian military installations in Syria, which could also escalate into a regional conflagration.

Fourth, Iran will have every reason to accelerate its ballistic missile program, which poses a greater danger not only to Israel, but also to US allies throughout the region. In addition, Iran will have further incentive to increase its financial support of extremist groups to destabilize the region, which it has and will continue to exploit.

Fifth, the unilateral withdrawal from the deal by the US will undoubtedly create a schism with US allies, Russia, and China and could foreclose any opening to modify the deal, which Trump failed to consider.

Finally, US credibility will be seriously tarnished with both friends and nemeses, especially at this juncture, when the US is preparing to work out a deal on denuclearization with North Korea's Chairman Kim Jong Un, who would be given a legitimate reason to doubt any American commitment to adhere to future agreements.

The advantages, had the deal been maintained

Iran's threat perception originates from its sense of encirclement, compelling it to pursue a defensive policy. Thus, I believe that Iran would have been willing to renegotiate various provisions of the deal to prevent it from acquiring nuclear weapons now or at any time in the future, only if it was assured that the new deal would first and foremost preserve the regime and that the **US would commit to not seeking regime change now or at any time in the future.**

Given that (other than Iran) there are six signatories to the deal and seven years to go before the first sunset clause expires, Trump, along with the United States' European allies, could have made every effort to enlist Russia and China to fully cooperate. Both powers would have supported a revised deal, as neither wanted the US to withdraw from the deal nor Iran to acquire nuclear weapons.

This would have compelled Iran to take seriously the collective demand, fearing that otherwise joint crippling sanctions will be reinstated, which Tehran wants to prevent at all cost. **Collectively**, they could have exerted far greater influence on Iran to modify the deal and mitigate the US' and regional allies' concerns.

New talks would not have been limited to fixing the current deal, but would have offered Iran a path for normalization of relations with the West. Iran exists and will continue to exist indefinitely. The US and the rest of the international community have every right to demand that Iran end all of its mischievous activities in the region. Similarly, Iran has also the right to govern itself as it sees fit, without fear and intimidation.

Revisiting the Iran deal would have provided a golden opportunity to change the regional dynamic, as long as Iran is ready and willing to play a constructive role to stabilize the region. This should have been the larger goal behind the search for a comprehensive and permanent new deal.

To that end, Tehran could have been required to commence talks about its ballistic missile program as a separate deal or in conjunction with the new talks to modify the current deal. Iran would have been under pressure to temper its bellicose rhetoric, support of violent extremist groups, and cyber hacking campaigns and to end the building of a network of partners and proxies—the "axis of resistance"—which raises regional tensions and could lead to military confrontations.

Moreover, Iran would have been compelled to ease the regional tension in the countries where it is directly or indirectly involved, by taking the initiative to bring an end to the horrifying wars in Yemen and Syria, and keeping Hezbollah and other extremist groups at bay. Iran could have also been induced to stop threatening Israel's existence to reduce the tension and prevent direct confrontation between the two countries, which in fact both sides want to avoid.

Notwithstanding the dreadful mistake of decertification, Trump can keep the deal on life-support if he does not immediately re-impose sanctions and gives the other five powers the time needed to work collectively with Iran and reach a new agreement—one that will chart a new course in the Middle East and potentially mitigate the multiple conflicts in which Iran plays a pivotal role.

Otherwise, we should all brace ourselves for intensified turmoil in the Middle East, thanks to the utter recklessness of Trump and Netanyahu, who failed miserably to realize how horrifying the consequences would be.

WHY US MUST EXPAND, NOT WITHDRAW, FORCES FROM SYRIA

May 29, 2018

I n early April, Trump stated that the US should withdraw its military forces from Syria. Secretary of Defense Mattis seems to have persuaded Trump to postpone this plan for at least six months, citing strategic necessity, with which I fully agree. Beyond that, however, US forces must not only remain in Syria, but be further augmented to make the US a credible player in shaping a permanent solution to the war that ravaged the country, ensuring the security of our allies and stabilizing the region.

We must carefully review the advantages and disadvantages of leaving or staying, especially now that the turmoil in the region is likely to intensify rather than subside in the wake of US withdrawal from the Iran deal. The reasons for staying and further boosting US forces in Syria are manifold.

First, the pull out of US forces within the next six months—at a time when Iran is in the process of establishing several permanent military bases in Syria, loaded with medium and long-range missiles that can reach any part of Israel—**is a recipe for war between Israel and Iran.** Although Israel has and will continue to attack Iranian military installations in Syria, the presence and further augmentation of US forces will in and of itself give credence to the United States' recent demands that Iran leave Syria and stop threatening Israel's existence with impunity.

Second, whether or not Iran continues to adhere to the terms of the nuclear deal, the American withdrawal from it would motivate Iran to **further destabilize the region**, support extremist groups, and accelerate its ballistic missiles program. The question is, will Iran end its malignant activities and walk away from the central pillars of its foreign and security policies, including its involvement in Syria and Yemen? There is no doubt that the continued and enlarged American military presence in Syria would force Tehran to think twice before it further entrenches itself in the country, fearing American retaliation that Iran cannot take lightly.

Third, for decades our allies in the region (the Gulf states, Jordan, and Israel) have and continue to **depend to various degrees on US protection of their national security**. It is true that the US has a huge military and naval presence in the Mediterranean and the Gulf, but America's beefed up presence in Syria, where the real battle for dominance between adversarial powers in the region is taking place, is central. Without American military presence, the US will not be in a position to influence the development of events after the defeat of ISIS. It will be left to Russia, Iran, and, to a lesser extent Turkey, to determine the future of Syria, when in fact American allies in the region will be adversely affected in one form or another by the nature of any outcome.

Fourth, the continuing military presence of the US and its further enlargement will **prevent ISIS from reemerging** in Iraq and Syria. No one should mistake the defeat of ISIS in the battlefield with its ideological durability. They have already emerged in many countries in the Middle East, North Africa, and Europe and remain a menace to America's friends and allies in the region. The United States' military presence on Syrian soil has both practical and symbolic implications that ISIS cannot ignore, given their experience in fighting US forces, which was the most significant factor that led to their ultimate defeat.

Fifth, nothing will deter the main antagonistic players in Syria—the Assad regime, Russia, Iran, and Turkey—other than a robust American military presence. These countries **understand the language of force better than anyone else**. I am not suggesting the US should ready itself to fight against any of these powers. The mere presence of the US, however, sends a clear message that it intends to play a weighty role in the search for a solution that will protect its own national interests and those of its allies.

Sixth, since the advent of the Obama administration and now under Trump, the US by its own inconsequential involvement has sent a clear signal that it has no geostrategic or security interest to be deeply involved in Syria's civil war. The US merely settled on providing marginal financial and limited military training to the rebels in their fight against the Assad regime. This indecisive approach was nothing but a dismal failure. **The absence of American military muscle in Syria has marginalized the US** while allowing Russia, Iran, and Turkey to disregard the US without suffering any consequences.

The absence of a robust American military presence in Syria allowed Iran to play a major role in the country and secure a contiguous landmass from the Gulf to the Mediterranean; gave an entirely free hand to Russia, making it the ultimate arbiter in the country; emboldened Turkey to conduct massive military incursions into Syria aimed at establishing a permanent presence in the country; and raised serious doubts about America's commitment to its allies' security in the region.

This dangerous slide cannot be reversed by simply bombing some of Assad's chemical facilities and storage, as Trump has done twice in the past because of Assad's use of chemical weapons against his own civilians. Although killing nearly four thousand Syrians over the past seven years with chemical weapons is atrocious and beyond the pale, what about the more than 500,000 who were mercilessly slaughtered by conventional weapons?

America's military absence is a factor, and no one who knows the dynamic of the conflict, the power plays, and the continuing volatility of the region can suggest otherwise. Even a cursory review of the conflicts currently raging in the Middle East suggests that the United States' stature is diminishing, and we are much worse off today than we were in the year 2003.

The disastrous Iraq War has massively destabilized the region and we are still suffering from its consequences. The war gave rise to the bitter Sunni-Shiite conflict, handed Iran a golden opportunity to entrench itself in Iraq and subsequently in Syria while playing a significant role in the civil war in Yemen, galvanized the emergence of ISIS, and thrust the Middle East into turmoil, the end of which is far from in sight.

Yes, history is instructive, and the US, regardless of its global geostrategic national interests, cannot involve itself in every conflict. That said, the US must not be paralyzed by past misguided policies. The US has moral and practical obligations to carefully examine each conflict on its own and determine its long and short-term ramifications if we act, and what would happen if we don't.

The US cannot impact the development of events in Syria without a credible and strong military backing to deter any adversary from acting in any way deemed inconsistent with US and our allies' interests. I hope that Secretary of Defense Mattis, who seems to have a clear grasp of the reality in Syria, will convince Trump to embrace this approach and prevail.

As long as America remains on the right side of history and upholds its moral obligations, it will reclaim its global leadership role, which is sorely lacking.

THE FUTURE OF THE EU IN THE
WAKE OF TRUMP'S BETRAYAL

July 19, 2018

My visit to Brussels last week during the NATO annual conference was nothing short of bewildering and dismaying. Trump's rampage against our most trusted and faithful allies sent shivers throughout the city, especially in the halls of the European Parliament where I spent considerable time talking to officials from different countries. They, and just about every other person I spoke with, were shocked to see and hear the President of the United States berating our closest allies, especially Chancellor Merkel of Germany and Britain's Prime Minister May. He treated them as if they were junior business partners who failed to pay their dues while reaping much of the profits. Trump's rage against them was appalling, displaying a complete lack of decency, if not outright hostility.

These are the seventy-year-old allies that stood by us through thick and thin, never wavered, demonstrated utter loyalty, willingly accepted American leadership, and took pride in an alliance that promoted peace and stability while safeguarding the principle tenets of democracy.

With unified resolve and unshakable commitment, they brought about the collapse of the Soviet Union, ushering in an unprecedented period of economic growth and prosperity, while ensuring the national security of every member state and their allies outside Europe.

These are the allies who were the first to respond to the 9/11 attack on New York and Washington by evoking NATO's Article V and stopped short of nothing to provide any aid and support to what they considered their most cherished ally—America—that stood by them in their hours of need throughout the Cold War and beyond.

These are the allies that joined the US campaign against Al-Qaeda in Afghanistan seventeen years ago, and as of this writing, they continue to stand shoulder-to-shoulder with the US even in an unwinnable war that has and continues to exact so much blood and resources. The alliance remains fast and steady in their determination to stand by the United States, which in turn has shown uncontested loyalty to its alliance with the European countries.

These are the allies that joined the US in the Iraq War, and despite how disastrous the war turned out to be, they never hesitated. They have sacrificed men, women, and treasure to the war efforts, and to this day they are still suffering from the consequences of this misguided war—a war that gave birth to ISIS and other violent extremist groups that have been terrorizing Europe while it struggles with waves of refugees flocking to its shores.

These are the allies who supported the US in its efforts to deal with wars and crises in the Middle East, Africa, and Eastern Europe. Regardless of how bad and misguided some of these efforts were, be that in Libya, Syria, Iraq, or the Balkans, they remain consistent in their commitment to stand by America.

Every American president from Truman to Obama honored and took pride in America's historic contribution to the rebuilding of Europe from the ashes of World War II, which led to the emergence of NATO and the European Union.

This was a testimony to America's greatness, shining as the beacon of democracy and human rights and inspiring scores of other nations to emulate it. America and our European allies stood together for what is right and moral, and made huge sacrifices to preserve the new exalted order.

That is, until Trump became the President of the United States. In short order, he shattered this most unique and successful alliance, questioned the value of NATO, and disgraced its leaders. He tore Europe apart and subjected it, along with America, to the whims of the West's harshest enemy, Putin's Russia.

Senator John McCain put it succinctly, stating that Trump made "a conscious choice to defend a tyrant" and presented "one of the most disgraceful performances by an American president in memory."[12] To be sure, Trump betrayed every principle and value the alliance has upheld, which raises a serious question as to what our allies should do now to save the alliance from being completely destroyed as a result of Trump's treachery.

It is hard to imagine that while sharing the stage with an enemy on foreign soil, Trump openly sided with Putin over his own intelligence community's findings about Russia's meddling in the election while overturning decades-long US foreign policy toward Russia only to serve his narrow political interests.

Trump's betrayal of our European allies will be remembered as the darkest chapter in the history of the NATO alliance, and it will not be rectified as long as Trump is in power. Trump's bullying of our most cherished allies last week in Brussels while displaying unreserved respect for the West's foremost nemesis—Putin—was unconscionably disgusting and outlandish, if not a betrayal.

To be sure, James Clapper, the former Director of National Intelligence, called Trump's acquiescence to Putin "an incredible capitulation," and former CIA chief John Brennan characterized it as "nothing short of treasonous."[13]

Due to this erratic behavior, Trump has now provided a historic opportunity for the EU to reassess its role and commitment to its alliance with the US. Whereas the EU must make every effort to preserve the integrity of the alliance, it must strive toward ending its psychological and emotional dependency on the US and anchor the alliance with America on a mutuality of strategic objectives.

That means the EU must be prepared to act unilaterally and independently when its collective national security interest is threatened, with or without the support of the US. The EU will be far more respected by the US and treated *as an equal* by assuming an independent posture, which must be sustained regardless of who occupies the White House.

To that end, the EU ought to develop its own vision of where it wants to be in the next fifteen to twenty years, and what measures it must take to preserve the integrity of the European alliance. The door will remain open for America's leadership under a sane and principled president who understands the far-reaching values of the alliance.

This time, however, the EU should build the political and defense mechanism with all that implies to stand on its own as Germany's Chancellor Merkel has recently stated, and accordingly develop a strategy that will lead it to the realization of such a vision in stages. The EU should obviously be prepared to take any corrective measure and rise to any challenge that may emerge.

Sadly, regardless of how long Trump may last, he has already caused incalculable damage to the Western alliance. The fact is there is a constituency that blindly supports such a misguided leader, which will undoubtedly outlast him and continue to impact American foreign and domestic policy.

As such, the EU cannot rule out potential American policies skewed in favor of "America first" that the Republicans will continue to embrace if they want to remain in power. To counter that, the EU needs, for obvious reasons, to continue to fully adhere to any agreements and treaties agreed upon, in defiance of Trump. The Paris Agreement on climate change and the JCPOA provide good examples.

Independently from the US, the EU ought to strengthen its military capability and acquire credible deterrence against Russia. As such, the EU must remain the most potent military force in Europe within NATO's framework and allocate all necessary funding to that end.

In this regard, the EU should reassess Turkey's reliability and trustworthiness as a member in the Organization and must not rule out kicking Turkey out as long as Ankara defies the NATO charter by its gross human rights violations and its cozying up to Europe's foremost nemesis—Russia.

The EU must also consolidate its institutions by reforming its constitution, particularly the decision-making process to enact timely and more effective policies. This is very important, especially now that it faces turmoil related to Brexit and internal political discord. Furthermore, it must develop a permanent financial structure that addresses the needs of member states experiencing financial difficulties, such as Greece.

The EU should freeze further expansion of its member states until such time when it has realized much of its reforms. Meanwhile, the EU ought to develop and nurture relations with all potential candidates for membership, particularly the Balkan countries, to stifle the ambitions of Turkey's Erdogan from luring these states into his Islamic orbit.

The EU needs also to focus on conflict resolution, especially in the Middle East and Africa, which have a direct and indirect impact on Europe. The EU has direct strategic and security interests to play an active role in the search for a solution to the conflicts in Libya (a byproduct of the European role in toppling Gaddafi) and Yemen and should certainly make continuing efforts to find a solution to the Israeli-Palestinian conflict, however elusive that may seem.

The EU ought to change the nature of the relationship with Africa from simple donor-recipient to playing a direct role in in the growth of underdeveloped African countries—not only because it has a moral obligation resulting from colonialism, but because such efforts serve the EU's own security interests.

A substantial part of the EU's extensive financial contribution to the African Union (over $3 billion since 2004[14]) should be devoted to sustainable development projects to provide job opportunities and empower local communities. This is the most effective way of addressing the root causes of violent extremism and migration, from which the EU suffers greatly.

Trump has become a marionette manipulated by a master puppeteer, Putin. He can no longer be trusted to serve either America's or our allies' interests. To be sure, Trump will face the judgment of the American electorate, hopefully sooner rather than later, and the historically indispensable alliance with our European partners will be restored.

THE DEAL OR THE DEBACLE OF THE CENTURY?

September 21, 2018

As we wait for Trump to unveil his plan to reach an Israeli-Palestinian peace agreement, he has in fact made the prospect of achieving "the deal of the century" far more remote than it was already. His recognition of Jerusalem as Israel's capital has enraged the Palestinians, who decided to suspend any further negotiations with his administration. Every subsequent punitive measure Trump has taken against the PA to coerce them to resume talks made matters only worse. Instead of enhancing the chances for a peace agreement, he severely undermined them.

Trump's recognition of Jerusalem as Israel's capital and relocating the American embassy from Tel Aviv to West Jerusalem could have dramatically advanced the peace process had he also stated that the US will also establish an American embassy to Palestine in East Jerusalem once a peace agreement is reached between the two sides.

In his statement, he left open the question of the final borders that separate East from West Jerusalem to be decided between the two parties. The Palestinians would have welcomed the American move had he also promised to establish an embassy to Palestine, which would have signaled that he was indeed committed to reaching a peace accord based on a two-state solution—but he never was.

Trump's unilateral action, however, did not simply remove the conflict over Jerusalem off the negotiating table, as he nonchalantly stated. It only suggested that he lacks any appreciation of the Palestinians' affinity toward Jerusalem. As a result, he made the prospect of finding a mutually accepted solution over Jerusalem extraordinarily difficult. Basically, Trump granted Netanyahu his greatest wish without demanding anything in return to push the peace process forward.

Cutting the financial aid from UNRWA was another major missed opportunity to resolve the Palestinian refugee problem. It is true that UNRWA's mandate should have been terminated decades ago, as it has directly and indirectly perpetuated the refugee problem. Everyone knows that the Palestinian refugees will never be able to exercise "the right of return," and everyone who investigated the problem would attest that the vast majority of the refugees themselves do not expect or want to return, even if given the choice.

That said: refugees have rights, which must be addressed if there is to be a solution to the Israeli-Palestinian conflict. Thus, instead of denying UNRWA future aid, Trump should have stated the obvious: that a solution to the refugee problem rests entirely on resettlement and/or compensation. To that end, Trump could have stated that UNRWA's functions should come to an end, say within two years, and in the interim, the US along with the EU and the oil-rich Arab states would raise an initial amount of $10 billion dedicated exclusively for refugee resettlement and/or compensation.

It is true that the Palestinians refuse to give in on the *principle* of the right of return, but this would become easier to address in the context of the resettlement/compensation process, and as hundreds of thousands of refugees resettle in their own country in the West Bank and Gaza. Current refugees in these areas are *de facto* internally displaced persons (IDPs), and their resettlement and/or compensation should begin there.

The third terrible mistake was Trump's decision to punish the PA by ending US financial aid (except for internal security) to force Abbas to come to the negotiating table. Here too, Trump has demonstrated a complete ignorance of the PA's mindset and Abbas's tenuous position at this particular juncture. True, the PA is in desperate need of financial aid, but for the Palestinians, Trump's punitive action did nothing but strengthen their resolve not to come to the negotiating table *crawling*.

The Palestinians have pride; they will struggle and even starve before they surrender to Trump's totally ill-advised action. Even if Abbas were to relent, I doubt very much that he could survive the ire of the Palestinians in the street, who would rightly feel bullied by Trump, and that their legitimate cause was trashed for money without yet any prospect of reaching a peace agreement with dignity.

Instead, Trump could have improved the chances for peace had he increased the financial aid and encouraged the PA to focus on building the infrastructure of a state. This, in combination with other measures, could have persuaded the Palestinians that Trump is serious, which would have doubtless made the PA far more receptive to his proposed peace plan.

Cutting $25 million in aid to Palestinian hospitals in East Jerusalem[15] may seem like an insignificant amount, but it's a huge sum for the underfunded hospitals that are in dire need of more financial aid. In which way could such an act possibly be seen as anything but mean-spirited and indifferent toward the sick and disabled Palestinians receiving essential, if not live-saving, medical treatment?

Ironically, many of the patients seeking medical help in these hospitals are those who are injured as a result of reckless, if not deliberate, injury inflicted by Israeli soldiers or settlers. By what logic then will depriving Palestinian hospitals of badly needed financial aid advance the peace process or compel the PA to beg for help?

In contrast to this inhumane act, Trump should have announced his intent to double the financial aid to these hospitals, to help them buy advanced medical equipment and attract more experienced and skilled doctors, which would have conveyed to the PA his concerns and empathy toward their needs.

Finally, ordering the closure of the Palestinian mission in Washington is probably the straw that broke the camel's back. Under any circumstance, a continuing dialogue with the Palestinians is necessary if for no other reason but to keep the diplomatic channels open for both practical and symbolic reasons.

How could the closure of the Palestinian mission help the peace process? This step is in total contrast to one of the main principles of conflict resolution. Leaving the Palestinian mission open would at a minimum suggest that not all doors are shut, especially following all other punitive measures that Trump has thoughtlessly taken.

The eerie thing about all this is that Netanyahu has been cheering Trump as if all the punitive measures are good for Israel. As much as the Palestinians are hurting and may well continue to suffer for many years to come, the longer the Israeli-Palestinian conflict persists, the greater the damage Israel will sustain.

Trump, more than any of his predecessors, has enabled Israel, especially under Netanyahu's leadership, to further entrench itself in the West Bank, deny the Palestinians their human rights, pass racist laws that openly discriminate against the Palestinians, and methodically chip away at what's left of a two-state solution.

We are still waiting for the unveiling of Trump's grandiose peace plans, which by all accounts is tailor-made to suit Netanyahu's vision that precludes a Palestinian state. As such, Trump's "deal of the century" will be recalled as the debacle of the century, condemning the Israeli-Palestinian conflict to decades more deepening distrust, intensified hatred, and bloodshed, which may well put an end to any prospect of a two-state solution.

AMERICA MUST NOT LIVE AND DIE BY THE GUN

November 9, 2018

When I woke up yesterday morning, I was shocked yet again to read about Wednesday's mass killing of twelve people during "college night" at a country music bar in southern California, sending hundreds fleeing in terror. I have young adult children who occasionally visit these types of bars, and I can only imagine how devastating and heart-wrenching it must be for any parent to lose a child to this heartless mass shooting phenomenon, which has tragically become routine.

All we hear from Trump and his stooges in Congress are hollow and insincere expressions of sorrow and condolences to the families of the victims whose lives are shattered. Like millions of citizens, I am offended by the callous way the Trump administration deals with this national disaster that robs the lives of more than three thousand innocent fellow citizens every single month.

To be sure, America is at war with itself, and the NRA is profiting from the slaughter of Americans by Americans. Our so-called lawmakers in Congress are benefitting from the political contributions the NRA generously hands out to these corrupt politicians, who couldn't care less that we are paying with our blood.

Every time the question of gun control is raised, the defenders of Wild West culture—of living by the gun—rush to invoke the Second Amendment, which supposedly grants every American the right to bear arms for self-protection. I say supposedly, because when this amendment was enacted, we were living in a different time under different circumstances and had a different responsibility to protect ourselves and our loved ones.

The Second **Amendment** of the United States **Constitution** reads: "A well-regulated Militia, being necessary to the security of a free State, the right of the people to keep and bear Arms, shall not be infringed." Today, we have "a well-regulated militia" in the form of the National Guard; we also have police forces to protect our inner cities, the FBI to investigate statewide and interstate crimes, and of course the military. The responsibility of each branch of our collective security is well defined, and they are accountable to a specific command structure.

Now given the changing order of our personal and collective security, the part of the Second Amendment that reads "the right of the people to keep and bear Arms, shall not be infringed," also needs to be reinterpreted. We are not calling for a total ban on gun ownership; we are calling for stricter gun control laws on the right to possess a firearm, including of course a background check of any individual who wishes to purchase a gun.

According to the Centers for Disease Control, there were thirty-nine thousand deaths from gun-related injuries in 2016. Of this, 456 were from mass shootings—the rest were fourteen thousand homicide deaths and twenty-three thousand suicides.[16] The gun lobby asserts that these statistics have little bearing on the number of people killed deliberately by mass shootings. True, but if guns were not readily accessible, how many of these people would have successfully committed suicide by stabbing or hanging themselves, or by swallowing deadly poison? While drowning, for example, is effective 66 percent of the time in attempted suicides, suicide by gun is effective 82 percent of the time.[17]

Since November 2016, ten mass shootings have taken place, resulting in 152 deaths. A mass shooting here is defined by the Congressional Research Service, where a shooter a) kills four or more people, b) selects victims randomly, and c) attacks in a public place. In a looser definition (four or more people shot but not necessarily killed at the same time and location, which includes incidents related to domestic violence and gang violence), 314 people have been killed in mass shootings in 2018.[18]

Just think, nearly one-third of the mass shootings that occur in the world have taken place in the United States: a country with 5 percent of the world's population has 31 percent of all public mass shootings.[19]

There is indisputable proof that the number of people who died of gunshot wounds in every single developed nation is minuscule when compared to the US. Take a look at some countries with strict gun laws; their **annual** rate of death by firearms speaks for itself. In the United Kingdom, with a population of fifty-six million, on average fifty to sixty are killed; in Germany with a population of 82.29 million, an average of 165; and in Japan with a population of 129 million, thirteen or (often) fewer are killed by guns.[20]

In Australia, before enacting strict gun control laws in 1996 following the deadliest mass shooting in Australian history, there were thirteen mass shootings in eighteen years. In the same time period following the legislation, there were zero.[21]

Let's set statistics aside. Every person that dies as a result of a gunshot is one person too many. How do you console a father or a mother who lost their child without even knowing why? What do you say to a parent whose child was just gunned down, to alleviate their agony and sinking soul? What sort of condolences and prayer can you offer to assuage the penetrating pain that sucks out the parent's heart? There are no words, no expressions, no prayer, no sympathy, and no condolences that can ease the consuming suffering and grief that a parent must endure.

The answer, Mr. Trump, is not placing armed guards in every restaurant, night club, bar, school, synagogue, church, amusement park, museum, movie theater, bank, hospital, store, hotel, train and bus station, and on every street corner. No, this is not how we should live our lives.

No, we cannot, and we will not succumb to your and Congress' whims to prevent effective gun control laws. And we will no longer live and die by the gun.

THE DEMOCRATS' VICTORY CAN
SAVE THE REPUBLICAN PARTY

November 15, 2018

The retaking of the House by the Democrats will soon allow them to exercise checks and balances and stop the Republicans from going down a slippery slope. Otherwise, the party would have slid into complete self-implosion as they blindly but willingly followed Trump's chaotic political agenda. During the past two years, Trump and his party have rendered the country a severe disservice with massive domestic and international implications. Partisanship became the norm, and the party's abdication of its oversight role over the executive branch has allowed Trump to pursue policies that defy logic and reality, to the detriment of the United States.

With the exception of a few Republican Congressmen who decided not to seek reelection, the vast majority of the Republican Party leadership have become totally subservient to, if not enslaved by, the president. They have remained largely silent about his regular maligning of our friends and allies, his racism and outbursts against people of color, his sweeping opposition to immigration, his Islamophobic attitude, his defiance of climate change, his deliberate polarization, his repeated lies and misleading statements, his shameless attacks on the press and any perceived or real opponents, his fear mongering, his vulgarity, and his demeaning attitude toward women.

Yes, the Republican Party lost its soul, and two more years in control of both the House and Senate would have caused irreparable damage to the US both internationally and domestically. Ironically, the Democrats' victory may well pull the Republican Party away from Trump's spell and save it from its own self-destructive path.

I believe that it will be a major mistake for the Democrats to even contemplate the impeachment of Trump, not only because it will not pass the Republican Senate, but because it will further galvanize his base and allow the Republicans in the House and Senate to regroup behind the president.

The fact that the House will soon be under Democratic control offers Republicans the chance to redeem themselves by working across the aisle to begin the process of healing a dangerously divided country. Under any circumstances, however, the Democrats must focus on four major crises facing the nation that have a direct and indirect impact on every American.

Healthcare:

Making healthcare a central issue in the midterm election was a winning strategy, precisely because healthcare is a fundamental issue for every American. Healthcare, to be sure, **is a basic human right** that must be granted by either the federal government or the state. It is nothing short of a travesty for any American, regardless of age and preexisting conditions, not to have accessible and reliable healthcare.

The Democrats must remain relentless in pushing for comprehensive healthcare legislation, particularly revising the ACA in the context of universal healthcare, and invite the Republicans to support it. The prospect for success and the potential for failure, should the Republicans decide to oppose it, will serve the Democrats' interests come 2020.

Immigration:

The source of America's greatness is in its people and their backgrounds, sets of beliefs, cultural riches, diversity, and differing resourcefulness that immigrants bring with them, which together made America not only great, but also unique. The Democrats must present all-encompassing immigration laws that will address the millions of undocumented immigrants, DACA recipients, asylum seekers, and the regular flow of legal immigrants, and finally pass the DREAM Act.

Regardless of Trump's disdain for immigrants of color, the demographic composition of America is changing. Black, Hispanic, and Asian Americans will comprise the majority within three decades,[22] a trend that Trump cannot stop, and his embrace of white supremacists is a stain on America. Republicans must make their choice, and the Democrats must press for what America stood for as the country of immigrants.

Climate change:

It is time for the Republican Party to wake up to the indisputable scientific evidence that climate change is a reality that must urgently be addressed. Indeed, only totally ignorant and morally corrupt people do not recognize that climate change is already upon us. The unprecedented ferocity of fires (particularly recently in California), hurricanes, tsunamis, rising sea levels, and pervasive destruction of the coral reefs are a direct result of climate change and are obvious for all to see.

Environmental deregulation is criminal and no Republican, including the president, has the right to contaminate our air, water, and land only to make the rich richer. The Democrats must make climate change a national emergency and leave no stone unturned to ensure that no business can financially benefit from deregulation, at the expense of the health and well-being of every American, who will suffer greatly from chronic diseases related to climate change. Rejoining the Paris Agreement will offer a good start.

Infrastructure:

The fourth thing the Democrats must focus on is the disastrous conditions of infrastructure throughout the country. Roads and bridges are crumbling, with over fifty-four thousand bridges rated structurally deficient;[23] more than two out of five interstate roads and highways are over capacity and can no longer accommodate the massive congestion, which is consuming more fuel and costing the economy $120 billion annually.[24] Thousands of small and medium-size towns are disintegrating and are in need of major revitalization. Moreover, the country's railway network is in sorry condition, vastly underfunded and cobbled together with freight and commuter rail lines, putting us to shame compared to countries like China, Japan, and most European states.

The Democrats must remain unyielding until infrastructure legislation passes. The Republican Senate will be hard-pressed not to work with the Democrats on such a critical bipartisan bill as 2020 hovers on the horizon.

The Democrats' focus on these four major national projects (as well as education and gun control) is central to maintaining the viability of the party. This is precisely what's needed to change the lives of ordinary Americans for the better, instead of demonizing the Republicans. The Democrats' victory in the House offers Republicans in the Senate an opportunity to redeem themselves by collaborating with Democrats on major issues that face the nation and saving their party from disintegration.

In 2020, the Democrats should be running on their achievements, or at a minimum, on their genuine efforts to deal with issues of great concern and urgency to the American people, and clearly demonstrate that the national interests take precedent over party politics.

A TWO-PRONGED POLICY NEEDED TO
STEM THE FLOW OF MIGRANTS

December 6, 2018

Dramatically slowing the flow of illegal immigration or even ending it will not rest on building walls, sending troops to the border, heartlessly snatching children from their mothers' arms, incarceration, deportation, or prosecution. A big part of the answer lies in economic development, mainly sustainable development projects, within the migrant's country of origin. Indeed, instead of building walls, we need to build the kind of bridges that can change the lives of other people for the better and give them hope. After all, the political destabilization in Central American countries was in part, if not to a great extent, precipitated by the United States, which makes America even more morally responsible to do something about it.

Beyond that, abject poverty and hopelessness breeds resentment and despondency and leads to gang violence and extremism, which is only the natural outcome of these subhuman conditions. Little will change unless the people, especially the youth, are given an opportunity to live a normal and productive life, develop a sense of belonging, and have vested interests in their work and self-worth.

The plight of three Central American countries tells the story behind the influx of immigrants flocking to our country from these and other countries.

Honduras is Central America's second-poorest country. More than 60 percent of the population lives in poverty, and it has one of the highest levels of economic inequality in Latin America. Poverty in Honduras is chiefly due to rampant crime, violence, political instability, corruption, and a significant susceptibility to hurricanes and droughts.

Guatemala has the largest economy in Central America, but despite recent growth, economic inequality and poverty have increased, particularly among the rural Indigenous population. Malnutrition and maternal mortality rates are among the worst in Latin America, especially in Indigenous areas. More than half of the population lives below the poverty line.

El Salvador has one of the lowest economic growth rates in Central America. Since the end of its civil war in 1992, the country has made progress in terms of political and social development, but high rates of crime and violence continue to threaten these gains. El Salvador is also vulnerable to adverse natural events, which is only made worse by extreme climate change.

In these countries, rural poverty places great stress on cities and ultimately propels immigration, and as long as it does, the enormous economic and political instability that it creates will continue.

Trump's demand of $20 billion to build a wall along the Mexican border is misguided, impractical, and a waste of precious resources that could change the lives of millions of people if invested wisely in these poverty-stricken countries. Does Trump know how cost-effective it is to promote people's projects within the country of origin?

A fraction of $20 billion would change the socioeconomic conditions in these countries. One billion dollars invested in economic development projects could provide food, drinking water, jobs, self-empowerment, and hope for better life for a million poor, displaced, and despairing people.

According to Dr. Yossef Ben-Meir, President of the High Atlas Foundation in Morocco and a twenty-year veteran in sustainable development, a $100,000 investment can establish a women's co-operative of approximately fifty members benefitting approximately 300-350 people. "The outstanding investment needed ends up being a relatively small proportion of the cost the nations that receive or repel migrants incur."[25]

In Guatemala, for example, WINGS Guatemala, an organization working on family planning in 2017 alone prevented over fourteen thousand unwanted pregnancies, ninety-five child deaths, and six maternal deaths, all with only $880,000.

It has unequivocally been shown that would-be immigrants strongly prefer to stay in their home communities if their basic needs are met and there are opportunities for growth. Under those circumstances, they work hard to ensure the sustainability of projects they choose and develop vested interests in their implementation and outcomes.

It should be noted that the principle of economic development is the same, be that in countries in South America or Africa; only the nature and the type of project differs from one country or community to another, depending on their special needs. Here is where we must invest, to give people a chance not only for their sake, but ours as well, because America flourishes when other people in far lands flourish too.

Economic investments and the implementation of sustainable development projects don't mean that all illegal immigration will stop. We still need a comprehensive immigration policy consistent with our tradition of receiving migrants with open arms—a sensible and companionate policy that governs all aspects of migration to America.

We should end DREAMers' painful instability by offering a path to citizenship to the nearly one million individuals who came to the US when they were children. They are Americans in their hearts and souls; they are here to stay, and we have a solemn obligation to remove any cloud of uncertainty about their future.

We must resolve once and for all the problem of the over twelve million undocumented immigrants who have been in the country for years and have become an integral part of America's social fabric. They should be assured that they will not be deported and will be offered a path to citizenship if they voluntarily register—a one-time amnesty program.

We must enforce established procedures to deal with refugees and asylum seekers, not ignore or completely violate them as the Trump administration has cruelly done—a decent process that allows safety for those who are escaping the horror of violence and would face certain death if turned back.

And finally, existing programs for legal immigration, including the Diversity Immigrant Visa Program, family reunification, and employment-based immigration, should be fully implemented. The Trump administration should be prevented from undermining these processes that have been in place for many years.

America has and must continue to welcome immigrants of all colors, denominations, and countries. Each and every new migrant, regardless of his or her background, brings with them the riches of their culture, talents, and skills and is ultimately economically beneficial to the United States, not a drain.

There is something magical about America. It is a country that has opened its doors to immigrants from the world over, and the wider the door has been open, the better and greater America has become. But sadly, Trump's racist, Islamophobic, and white supremacist DNA has made an even greater mess of the already unsavory, incoherent, and partisan policy and methods in addressing the problem of immigration.

The solution to illegal immigration must be based on a two-pronged policy. First, America must invest in economic development projects *through private entities* to alleviate poverty and substantially reduce violence, which would also encourage other countries to invest. Second, it must develop a comprehensive immigration policy consistent with our tradition and moral obligation to extend our hands to those whose only sin is escaping the horrors of war, violence, and starvation.

The simultaneous implementation of this two-tiered policy would, within a relatively short period of time, significantly reduce the influx of migrants to our borders while developing the socioeconomic conditions to allow the inhabitants of these countries to stay put and build a hopeful future in their homeland.

IT'S TIME FOR CONGRESSWOMEN
TO TAKE THE LEAD

December 13, 2018

The election of a record number of women to Congress is significant in that Congresswomen are more likely to focus on socioeconomic and gender-based issues that have largely been either ignored or resisted by a predominantly male Congress. The fact that nearly 25 percent of the House and Senate are now women means their voices can no longer be ignored, as they will have the power to block any legislation that are inconsistent with their set of beliefs and priorities, within their own party. As such, women legislators can be extraordinarily effective because they were elected largely on the premise they would be focused on socioeconomic issues of great concern to their constituents.

Women are more attuned to these issues for several reasons, including social conditioning and culture, where the expectation is on women to be primary caregivers. Additionally, women's role as part of a marginalized community makes them more empathetic to injustices, as women have a long history of being treated as second-class citizens.

There are numerous significant issues that sadly have not been effectively addressed by either the Democrats or Republicans over the past ten years, which Congresswomen can now focus on. Although some such legislative initiatives may take place under a Democratically-controlled House, the Republican Senate is unlikely to adopt them. Nevertheless, the mere fact that these issues are debated in the House will engender important public support, which will significantly aid the Democrats in the run-up to the 2020 elections.

Child poverty: Legislation should be introduced by Congresswomen to deal with the growing travesty of 6.5 million children living in extreme poverty throughout the United States. Many of these children go to sleep hungry, live in squalor, and are unable to attend school on a regular basis. It is hard to fathom that this terrible phenomenon exists in the United States, one of the richest countries in the world.

Appropriating the necessary funding to tackle this issue over a period of three to five years is critical, not only for the children themselves, but for

America as a country. Indeed, the difference between a poor and uneducated child versus a better fed and educated one has serious social and political repercussions that we cannot afford to ignore.

Equal pay for equal work: Congresswomen should introduce legislation to close the gender pay gap in the workplace. There is absolutely no reason why women who perform equal tasks to any man should receive a considerably lower salary or be passed over for promotions solely based on gender.

The statistics in this regard are startling. On the whole, white women earn only 80 cents to every dollar a man makes; African American women earn 61 cents, Native American women earn 58 cents, and Hispanic women earn only 53 cents to every dollar a man makes.[26] Similar pay disparities exist between white men and men of color.

This issue should be debated to create public awareness, and legislative guidelines should be provided to promote equality and forge an easier legal path for aggrieved women in this area in order to rectify the discrimination.

Reproductive rights: Another issue of great concern to women is the absurdity that a predominantly male Congress presumes it has the right to determine what women can or cannot do with their bodies. A woman's decision to bear children should be her and *only* her prerogative with no outside interference, other than within the family. Prohibiting, cutting funding, and preventing access to Planned Parenthood must totally be outside the domain of federal legislation.

For the Republicans, preventing women from determining their own reproductive future because they seek the political support of evangelicals and other conservative groups borders on insanity. Congresswomen must bring this issue to the fore now, specifically because the current Republican Senate's disgraceful rejection of any reform in this regard can now be challenged by House Democrats. Congresswomen must fight to ensure that *Roe v. Wade* is never tampered with.

Minimum wage: Congresswomen should fight to raise the minimum wage. It is simply incomprehensible that since 2009, the federal minimum wage (which was "designed to create a minimum standard of living to protect the health and well-being of employees"[27]) has not been raised from $7.25. The annual sum of this for a full-time employee would roughly be $11-12,000 after taxes, which is below the poverty threshold. To suggest that a family of four, with both parents working, can survive on this amount is unfathomable.

The Republican Party, which passed major tax cuts that provided billions to the rich, pretends that those benefits will trickle down to the poor, who have basically received no benefit whatsoever, and yet those legislators still resist raising the minimum wage. Congresswomen ought to push for legislation to increase the minimum wage to $15, which will allow the poorest to have three meals a day, rather than go to sleep hungry.

Gun control: Congresswomen should push for gun control laws to end the epidemic of mass shootings, homicide, and suicide by firearms, which kill on average thirty-nine thousand people per year.[28] In the United States, it's estimated there is in excess of 390 million firearms, more than one for every American.[29] It's time to wake up to this miserable reality. New Congresswomen, such as Lucy McBath of Georgia's Sixth District, who ran on a gun reform platform, can make this a top priority.

The answer to gun violence is certainly not arming teachers or placing armed guards in every private or public institution. As it is, the current level of security feels like a military camp everywhere one goes. What needs to be done is to make background checks required, support gun buyback programs, restrict private sales of weapons, reinstate the federal assault weapons ban, remove restrictions on suing gun manufacturers, pass campaign finance reform to limit campaign contributions from lobbyists including the NRA, and raise the age to purchase a weapon, to twenty-one at a minimum, but ideally to twenty-five years old.

Opioid addiction: Women legislators should introduce legislation to provide states with specific funding to battle the epidemic of opioid addiction, which disproportionately affects women. In 2017, nearly seventy-two thousand Americans died from overdoses, more than any previous year.[30]

Some steps to combat addiction include providing funding for access to treatment, tightening FDA rules on prescription drugs, introducing campaign finance reform limiting contributions from pharmaceutical companies, providing job opportunities and education, and ending the "war on drugs," which accomplished nothing and created a false sense that we were actually combating drug crimes.

Prison reform: Another shameful reality is that in the United States, over two million people are in prisons and the conditions under which many are held are appalling. Sixty-six percent of all prisoners are non-violent offenders, hundreds of thousands are in prison for misdemeanors, and one in five prisoners are locked up for minor drug offenses.[31]

This prison system costs $182 billion each year. More than fifty thousand women are in prison for non-violent offenses; most incarcerated are the mothers of children under eighteen.[32] Their sentences should be reviewed and either dramatically reduced or immediately released. Concurrently, programs should be established to provide guidance, job opportunities, education, and transitional housing.

Moreover, juvenile detention centers should be primarily rehabilitative, not punitive, and professional training should be given. The failure of previous administrations of either party to deal with this is unforgiveable. Women legislators ought to raise this issue because it has a major impact on family stability, providing a more positive future and beginning the process of healing communities.

None of the above suggests that women legislators should not be involved in defense and foreign policy. But since most Congressmen from both parties have miserably failed to address these critical social issues, Congresswomen must now take the lead and use their newly found power to make a real difference in the lives of millions of Americans.

TRUMP'S NEW YEAR'S GIFT TO PUTIN, ROUHANI, AND ERDOGAN

December 21, 2018

Trump's decision to withdraw US forces from Syria is extremely reckless and is bound to backfire in more than one way. To make such a decision, which has major implications that directly and adversely affect our allies in and outside the region, through a simple tweet *and* against the advice of his senior advisors is nothing short of outrageous. This is the most valuable New Year's gift that Trump could possibly give Russia, Iran, Hezbollah, and Turkey. What on earth did he base his decision on? From every angle we examine it, there seems to be absolutely no good that could possibly come out of it.

In fact, our forces should not only remain in Syria but be further augmented to secure our and our allies' short- and long-term national interests throughout the region. The reasons for staying and even further boosting US forces in Syria are manifold.

The pullout of US forces at a time when Iran is in the process of establishing several permanent military bases in Syria, loaded with medium and long-range missiles that can reach any part of Israel, is a recipe for war between Israel and Iran. The American withdrawal will motivate Iran to further destabilize the region; support extremist groups, especially Hezbollah; and accelerate its ballistic missiles program. More importantly, it will allow Iran to secure a contiguous landmass from the Gulf to the Mediterranean.

Every military observer strongly suggests that the continued American military presence in Syria would force Tehran to think twice before it further entrenches itself in the country, fearing American retaliation that Iran cannot take lightly.

For decades, our allies in the region (the Gulf states, Jordan, and Israel) have and continue to depend to various degrees on US protection of their national security. The US military presence in Syria is central and without it, Russia, Iran, and Turkey would further destabilize the region and force America's allies to suffer the consequences from the vacuum that we would leave behind, which our adversaries would be quick to fill.

Furthermore, Trump's claim that ISIS has been defeated and that our mission is accomplished is nothing but a bald-faced lie. ISIS is still very much alive and the US military presence in Syria has both practical and symbolic implications that cannot be ignored. It is estimated that between fifteen and twenty thousand fighters remain in the region, and scores of sleeper cells exist throughout the Middle East and Europe. But sadly, given Trump's domestic troubles, he is desperate for a win, however presumptuous and uncanny, just before the end of the year. Only a sick person, such as this president, would sell his country down the river to satisfy his inflated ego.

More troubling than anything else, Trump shamelessly betrayed one of our closest allies in the fight against ISIS—the Syrian Kurds (YPG). By his unconscionable decision, he left their fate to the butcher of Ankara—Erdogan—who is determined to battle the Syrian Kurds into submission while aiming to establish a permanent presence in the country.

Nothing will deter the main antagonistic players in Syria—the Assad regime, Russia, Iran, and Turkey—other than a robust American military presence. For these countries, the mere American presence sends a clear message that in regards to Syria, the US intends to play a significant role in the search for a solution to the civil war that will protect not only its own national interests, but also those of its allies.

America's military absence is a factor, and no one who knows the dynamic of the conflict, the power plays, and the continuing volatility of the region can claim otherwise. Even a cursory review of the conflicts currently raging in the Middle East suggests that the United States' stature is diminishing, and we are much worse off today than we were in 2003.

The absence of American military muscle in Syria would further marginalize the US while allowing Russia, Iran, and Turkey to disregard the US without suffering any consequences and give Russia an entirely free hand, making it the ultimate arbiter in the country.

History is instructive, and the US, regardless of its global geostrategic national interests, cannot involve itself in every conflict. That said, the US must not be paralyzed by past misguided policies. But if we must withdraw our forces from any country, after seventeen years it should be Afghanistan, where we are fighting a simply unwinnable war, no matter how much money and manpower we continue to dedicate to the war effort against the Taliban.

The US cannot impact the development of events in Syria without a credible and strong military backing to deter any adversary from acting with impunity in any way deemed inconsistent with the United States' and our allies' strategic interests.

Trump's haphazard and thoughtless decision to withdraw forces from Syria points only to his abdication of the United States' moral responsibility, not to speak of its global leadership, which has been dangerously waning under his disastrous policies.

Notes

1   Mitt Romney, Facebook post, Aug. 18, 2017, 9:12 a.m., https://www.facebook.com/mittromney/.

2   Jon Henley, "Angela Merkel: EU cannot Completely Rely on US And Britain any More," *The Guardian*, May 28, 2017, https://www.theguardian.com/world/2017/may/28/merkel-says-eu-cannot-completely-rely-on-us-and-britain-any-more-g7-talks.

3   "Rating World Leaders: 2018," *Gallup*, 2018, https://www.politico.com/f/?id=00000161-0647-da3c-a371-867f6acc0001.

4   "Key Statistics," *Brady Campaign to End Gun Violence,* accessed February 15, 2018, https://www.bradyunited.org/key-statistics; "iCasualties Iraq," *Iraq Coalition Casualty Count,* accessed February 15, 2018, http://icasualties.org/.

5   Jugal K. Patel, "After Sandy Hook, More than 400 People have been Shot in over 200 School Shootings," *New York Times*, Feb. 15, 2018, https://www.nytimes.com/interactive/2018/02/15/us/school-shootings-sandy-hook-parkland.html.

6   Ricardo Torres-Cortez, "Sheriff: Person of Interest Part of Strip Shooting Probe; Paddock had Child Porn," *Las Vegas Sun*, Jan. 19, 2018, https://lasvegassun.com/news/2018/jan/19/sheriff-to-provide-update-about-strip-mass-shootin/; "Florida School Shooting Ranks among America's Deadliest," *CBS News*, accessed Feb. 15, 2018, https://www.cbsnews.com/news/florida-school-shooting-ranks-among-americas-deadliest/.

7   Jane Onyanga-Omara, "Gun Violence Rare in U.K. Compared to U.S.," *USA Today*, Jun. 16, 2016, https://www.usatoday.com/story/news/world/2016/06/16/gun-violence-united-kingdom-united-states/85994716/; Kevin Quealy and Margot Sanger-Katz, "Comparing Gun Deaths by Country: The U.S. is in a Different World," *New York Times*, Jun. 13, 2016, https://www.nytimes.com/2016/06/14/upshot/compare-these-gun-death-rates-the-us-is-in-a-different-world.html.

8   Maggie Fox, "No Mass Shootings in Australia in 20 Years: How did They do It?," *NBC News*, Jun. 22, 2016, https://www.nbcnews.com/health/health-news/no-mass-shootings-australia-20-years-how-did-they-do-n597091.

9   "Response by HR/VP Mogherini Regarding Israeli Prime Minister Netanyahu's Presentation on Iran," European Union External Action, Apr. 30, 2018, https://eeas.europa.eu/headquarters/headquarters-Homepage/43768/response-hrvp-mogherini-regarding-israeli-prime-minister-netanyahu%E2%80%99s-presentation-iran_es.

10 "Mattis Breaks with Trump, Says Iran Nuclear Deal Includes 'Robust' Verification," *Haaretz*, Apr. 26, 2018, https://www.haaretz.com/middle-east-news/iran/mattis-says-iran-nuclear-deal-includes-robust-verification-1.6032581.

11 Parisa Hafezi, "Iran Says will Not Renegotiate Nuclear Deal, Warns against Changes," *Reuters*, May 3, 2018, https://www.reuters.com/article/us-iran-nuclear-usa/iran-says-will-not-renegotiate-nuclear-deal-warns-against-changes-idUSKBN1I41CO.

12 Katie Reilly, "John McCain Calls Trump's Press Conference with Putin 'One of the Most Disgraceful Performances by an American President,'" *Time*, Jul. 16, 2018, https://time.com/5339932/john-mccain-statement-trump-putin-meeting/.

13 "US Lawmakers Blast 'Shameful' Trump after Helsinki Summit with Putin," *France24*, Jul. 17, 2018, https://www.france24.com/en/20180717-usa-russia-lawmakers-blast-shameful-trump-helsinki-summit-putin-republicans-democrats.

14 "Financing the Partnership," *The Africa-EU Partnership*, accessed Jul. 16, 2018, https://africa-eu-partnership.org/en/about-us/financing-partnership.

15 "Trump Cuts $25 Million in Aid for Palestinians in East Jerusalem Hospitals," *Reuters*, Sep. 8, 2018, https://www.reuters.com/article/us-usa-palestinians-hospitals/trump-axes-25-million-in-aid-for-palestinians-in-east-jerusalem-hospitals-idUSKCN1LO0O0.

16 German Lopez and Kavya Sukumar, "Mass Shootings since Sandy Hook, in One Map," *Vox*, accessed Nov. 8, 2018, https://www.vox.com/a/mass-shootings-america-sandy-hook-gun-violence.

17 "Lethality of Suicide Methods," *Harvard T.H. Chan School of Public Health*, accessed Nov. 8, 2018, https://www.hsph.harvard.edu/means-matter/means-matter/case-fatality/.

18 A.J. Willingham and Saeed Ahmed, "Mass Shootings in America are a Serious Problem – And these 9 Charts Show Just Why," *CNN*, Nov. 6, 2017, https://www.cnn.

com/2016/06/13/health/mass-shootings-in-america-in-charts-and-graphs-trnd/index.html.

19   Ibid.

20   Onyanga-Omara, "Gun Violence Rare in U.K. Compared to U.S."; Quealy and Sanger-Katz, "Comparing Gun Deaths by Country."

21   Fox, "No Mass Shootings in Australia in 20 Years."

22   William H. Frey, "The US will Become 'Minority White' in 2045, Census Projects," *Brookings Institution,* Mar. 14, 2018, https://www.brookings.edu/blog/the-avenue/2018/03/14/the-us-will-become-minority-white-in-2045-census-projects/.

23   "Over 54,000 American Bridges Structurally Deficient, Analysis of New Federal Data Shows," *American Road & Transportation Builders Association,* 2018, https://www.artba.org/2018/01/29/54000-american-bridges-structurally-deficient-analysis-new-federal-data-shows/.

24   "Road Infrastructure," *2017 Infrastructure Report Card,* accessed Nov. 12, 2018, https://www.infrastructurereportcard.org/cat-item/roads/.

25   Dr. Yossef Ben-Meir in discussion with the author, December 2018.

26   "The Simple Truth about the Gender Pay Gap," *American Association of University Women,* accessed Dec. 10, 2018, https://www.aauw.org/resources/research/simple-truth/.

27   "Minimum Wage," *Legal Information Institute, Cornell Law School,* accessed Dec. 10, 2018, https://www.law.cornell.edu/wex/minimum_wage.

28   Lopez and Sukumar, "Mass Shootings since Sandy Hook."

29   Christopher Ingraham, "There are More Guns than People in the United States, According to a New Study of Global Firearm Ownership," *Washington Post,* Jun. 19, 2018, https://www.washingtonpost.com/news/wonk/wp/2018/06/19/there-are-more-guns-than-people-in-the-united-states-according-to-a-new-study-of-global-firearm-ownership/.

30   Andis Robezneiks, "Women Bear Greater Burden of Opioid Epidemic," *American Medical Association,* Jun. 27, 2017, https://www.ama-assn.org/delivering-care/opioids/women-bear-greater-burden-opioid-epidemic; "Overdose Death Rates," *National Institute on Drug Abuse,* accessed Dec. 10, 2018, https://www.drugabuse.gov/drug-topics/trends-statistics/overdose-death-rates.

31   Peter Wagner and Wendy Sawyer, "Mass Incarceration: The Whole Pie 2018," *Prison Policy Initiative,* Mar. 14, 2018, https://www.prisonpolicy.org/reports/pie2018.html.

32   Aleks Kajstura, "Women's Mass Incarceration: The Whole Pie 2018," *Prison Policy*

Initiative, Nov. 13, 2018, https://www.prisonpolicy.org/reports/pie2018women.html; Wendy Sawyer, "The Gender Divide: Tracking Women's State Prison Growth," *Prison Policy Initiative,* Jan. 9, 2018, https://www.prisonpolicy.org/reports/women_overtime.html.

2019

THE TALIBAN AND THE US:
ACCEPTING THE INEVITABLE

January 31, 2019

T he longest war in American history *may* come to an end following an agreement in principle between the US and the Taliban, which was recently concluded in Doha. It is significant in that it is the first time the US and the Taliban negotiated face-to-face, the negotiations were made public, and the principle accord that was reached addressed the two most important requirements that each side demanded from the other: the Taliban agreed to prevent any militant group like al-Qaeda from using Afghan territory to plan attacks on the US and its allies and, in return, the US-led military coalition agreed to withdraw their forces from the country.

Notwithstanding the importance of the agreement, there are many hurdles that must be overcome before a final and permanent accord is struck. Both sides need to demonstrate willingness to compromise in dealing with some of the crucial aspects of the agreement where other players, especially the current Afghan government, have a stake in the outcome.

Moreover, given the distrust between the two sides and the heavy toll the war exacted over seventeen years of fighting, reaching a sustainable deal necessitates sequential steps. In addition, they need a negotiating process to which both sides must fully adhere to engender mutual trust and mitigate the psychological impediments that have eluded them from reaching an agreement in the past.

The framework of the agreement: The understanding between the two sides is that they must agree on all conflicting issues as a prerequisite to reaching a comprehensive agreement. Although this obviously is necessary, it will be a mistake to link each pending issue to another instead of "banking" each agreed-upon issue and building on them. That is, even if a serious disagreement were to emerge over a given conflicting issue and the talks break down, once negotiations resume, they would not start from scratch. This would also help in maintaining some momentum, as the two sides will have already developed a vested interest in the negotiating process.

Sequencing: It will be extremely important to agree on a process that would establish a sequential order of specific steps to be taken by one side and reciprocated by the other. This process should begin by requiring the Taliban to declare a ceasefire, against which 10-15 percent of American troops will be withdrawn. This should be followed by an interest-based negotiation between the Taliban and the central government to reach a lasting political solution, against which another segment of American forces will be pulled out. The sequential *quid pro quo* on many issues still to be negotiated will cement the negotiating process and ensure the desired outcome.

Security: A long-term security arrangement must be established to ensure that security is maintained throughout the country during the withdrawal process of US forces and beyond. Afghan military forces and the Taliban need to cooperate in this regard, which will not be easy to accomplish. That said: it is hard to imagine any agreement that would not entail such cooperation, which is central to the future security and stability of the country.

Additionally, they must agree to fully collaborate on a monitoring regime, which would include international observers to ensure that Afghanistan is not used as a terrorist base. It is important to note that the Taliban and Afghan forces still see each other as sworn enemies, and it will take a process of reconciliation for a period of time to ensure continuing cooperation between the two sides.

The participation of the tribal chiefs: The success of any agreement in the long-term would require the full support of tribal heads, as they exert tremendous power on their tribes, and by extension on the Taliban. In a long conversation I had recently with a Pashtun tribal chief, Ajmal Khan Zazai, he fervently asserted that without the support of the tribes, no agreement could endure, given that the country has long been a tribal society. Convening a meeting between the tribal heads to endorse the peace agreement will be necessary to give it legitimacy and bolster its sustainability.

Reconciliation between the government and the Taliban: Currently, the Taliban refuses to directly engage with the central government. President Ghani insists that a final agreement must protect the rights and values of Afghans that cannot be disputed, such as national unity and sovereignty, territorial integrity, and the central role of the government. Additionally, the role of civil society, the rights of other ethnic groups, women's rights, and a consensual representative government must be protected. Given the bitter history of the conflict, this type of political settlement will not be easy to achieve, as it would also require the support of a cross-section of the Afghan population.

Based on what we know, as the Taliban no longer seeks a monopoly on power or an Islamic caliphate, an agreement is entirely possible. Both sides understand that full cooperation between them is *sine qua non* to ending hostilities and securing a lasting solution.

Pakistan's role: Pakistan has always played a direct and indirect role in the Afghanistan war, as the country has considerable stakes in the stability and security of Afghanistan as a neighbor. For years, Pakistan provided a refuge for Taliban fighters, where they staged terror attacks against Afghan and coalition forces.

Knowing though that the US is bent on withdrawing its forces sooner than later, Pakistan wants to ensure that its own security is not compromised, strengthen ties with the US and benefit financially, and prevent Indian influence in Afghanistan while enhancing its own. To be sure, Pakistan wants to strengthen its position regionally, and prevent Iran from meddling in the internal affairs of Afghanistan as well.

International funding: After seventeen years of death and destruction, Afghanistan needs billions in financial aid for reconstruction, rehabilitation, infrastructure, schools, hospitals, and housing. Indeed, any peace agreement will collapse under continuing economic distress. The US and the EU in particular must provide significant financial aid to help the country stand on its own feet. Indeed, instead of continuing to spend billions on the war effort, US financial assistance will be of better use in reconstruction efforts.

Allowing for more time: Many hurdles are still in the way of reaching a sustainable peace in Afghanistan, but to prevent such potential obstacles from scuttling a lasting deal, the Trump administration should give time for the current negotiations to settle several intractable time-consuming issues and to develop a shared political vision for the future of the country.

Ironically, following the 9/11 attack seventeen years ago, the Bush administration demanded that the then-Taliban government prevent any violent extremists, such as al-Qaeda, from planning attacks against the US, which the Taliban refused, leading to the Afghanistan war. Sadly, it took the death of twenty-three hundred American soldiers and tens of thousands of Afghans and more than a trillion dollars to accept the inevitable by reaching today's agreement, which is based on the very same principles.

It will be tragic if either the US or the Taliban squanders this initial agreement, because the alternative is more death and destruction. Although the US must end this consuming war, it should not withdraw precipitously and leave swirling instability in its wake, which will severely undermine US geostrategic interests.

TRUMP MUST NEVER LISTEN TO
THE WARMONGER BOLTON

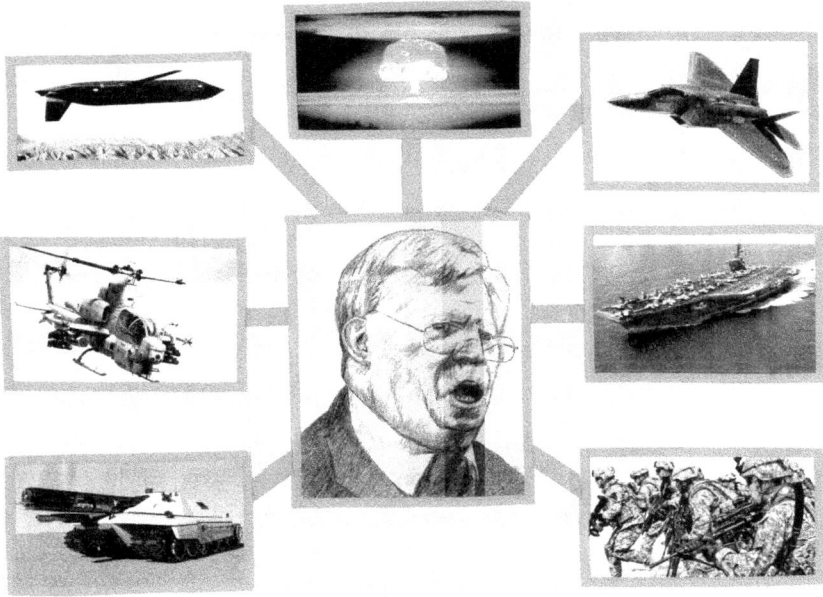

May 23, 2019

Waging a war against Iran, or even thinking of doing so, is sheer madness. Trump has thus far wisely rejected warmonger National Security Advisor John Bolton's outrageous advice. Waging another war in the Middle East, this time against Iran, would have not only disastrous consequences for the US, but would also engulf our allies in a war in which they would suffer incalculable human losses and destruction. Bolton was the architect behind the devastating war in Iraq in 2003, which inflicted more than five thousand US casualties and a cost exceeding $2 trillion, allowed Iran to entrench itself in Iraq, and gave way to the rise of ISIS.

The Iraq War would be child's play compared to a war against Iran, which would put up a fight far worse than all of the wars in the Middle East since 1948 combined. Much of the Middle East would be in flames. American casualties would be many times that of the Iraq war.

Trump should never listen to Bolton, who is strongly influenced by Crown Prince bin Salman and Netanyahu, who seem to encourage him to attack Iran. They are dangerous men who want to prevail over Iran at the expense of the United States by dragging it into an unwinnable war. No matter how much death and destruction Iran would suffer, it is here to stay. To think that regime change in Iran, as Bolton and Pompeo continue to advocate, would usher in a democracy is an illusion that will never materialize.

The US efforts to establish democracies in Egypt and Libya in the wake of the Arab Spring offer glaring examples of the United States' dismal failure. To resolve the conflict with Iran by toppling the clergy through the use of force is not the answer. Iran technically will lose such a war, but that in no way guarantees that regime change and democracy will follow. The answer lies through negotiation and only negotiation, until all conflicting issues that separate the US and its allies from Iran are settled peacefully.

Israel's and Saudi Arabia's concerns about Iran acquiring a nuclear weapon and whether it would severely compromise their national security are exaggerated at best and unfounded at worse. Even if Iran acquires such weapons, Tehran will not use them preemptively or in retaliation to a conventional attack on its nuclear facilities and high-value military assets. If Iran is actively seeking nuclear weapons, it is doing so strictly for defensive purposes, just like Israel, Pakistan, North Korea, and India.

No one knows better than the Revolutionary Guard and the clergy in Tehran that using nuclear weapons for either defensive or offensive attacks is tantamount to suicide. Israel as a nuclear power will always maintain second-strike capability and will not hesitate for a moment to respond in kind and inflict unacceptable damage from which Iran could suffer for decades.

Like any other country, Iran wants to live and prosper in peace. Yes, it has been and still is involved in many nefarious activities throughout the region. And yes, it has the ambition of becoming the region's hegemon. But, in the final analysis, Iran will weigh the benefits versus the disadvantages that it can garner by being a constructive player in the Middle East.

However, Iran will fight with all its might against regime change imposed on it by a foreign power or otherwise. The Iranian government, led by the clergy, has every right to govern itself in any manner it chooses. Its current military preparations are only in response to US threats to use force to effect regime change. Tehran has in no way any offensive designs in mind, and Bolton cannot fool anyone otherwise. I give credit to Trump for resisting Bolton and Secretary of State Pompeo's adventurous streaks.

Certainly, Iran's behavior is not acceptable. Iran must stop threatening Israel and other countries in the region, and disabuse Netanyahu in particular of the notion that Tehran is out to destroy Israel. A resolution to the Israeli-Palestinian conflict will also disabuse Iran from using that conflict to justify its enmity toward Israel.

There is no better or more urgent time than now for the EU to interject itself in an effort to ameliorate the growing tension between the United States and Iran. The EU should initiate behind-the-scenes negotiations with Iran and agree with the US on a joint cohesive strategic plan to mitigate the conflict with Iran. The new negotiations should be based on a *quid pro quo* aiming to achieve a comprehensive deal in stages that could lead to a permanent solution.

Every conflicting issue should be placed on the table. Iran must stop meddling in the affairs of other states, freeze its research and development of ballistic missiles, and end its support of extremist groups such as Hezbollah and waging of proxy wars in Yemen and Syria. In return, the EU and the US should offer Iran a path for normalizing relations and removing sanctions, and assure it that the West will not seek regime change.

This kind of cooperation and high level of transparency will serve the objective of reaching regional stability from which Iran can benefit greatly, instead of continuing its nefarious activities that invite even more severe sanctions, and potentially a devastating war.

Neither Tehran nor Washington want war, and every party directly or indirectly affected by the conflict with Iran—especially Israel, Saudi Arabia, and the other Gulf states—will greatly benefit from a new, peaceful agreement with Iran.

Trump must not engage the United States in another war in the Middle East. We have paid and continue to pay dearly for the Iraq and Afghanistan wars, and we are still fighting the latter. Of all the promises that Trump made in his political campaign for the presidency, preventing another war is the one promise he must keep.

TRUMP'S EMBRACE OF WHITE SUPREMACY IS POISONING AMERICA'S SOUL

August 6, 2019

Within thirteen hours, two mass shootings took place—in El Paso, Texas and Dayton, Ohio—killing thirty-one innocent people and injuring twice as many. We normally hear about these horrifying incidents, express sorrow and bewilderment, talk about gun control, and move on. Politicians, including Trump, dispatch their old and tired expressions of condolences and offer prayers to console the bereaved families of the victims. But then we go about our daily routine, knowing that the next mass shooting looms as if it were a natural phenomenon like a thunderstorm, in the face of which we can do nothing. And tragically, the vicious cycle continues.

This time, however, something far more sinister and profoundly troubling is at play. Race, guns, and immigration were so artfully combined by a racist president who is sworn not to pass meaningful gun control laws to please his base, promotes racism to divide the country, and calls Hispanic immigrants "invaders" to make them targets. During the past few months, Trump spent over a million dollars on Facebook ads with the word "invasion" in big letters to spread fear among his constituents and create an atmosphere ripe for violence against people of color.[1]

In the first 216 days of this year, 251 mass shootings took place—killing over 520 people and injuring at least two thousand.[2] Is it just a coincidence that of the ten worst mass shootings in American history, five took place since 2016?[3] Can anyone suggest that Trump has nothing to do with it? Leave it of course to Trump to blame the press, mental illness, and even video games for being behind the frequency of mass shootings.

Darker and more ominous days await us. Mass shootings cannot be addressed in isolation, but only in the context of the general environment in which we are living. The country is politically divided, our values are being stomped on, racism is consuming our social fabric, white supremacists are parading their bigotry with pride, and the president is contributing to the epidemic of gun violence by spreading hate to promote his political agenda.

When a president makes racism and bigotry the order of the day, and Republican leaders condone it by virtue of their silence, it poisons our social and political organs and defies the very premise on which this country was founded.

The mass shooting in El Paso was explicitly motivated by hate, claiming there is a "Hispanic invasion of Texas."[4] It was a hate crime targeting Hispanics, whom Trump sees as alien, rapists, and criminals who take away jobs, sap public resources, and above all change the color of the country. This is the message that Trump is conveying to his white supremacist followers, that America is becoming "browner" and that something must be done to prevent that from happening, all while pointing the finger at Hispanic immigrants as the culprits.

True, mass shootings have occurred before and may continue for years after Trump leaves office. The degree to which mass shootings slow or escalate, however, depends not only on the passage of strict gun control laws, but also on the action or inaction of Trump and the Republican Party, because they must bear the full responsibility for the sorry state of affairs in which we find ourselves. I do not hold my breath waiting for our racist-in-chief to do anything about it.

In fact, the precise opposite will happen. At a time of looming elections, Trump will continue to drum up his racism and dehumanization of immigrants and use toxic language against anybody who looks Hispanic. He believes that fomenting social division is a brilliant strategy to nurture his white supremacist base, which listens to him and follows his preaching. The shooter in El Paso echoed precisely Trump's sentiment. And while Trump is talking about some gun control legislation, neither he nor his submissive Republican Senate will consider or debate any such laws that may alienate any segment of his followers.

While the Democratic candidates for president continue to bicker about healthcare, taxes, and climate change, however important these issues maybe, they have not only ignored the need for gun control laws, but more importantly failed to address where the country is headed under Trump's watch. Whereas they labeled Trump as a racist, they have not focused on the implications of his racist utterances and how devastatingly that impacts America's social cohesiveness and tolerance, which is the moral glue that keeps the country together.

The Republicans, on the other hand, seem to have totally abdicated their moral responsibility and resolved to enable Trump and use him to promote their socio-political and economic agenda. The fact that America's international standing is at an all-time low and domestic social disintegration is alarmingly unfolding does not seem to bother the Republicans, who put their personal and party interest above the nation's.

Just imagine what might happen if Trump loses the next election? Having polarized the country politically to the degree that he has, his poisonous rhetoric against people of color, concoction of a Hispanic invasion, alignment with white supremacists, and catering to his base have created an extraordinarily ominous environment that invites extremism and violence.

Although at this juncture enacting gun control laws remains critically important, they are not enough to remedy the damage that Trump has done to America. Under his watch, America has lost its soul. He has sown hatred, nurtured divisiveness, and pitted one segment of the American people against the other. Antisemitism has reached a new high, people of color are targets of disdain and discrimination, corruption and obstruction of justice is at the top, and alas, mass shootings are further escalating.

Trump will be damned by history for tearing the country apart, and as long as he is in power, we should expect that America's values and its moral standing will continue to degrade potentially to a point of no return.

Trump is dangerous, and the American public must unseat him to save America's soul before it's too late.

NOT ACTING ON CLIMATE
CRISIS IS AT OUR PERIL

August 14, 2019

C limate change is real and visible for all to see. The scientific evidence is overwhelming, and denying that climate change is already upon us, especially as the president and his party does, flies in the face of the indisputably dire consequences that will be inflicted on all humanity. The Intergovernmental Panel on Climate Change's (IPCC) special report is the final call—the most extensive warning yet on the risks of rising global temperatures and its far-reaching implications.

The US is the second-largest polluter in the world, and more than any other country it bears the responsibility to cut down on gas emissions. Moreover, the IPCC says that limiting global warming to below 1.5 degrees Celsius (2.7 degrees Fahrenheit) will require "rapid, far-reaching and unprecedented changes in all aspects of society."[5] It will be very expensive, but the window of opportunity isn't yet closed. We must act now to avert the catastrophic impact of climate crisis before it is too late.

There are today fifteen hundred oil and gas firms listed on stock exchanges worldwide—together they are worth over $4.5 trillion.[6] With everything we are doing to transition to green sources energy, fossil fuels—primarily petroleum, natural gas, and coal—still provide 80 percent of the energy consumed in the US.[7]

Michael E. Mann, a noted climatologist and geophysicist, observes that the science he and his colleagues does is "a threat to the world's most powerful and wealthiest special interests."[8] This explains the self-serving denials of people like Trump, who choose to ignore that there is a looming disastrous climate crisis.

Mann further argues that the fossil fuel industry uses its immense resources to discredit the science and scientists, running a disinformation campaign on a global scale to mislead the public and policymakers alike. He calls this "the most villainous act in the history of human civilization, because it is about the short-term interests of a small number of plutocrats over the long-term welfare of this planet and the people who live on it."[9]

California offers one glaring example of climate change. Presently, the average wildfire season is seventy-eight days longer than it was in 1970. Climate change has led to hot and dry conditions that increase the activity of wildfires. The average burned area is now much larger—by as much as 600 percent in some types of forest.[10]

Temperatures, soil moisture, and the presence of trees and other forms of fuel are all factors that impact the risk of wildfires—and they are also factors with strong direct or indirect links to climate variability and climate change. Canada currently spends $1 billion every year to fight fires; five times what it spent in the 1990s.[11]

Tragically, climate refugees and IDPs are just another facet of this crisis. People are forced to leave their homes due to "sudden or gradual alterations in their natural environment"[12]—these alterations may be due to sea-level rise, extreme weather events (like hurricanes such as the one that battered Puerto Rico), or drought and water scarcity. The disappearance of Lake Chad in West Africa due to desertification has fostered armed conflict, which has driven more than four million people into camps.[13]

In the United States itself, climate change has caused a large number of IDPs. Ninety percent of the population of Paradise, CA (which was mostly destroyed in last fall's Camp Fire) has not yet been able to return to their homes.[14] According to the Internal Displacement Monitoring Center, over 1.2 million people within the US were displaced in 2018 alone due to natural disasters, many of which are amplified by climate change.[15]

One of the big problems is that climate refugees do not have any officially recognized definition or protections. The most vulnerable regions are sub-Saharan Africa, South Asia, and Latin America; studies show that by 2050, nearly 150 million people from these regions could be displaced due to climate change.[16]

Sadly, under Brazil's far-right president, Jair Bolsonaro, the Amazon rainforest is being cut down at an alarming pace. Protections that were in place for the past two decades are no longer enforced and the deforestation rate has risen drastically, as the *New York Times* reports.[17] In fact, the clearing and burning of forests accounts for roughly eighteen percent of all global greenhouse gas emissions due to human activity.[18] Massive deforestation is systematically eliminating one of the best resources our planet has for absorbing carbon (trees themselves, which process carbon dioxide into oxygen), which means that what we are witnessing in the Amazon and elsewhere is a major blow against the efforts to reduce anthropogenic climate change.

Rainforests are home to the highest concentration of plants and animals found anywhere on Earth. Their rampant destruction is a human tragedy, as we are undoubtedly erasing from the Earth species that are still unknown to science.

Along with the rainforests, coral reefs are among the most biodiverse ecosystems found on the planet, protect coastlines, provide habitat and shelter to countless marine organisms, and are now dying at a horrifying rate. Twenty-seven percent of monitored reefs have been lost, and over 30 percent are at risk of being lost within the next few decades.[19]

The reasons for this unfolding tragedy are clear enough. Coral mining, overfishing, blast fishing, pollution, warming oceans, and ocean acidification are among the major contributing factors. Sylvia Earle, an American marine biologist and former chief scientist of the National Oceanic and Atmospheric Association, pointedly observes that "Half the coral reefs are still in pretty good shape, a jeweled belt around the middle of the planet. There's still time, but not a lot, to turn things around."[20]

The Financial Times says "the world is on track to overshoot the targets of the Paris climate agreement" and the temperature will rise by 3 degrees Celsius by the end of the century, a level that would disrupt life around the planet.[21] The EPA knows everything stated in this article and some, but Trump and his operatives in Congress refuse to face the climate crisis as it does not serve their twisted economic agenda. Indeed, environmental deregulation is criminal and **no** Republican, including the president, has the right to contaminate our air, water, and land only to make the rich richer.

Being in control of the House, the Democrats must now make climate change a national emergency. They must insist on restoring environmental regulations by attaching them to future spending bills. They must leave no stone unturned to ensure that no business can continue to financially benefit from deregulation at the expense of the health and well-being of every American, who will suffer greatly from chronic diseases related to climate change.

Moreover, every state of the union that has not joined the twenty-four states in the US Climate Alliance should do so immediately and enact similar rules and regulations to address climate change hazards, consistent with the Paris Agreement.

Climate change equally impacts Democrats and Republicans alike; young and old; white and persons of color; men, women, and children; and every species. Those who are running for office, including the presidency, must be warned that unless they publicly commit to support any and all measures to address climate change, they will be held accountable and denied the votes they need to be elected.

Certainly, by defeating Trump in the next election and winning back the Senate, the Democrats, hopefully with the support of some Republicans, will be able to avert the catastrophic impact of climate change while there is still time.

THE DISGRACEFUL PRESIDENT AND THE CONTEMPTIBLE PRIME MINISTER

August 19, 2019

Much has been said and written about Trump's disgraceful pointed "advice" to Prime Minister Netanyahu not to allow two duly elected Muslim Democrat congresswomen, Rashida Tlaib (MI) and Ilhan Omar (MN), to enter Israel. Netanyahu, like a poodle, simply obeys his master's command without as much as giving it a second thought, while ignoring the far-reaching implications of his egregious act. For whatever it's worth, let me add my voice.

Here we have a president or a so-called one

whose racism has long since been established.

Never missed an opportunity to demonstrate his loathing and disdain

toward people of color—Hispanic, Black, and Muslim in particular.

His disgraceful behavior is always on display,

as he engenders sick satisfaction from arousing hatred and division.

Though his enmity toward the Democrats is engrained,

to show this much disgrace goes beyond the pale of indignity and shame.

He has disgraced himself.

Disgraced the office of the Presidency.

Disgraced the House of Representatives.

Disgraced ordinary Americans and even many of his adherents.

Disgraced the Jewish community.

Disgraced our allies who believe in sovereignty.

And it all comes down to a man who throws his weight around,

to cover for his own weakness, frailty and brazen audacity.

Netanyahu would not have shown weakness by allowing Tlaib and Omar entry,

but strength, dignity, and respect for the office they hold.

For the American Congress, whose unwavering backing of Israel
stands unique in the annals of bilateral congressional support,
and stood fast by the country that shared their values.
A country that would have stood alone in adversity and existential
threat.
But America—Democrats and Republicans alike,
together never waver, hesitate, or vacillate,
because Israel was not seen just an ally, but a partner.
A partnership that withstood the test of time.
A partnership that helped Israel to grow and prosper.
A partnership that made Israel safe and secure.
A partnership that has become a model for an inimitable relationship.

And here comes Netanyahu—a political animal,
who would sell his mother (and deliver her) only to stay in power!
Now that he is running for his political life,
he sees Trump as his savior.
Never mind that Trump does not really give a damn about Israel.
Never mind that Trump sees Netanyahu as a stooge to serve his sin-
ister agenda.
Never mind that he set up Netanyahu against the Democrats.
Never mind that he broke all diplomatic protocols.
Never mind that he undermined Israel's freedom to choose.
Never mind that he made Israel subservient to his whims.
But then, Netanyahu was not only happy but eager too to do Trump's
bidding.

This is how Netanyahu showed his contempt.
His contempt of what Israel stands for.
Contempt of the American Jewish community.
Contempt of the House of Representatives.
Contempt of political etiquette and culture.

Contempt of those with viewpoints that do not align with his.

Contempt of two Congresswomen who criticize Israel's policy toward the Palestinians.

Contempt of people of color.

Contempt of the office of the Prime Minister.

This is the Netanyahu that has lost any sense of common decency.

For nothing matters to him, no country, no party and no civility.

Netanyahu and Trump are made of the same cloth

Narcissists, self-absorbed, egomaniac, xenophobic, and

yes, with insatiable lust for ever more power

while selling their countries down the river.

Netanyahu has lost an invaluable opportunity

to show hospitality—and welcome the two Congresswomen.

To listen to their grievances and concerns.

To explain the nature of the conflict with the Palestinians.

To elucidate why Israel opposes the BDS movement.

To demonstrate what Israel is all about.

To suggest how the Israelis and the Palestinians can live in peace and harmony.

To invite them to be a part of a process of reconciliation.

To become emissaries of peace and amity.

But then, this is not what Netanyahu stands for or believes in.

He is a nationalist who stains Israel's reputation.

He is a racist and a bigot who has long since lost his bearings.

He is destroying Israel's democracy brick-by-brick.

He is a criminal and soon to be tried for abuse of power and breach of trust.

He betrayed his countrymen, betrayed the state.

Betrayed the American Jewish community,

while succumbing to the whims of a would-be a dictator.

And with deep sorrow, the once-cherished US-Israel relationship
may never be the same.
Because these two wicked men
have adopted disgrace and contempt
that deservedly bonded them together.

FOR THE US AND IRAN, WAR IS NOT AN OPTION

September 5, 2019

T rump's decision to withdraw from the JCPOA (or Iran deal) was sadly based on a lack of understanding of its importance and potential contribution to a future nuclear-free zone in the Middle East. Even without knowing the nuances of the deal, Trump's decision to withdraw from it was based on his pledge to do so when he was campaigning for president and his determination to undo President Obama's signature achievement. Moreover, Prime Minister Netanyahu, who vehemently opposed the deal, was able to persuade Trump to abrogate it with the full backing of American evangelicals, whose political support Trump needs.

From the onset, the Obama administration understood that the Iran deal would substantially slow Iran's nuclear development program in a number of stages for ten to twenty-five years. None of the signatories to the deal believed that Iran would necessarily abandon its ambition to acquire nuclear weapons. Nevertheless, they all agreed that during this period, continuing efforts must be made by all parties to build on the deal to prevent Iran from acquiring nuclear weapons and normalize its foreign relations.

By allowing Iran to reap political and economic benefits through the removal of the sanctions and normalization of relations with the US and its allies, and being assured that the US has no design toward regime change, Iran would feel secure while enjoying a thriving economy. This would mitigate its external threats and render the acquisition of nuclear weapons unnecessary, and in fact undesirable, as it would once again isolate Iran and subject it to new crippling sanctions, severely undermining the progress it had made in the interim.

The development of events since the US withdrew from the deal made Trump and Netanyahu realize that the withdrawal was a mistake. Iran assumed an even harder line, refused to end its nefarious activities, and continues to weather the nearly crippling sanctions. Netanyahu's hope that Trump would potentially attack Iran's nuclear facilities and bring about a regime change failed to materialize, and his optimism that Iran will succumb in the face of sanctions turned out to be misplaced.

Realizing the potentially dire consequences of a war with Iran, Trump is determined not to initiate any hostility against Tehran. Following Iran's downing of an American spy drone in June, Trump rescinded his order to retaliate against Iranian targets, fearing unnecessary escalation. Iran's resiliency and its readiness to counter any American attack, even at the expense of suffering major loses and destruction, persuaded Trump, to the chagrin of Netanyahu, that only negotiations would solve the conflict with Iran.

Moreover, although technically the Europeans continue to adhere to the deal, a significant reduction in trade with Iran has occurred due to US pressure, even though the Europeans want to preserve the deal and view it as an instrument to contain crises in the region. If this trend continues, Iran will have no incentive to continue to largely adhere to the provisions of the deal and may well walk away, because it refuses to abide by a deal that increases its sense of vulnerability.

That said, given the changing circumstances, it has become impossible to enter into new negotiations unless a new atmosphere is created that would not be seen or interpreted as surrender—which Iran will never allow to happen. President Rouhani's demand that the sanctions be lifted as a precondition toward renewed negotiations is a non-starter. Instead, entering new talks should be unconditional. A revised deal should be based on the original one and be structured to restore Iran's confidence and prevent any future aggression against it by any power from within or outside the region.

The involvement of a "trusted" third party is particularly important because the Iranians do not trust Trump—not only because of his withdrawal from the deal, but because of his reversal of positions and public disdain toward Iran.

France, which assumed upon itself a mediating role between the US and Iran, is most suited to continue with its efforts to pave the way for direct US-Iran talks without asking Iran for any concessions that may appear to be a weakness. France will also be in a position to help mitigate any roadblocks that are bound to arise throughout the negotiating process with the following prerequisites in place.

The condition for new negotiations

Contrary to statements made by National Security Advisor John Bolton and Secretary of State Pompeo openly calling for regime change in Iran, Trump must make it clear that his administration does not seek regime change in Tehran. This is the most critical issue for the regime, and anything else is secondary. Indeed, Iran agreed to the deal not only because of the sanctions, but also because the deal provided it with guaranteed security, which is the preservation of the regime.

Trump should reiterate his willingness to enter into direct and unconditional negotiations because, given the current circumstances, direct talks remain the only viable option. By conducting face-to-face talks, some of the distrust, which runs deep, can be mitigated between the US and Iran. Knowing that the new negotiations could not possibly ignore the original deal, Trump needs to publicly state that the US intent is to have an *improved* agreement that *reflects the interests of both sides.*

Both sides must stop any and all acrimonious public statements against the other. To be sure, conducting negotiations under conditions of mutual verbal hostility and threats will only reinforce their suspicion over the other's real intent.

Since the primary conflict is between the US and Iran, no other signatory to the deal, other than France as a mediator, should participate in the new talks. Russia and China have their own axes to grind, and given their increasingly tense relations with the US, they may hinder rather than help US efforts to strike a new deal.

Both Iran and the US must avoid any provocations in preparation for and certainly during the negotiations. The seizure of ships or the downing of another drone by either side would badly disrupt the negotiations, if not torpedo them altogether.

Addressing Iran's nefarious activity

Iran needs to understand that meddling in the region raises major security concerns, as it continues to be involved in nefarious activities. Thus, to reduce threat perception and prevent future action against it, Iran must agree to address other major issues, albeit on a separate track from the nuclear talks. This includes Iran's support of extremist groups such as Hezbollah and Hamas, its funding of terrorism and subversion, its direct involvement in Yemen's civil war in support of the Houthis, its use of Shiite militias to fight its proxy wars in Syria, and its repeated threats against Israel.

Aside from that, Iran must agree on limiting its development of ballistic missiles, which is of great concern to the countries in the region and runs against several UN resolutions. In addition, Iran should be required to provide a full account of its nuclear history and present all information pertaining to its nuclear facilities and equipment, as was uncovered by the archives seized by Israel, along with the technology and materials that it has hidden from the international monitors.

Considering the Iranian psychological disposition and how the regime views itself, it would be naïve to assume that applying maximum pressure through sanctions would bring Iran crawling to the negotiating table. Iran is a proud nation; it seeks respect and would not cave to threats, irrespective of the suffering it may endure.

Thus, since both the US and Iran want to avoid war, the only viable option remaining rests on negotiations. What is needed is the creation of conditions for new talks that are conducive to reaching a new deal that would allow Iran to save face and allow Trump to claim that he exacted a much better deal than Obama.

CLIMATE CHANGE: A WORLDWIDE
CATASTROPHE IN THE MAKING

September 25, 2019

I could not possibly applaud enough the young men and women who flooded the streets in hundreds of cities around the world demanding their governments take immediate and long-term action to combat climate change. By the same token, I could not condemn and denounce more vehemently Trump and many of his ilk, like Bolsonaro of Brazil, for their criminal disregard of the catastrophic peril that climate change represents. By denying the threat that climate change poses and its devastating harm to countless living creatures, they are systematically undermining any chance we still have of avoiding a terrible catastrophe, including a mass extinction of species the likes of which the modern world has never seen.

On Monday, the United Nations Climate Action Summit revealed how far presidents and prime ministers are willing to go. More than sixty countries announced tangible plans to reduce emissions and help the countries most vulnerable to climate change to manage the terrible consequences of global warming.

Yet, since the beginning of his administration, Trump has undermined environmental protections, by his withdrawal from the Paris Agreement on climate change, his refusal to attend the G7 special meeting on climate change, his cutting back on the regulation of methane emissions, the freezing of antipollution and fuel-efficiency standards for cars, and his weakening the Endangered Species Act, while allowing gas drilling and offshore oil in all coastal waters off the United States.

To have a better understanding of the unfolding disasters precipitated by climate change, let us examine the following, which are not new revelations but point out some of the far-reaching implications of climate change that no country can afford to overlook.

The rainforests are a crucial bulwark against climate change because they act as a carbon sink, absorbing carbon dioxide out of the atmosphere. The rampant deforestation that is occurring in the Amazon and elsewhere (including Indonesia, Thailand, and the Democratic Republic of the Congo) is effectively eliminating one of the most powerful resources we have for combatting global warming.

When Brazilian president Jair Bolsonaro was elected in October 2018, he came to power intending to open the Amazon basin to business interests. He cut the budget of Brazil's environmental enforcement agency by $23 million, and essentially encouraged cattlemen, agribusinesses, and loggers to exploit and deforest an ever-growing amount of Amazon land. Small wonder then that fires in Brazil are up 85 percent this year compared to the previous year.[22]

Although it is certainly a good thing that European leaders recognize the calamity resulting from the burning of the Amazon rainforest, the pathetic $20 million the G7 has allocated for fighting these fires is a paltry sum considering the enormity of the disaster.[23] This sum of money does not match the urgency expressed by the G7 leaders—do they really understand the magnitude of the disaster that is unfolding in front of our eyes? Presently, an area about one and a half times the size of a football field is being destroyed each and every minute of each and every day.[24]

The systematic destruction of the rainforest is not limited to Brazil. The Democratic Republic of the Congo has seen a loss of roughly 2,700 square miles of forest every year since 1990, an annual reduction of 0.23 percent.[25] That is a forest area slightly larger than the size of Delaware that is destroyed annually. The rainforest in the Congo Basin is the largest in Africa, second only to the Amazon Basin in size. Many of the wildlife species are threatened by illegal logging, including the lowland gorillas and chimpanzees. Forest elephants have seen their numbers decline by 62 percent.[26]

War, ethnic conflicts, deteriorating economies, and climate change have forced millions across the world to flee their homes. Over 1.6 million individuals were still internally displaced by the end of 2018, and 3.5 million refugees reached Europe between 2015 and 2018, mostly from Asia, Africa, and the Middle East.[27] Tragically, climate refugees and IDPs are just another facet of this crisis.

Climate refugees are people forced to leave their homes due to "sudden or gradual alterations in their natural environment."[28] The most vulnerable regions are sub-Saharan Africa, South Asia, and Latin America; studies show that by 2050, nearly 150 million people from these regions could be displaced due to climate change.[29]

Coral reefs are also dying at a horrifying rate as a result of global warming. Twenty seven percent of monitored reefs have been lost and over 30 percent are at risk of being lost within the next few decades.[30] Coral mining, overfishing and blast fishing, pollution, warming oceans, and ocean acidification are among the major contributing factors to this unfolding tragedy. Former chief scientist of the National Oceanic and Atmospheric Association and notable marine biologist Sylvia Earle notes that "Half the coral reefs are still in pretty good shape, a jeweled belt around the middle of the planet. There's still time, *but not a lot*, to turn things around."[31]

Factory farming is contributing directly to global warming. Over forty-five billion animals worldwide—including cows, chickens and pigs—are restricted to Confined Animal Feeding Operations (CAFOs).[32] These CAFOs release massive amounts of greenhouse gasses, surpassing even the entire global transportation industry. According to the Food and Agriculture Organization of the United Nations, animal agriculture is responsible for 18 percent—nearly one-fifth—of all human-induced greenhouse gas emissions.[33]

Factory farming is also indirectly intensifying climate change through deforestation. In fact, clearing land for feed crops and grazing releases up to twenty-eight million tons of carbon dioxide per year globally.[34] As Jonathan Safran Foer, author of *Eating Animals*, states, "We *know*, at least, that this decision [ending factory farming] will help prevent deforestation, curb global warming, reduce pollution, save oil reserves, lessen the burden on rural America, decrease human rights abuses, improve publish health, and help eliminate the most systematic animal abuse in world history."[35]

Climate change equally impacts Democrats and Republicans alike; young and old; white and persons of color; men, women, and children; and every species. Those who have brought us face-to-face with this horrifying reality must now realize that their time is up. Climate change is real, and the plethora of scientific evidence is indisputable. This is a calamity in the making—all nations that care must wake up before it is too late.

All the power to the young Swedish student Greta Thunberg who bravely stood before the UN special session on climate change and forcefully stated that, "You have stolen my dreams and my childhood with your empty words. And yet I'm one of the lucky ones. People are suffering. People are dying. Entire ecosystems are collapsing. We are in the beginning of a mass extinction, and all you can talk about is money and fairy tales of eternal economic growth. How dare you!"[36]

AN ACT OF BETRAYAL AND INFAMY

October 11, 2019

Trump's decision to withdraw American forces from Syria may well be remembered as one of the most egregious and inhuman disasters that he ever took since coming to power. For a President of the United States to make such a critical decision with so many implications, simply based on a conversation with Turkish President Erdogan, not only shows his shortsightedness and total lack of strategic approach, but also his inability to appreciate how that will adversely affect our friends and please our foes. We are already witnessing the unfolding disaster, and there are no words to explain how and by what logic the President of the United States in particular can take such critical steps, knowing how disastrous the repercussions of his actions would be.

We are already witnessing the humanitarian disaster that has been inflicted on the Kurdish community in Syria. They are the very same Kurds who have fought courageously and valiantly against ISIS and suffered thousands of casualties, demonstrating their commitment to fight to the end, at which they have largely succeeded. The last thing that any Kurdish fighter could imagine is for the United States to betray them, having demonstrated their loyalty at a terrible cost with horrifying losses.

It is true, of course: the Kurds have not merely fought to support the US or other allies' efforts in the war against ISIS, but also for their own self-defense, protecting their land and people. And now, they are fleeing by the thousands—nearly sixty-five thousand have already fled, and aid groups expect as many as 450,000 to flee.[37] More than three hundred have already been killed by the vicious and ruthless Turkish military under the fanatic and zealous orders of Erdogan.[38]

Interestingly, while Republicans have thus far accepted and even embraced Trump's follies on scores of domestic and international issues, they have not done or said hardly anything against his repeated egregious actions, lies, misstatements, and self-indulgence. This time, they finally raised their voices and condemned the precipitous withdrawal from Syria. They understood how dire the regional consequences would be in particular for America's allies throughout the Middle East.

No single ally in the region and elsewhere will be able to trust the United States under Trump to do anything on their behalf, let alone take any critical steps that might be needed to protect their national security. Senator Lindsey Graham (R-SC), one of Trump's fervent backers, stated "The president has abandoned the people who helped us destroy ISIS, chaos is unfolding, and when I hear the president—'We're getting out of Syria'—my statement to you is this is worse than what Obama did [in withdrawing from Iraq]."[39]

The Middle Eastern countries who have direct or indirect interest and concern about what's happening in Syria, especially Saudi Arabia and Israel, certainly feel abandoned. They know firsthand that the result of the American withdrawal from Syria will have serious national security implications for them, as it will affect their long-term geostrategic calculus in a region with continuing upheaval.

Netanyahu has expressed Israel's concern over the situation, stating, "Israel strongly condemns the Turkish invasion of the Kurdish areas in Syria and warns against the ethnic cleansing of the Kurds by Turkey and its proxies. Israel is prepared to extend humanitarian assistance to the gallant Kurdish people."[40] Erdogan's office lashed out, with communications director Fahrettin Altun replying, "Empty words of a disgraced politician looking at many years in prison on bribery, fraud and breach of trust charges."[41]

The reaction of the European community, and scores of other countries throughout the world, has been one of disbelief. French President Emmanuel Macron, taking stock of the situation, warned that "Turkey is putting millions of people at humanitarian risk. In doing so, Turkey will be responsible in front of the international community for helping Daesh (so-called Islamic State) building a Caliphate."[42]

For Trump to take this kind of action that directly impacts the European interests in the region, without any consultation, amounts to betraying our closest European allies. Trump never understood that because of Europe's proximity to the region, it would be affected directly and indirectly by the regional turmoil. For that reason, they have fought side-by-side the United States in the Middle East and Central Asia, even though at times they disagreed with the American strategy. They made these sacrifices and commitments to preserve the alliance with the United States and the integrity of NATO.

Needless to say, the countries that benefit the most from this ill-fated decision by Trump are Turkey itself, Russia, and Iran. Turkey's invasion of Syria will simply not end by defeating the Kurds; Erdogan will ensure that Turkey remains permanently in Syria, as this was all along part of his sinister strategic ambition.

Iran will further entrench itself in Syria, and regardless of what Israel will do or say, there will be no prospect of Iran leaving, knowing the United States will not only refrain from using any military force to oust Iran, but it will no longer have much say about the future of Syria itself. Moreover, there is no other power that could compel Tehran to abandon its strategic interest in Syria under almost any circumstances, which terrifies the Israelis.

Russia, which has been entrenched in Syria for five decades, has worked closely with Iran and Turkey. It should be noted that Putin, Erdogan, and Rouhani have met several times in the last eighteen months and developed their own scheme about Syria's future. It is quite clear that Putin and Rouhani certainly supported Erdogan's invasion, which explains why neither Russia nor Iran have not said one word about Turkey's gross transgression.

It is no secret that Trump's decision was also largely motivated by his financial interest in Turkey, which goes back many years to 2012, with the opening of Trump Towers in Istanbul. To think though, that the President of the United States would sell America's interests and abandon its allies for the sake of personal financial gain is not merely outrageous, but criminal. To me, this amounts to nothing less than treason.

TRUMP'S DISGRACEFUL LETTER TO ERDOGAN

October 18, 2019

There is no wonder that every person and news outlet that saw Trump's letter to Turkey's President Erdogan thought it was a joke. When it was confirmed that the letter was indeed authentic, bewilderment and disbelief struck everyone who read it, as no US president has ever written such a disgraceful letter, which will be remembered in infamy.

Trump starts the letter by stating, "Let's work out a good deal!" Yes, a good deal, just like another shady real estate transaction based on a wicked *quid pro quo*. Only a psychopath would forget that he gave Erdogan the green light to invade Syria to kill, destroy, and pillage the same Syrian Kurds who were America's most trusted allies in the fight against ISIS and suffered more than ten thousand casualties. Throughout the war they remained steadfast as an ally, believing that the US would always watch their back, but they were crushingly disappointed.

"You don't want to be responsible for slaughtering thousands of people," Trump goes on to say in his infamous letter. Since when has Erdogan ever been concerned about slaughtering anyone that stood in his way, especially the Kurds whom he hates with a vengeance and has been planning for more than two years to attack and massacre—men, women, and children?

Then Trump stated that "I don't want to be responsible for destroying the Turkish economy – and I will. I've already given you a little sample with respect to Pastor Brunson." First, Trump tells Erdogan to go ahead and wreak havoc on our allies, but then warns Erdogan that he will destroy the Turkish economy if Erdogan does not heed his demand. Well, if this isn't the nature of a mentally disturbed individual, then I don't know what is.

Trump then proceeds by saying that "I have worked hard to solve some of your problems." The question is: what has Trump worked so hard on with Erdogan when the two hardly ever see eye-to-eye? There is one exception though. Trump envies the Turkish dictator who has been ruling his country with an iron fist: subjugating, jailing, pillaging, and purging his own people with absolutely no qualms and no misgivings. Yes, Trump would love to rule over the US and terrorize the Democrats into submission just like Erdogan, if he only had his way.

"Don't let the world down," Trump continues. What is that supposed to mean? Erdogan has let down the US, all NATO member states, and every institution Turkey is a member of or has any affiliation with. Erdogan is a criminal and has committed crimes against humanity. But then, what is there to say? Erdogan, after all, is a byproduct of the Ottoman Empire, which committed genocide against the Armenians and the Greeks, but he conveniently denies that, even though the historic records are irrefutable.

Trump goes on to say that "General Mazloum is willing to negotiate with you, and he is willing to make concessions that they would never have made in the past." What is there to negotiate? Erdogan has been given a free hand all along. He has been killing his own Kurds for decades; he defied Trump previously by buying the Russian S-400 air defense system; he is interfering in the internal affairs of many countries, especially in the Balkans and the Middle East; and he is ignoring his Western allies, showing them his middle finger with a smirk on his face.

Now Trump dispatches his Secretary of State Pompeo and Vice President Pence to cajole Erdogan and beg him to agree to a ceasefire while granting him everything he wished for. With the green light given by Trump, Turkey invaded northeastern Syria with the purpose of establishing a "safe zone" for displaced Syrians, but more importantly to push out the Kurdish fighters who are viewed by Ankara as a security threat. In the main, however, Ankara's goal is to prevent the establishment of an independent Kurdish state in Syria that could evoke a renewed drive by Turkey's Kurdish minority to seek independence.

Just think about what actually happened. Here you have the President of the United States, no less, pleading for cessation of hostilities instead of *demanding*, in no uncertain terms, that Erdogan *pull out his forces immediately from Syria or face dire consequences.* Erdogan, however, seems to take Trump for granted, feeling assured that the straw man in the White House will not take any punitive action not only because he lacks strategic thinking but because of his cowardice.

Trump stated that Pence and Pompeo scored a victory, when in fact it was Erdogan who emerged victorious. Erdogan succeeded in outmaneuvering Trump at every turn, with the US caving into giving Erdogan everything he wanted. Trump ceded ground in Syria, including US military bases, and also agreed to lift the sanctions. The ceasefire may have stopped the killing of the Kurds, but no ceasefire will erase the United States' betrayal of them. The price that the US will end up paying will be hard to imagine.

Next Trump goes on to say that "History will look upon you favorably if you get this done the right and humane way. It will look upon you forever as the devil if good things don't happen." Will history ever look at Erdogan favorably? The so-called man whose despicable personality supersedes only his ruthlessness and brutality? Erdogan, who took pleasure in the ethnic cleansing of the Kurds, personifies the devil itself and is simply incapable of doing anything, as Trump puts it, "the right and humane way."

Finally, Trump preaches to Erdogan, saying, "Don't be a tough guy. Don't be a fool!" Well, Trump is simply looking at himself in the mirror. He is the one who tries to play the tough guy, and he is the real fool who occupies the White House.

"I will call you later." This is how Trump ends the letter. Call Erdogan for what, just to tell him "Don't worry, I still believe that my decision to pull out our troops from Syria was the right decision. You, Erdogan, just go ahead and do what you need to; just don't make too much noise and don't brag about it. Leave the bragging to me."

THE BUTCHER OF ANKARA'S VISIT
TO THE HOUSE OF LIES

November 8, 2019

Trump's inviting of Turkey's President Erdogan to Washington comes at a peculiar time when the House of Representatives is pursuing the impeachment inquiry against Trump and when Erdogan is preoccupied with his invasion of Syria and the growing frustration of the Turkish public with his ruthless domestic and adventurous foreign policy. The question is: what message will Erdogan's visit send to both the United States' friends and foes?

Our adversaries will bask in the notion that the US is no longer guided by any moral principles. Inviting Erdogan to Washington, when Kurdish blood is still fresh on his hands, only confirms that Trump has no scruples and that under his leadership today's friends may well become the enemies of tomorrow. Our friends, on the other hand, are bewildered as to why the US would accord a formal visit to the White House to a brutal leader such as Erdogan, who has committed gross human rights violations against his own people and in particular against both Turkish and Syrian Kurds.

Speculation about what might come out of Trump and Erdogan's meeting abounds, but mine is that nothing of substance will emerge from their face-to-face encounter other than each trying to reap some personal gains. Indeed, Trump is solely for Trump, and Erdogan's narcissism is surpassed only by Trump's inflated ego and pathetic self-indulgence.

Erdogan's eagerness to visit the White House is motivated by a number of "sober" considerations: for Erdogan, the visit demonstrates to his own public that he enjoys the support of the US while showing off that he is a world leader upon whom even the US would accord the status and respect that other prominent head of states deserve, such Germany's Merkel and France's Macron.

Moreover, the visit will embolden Erdogan to continue his rampage against his own Kurds and displays a lack of concern by the US about his gross human rights violations. The visit will further demonstrate that the US is conceding to Erdogan's growing friendly relations with Russia and forgetting altogether Ankara's purchase of the Russian S-400 air defense system, even though it severely compromises NATO's sensitive technology and intelligence.

Sadly, and most troublingly, the visit clearly suggests that Trump is careless about Erdogan's sinister design to decimate the Syrian Kurdish opposition, the YPG, and their comrades in arms, the Free Syrian Army (FSA), and maintain a permanent foothold in Syria, which will only intensify regional conflicts and instability.

For Trump, Erdogan's visit offers another stunt to distract the American public's attention from his compounding daily troubles for at least a short period of time. Given the outrage by both Republicans and Democrats following his precipitous decision to withdraw our forces from Syria, Trump wanted to demonstrate that his decision was the right one. After all, there is a ceasefire in place and US forces are protecting Syria's oil fields, which he cynically views as an advantage, regardless of the fact that hundreds of our closest allies—the Syrian Kurds—have already been killed by Turkish forces and tens of thousands are internally displaced.

Moreover, given that Trump is mostly a façade with no substance, he is desperately eager to demonstrate that he is, in fact, actively engaged in foreign affairs in the search for a solution to various conflicts in the Middle East, including the Turkish-Kurdish conflict. And while he is at it, he wanted to prove to his base that he is the most powerful man and leaders will come from every corner of the world to rub shoulders with him, which also satisfies his ego.

However inconsequential Erdogan's visit to the White House may be, it is worrisome in that Erdogan has succeeded in effectively sidelining the US from having much of a say about Syria's future. Syria's fate is now in the hands of Russia's Putin, Iran's Rouhani, and Erdogan himself. For all intents and purposes, Trump dumped Syria in the lap of these three leaders, whose main objective is to push the US out of the Middle East as each wants to pursue his own agenda in the region without American intervention.

To be sure, the Turkish butcher Erdogan and the notorious liar Trump found their match, and they have no shame and no remorse about the extent to which they use each other to advance their interests.

The visit will end the same way it started. Nothing of any substance will come of their unceremonious meeting, as neither has anything to offer the other and will largely maintain their implicit mutual disdain toward one another for as long as they remain in office.

ENDING US-IRAN IMPASSE RESTS ONLY ON FACE-TO-FACE NEGOTIATIONS

December 12, 2019

Even a cursory review of the turmoil sweeping the Middle East points to Iran as one of the main culprits behind most of the conflicts that have and continue to destabilize the region. We find Iran directly involved in the civil war in Yemen, it equips and supports Hezbollah in Lebanon and exerts huge political influence in Iraq, significantly contributing to the unrest in that country. Moreover, Iran maintains a strong military presence in Syria, opening a third front to threaten Israel, and it is beefing up Hamas's arsenals and defenses against the Jewish state. Finally, Iran enlists, finances, and trains militias and an array of jihadist and terrorist organizations to do its bidding on all fronts.

There is no doubt that ending the impasse between the US and Iran would markedly reduce tension and mitigate some other conflicts in the region, as the discussion between the two sides, according to US sources, would not be limited to Iran's nuclear program. The US would insist on discussing some of Iran's nefarious activities, such as its support of jihadist groups and missile development, albeit on a separate track, with linkages to ensure that the benefits Iran acquires from a new nuclear deal are compensated by Tehran's demonstrable actions as a constructive regional player.

The question is how we go about finding such an accord and what will in fact bring the Iranian government back to the negotiating table without losing face in the eyes of its own public. To that end, we need to explore five different scenarios; through a process of elimination, we will definitively conclude that face-to-face negotiations between the US and Iran remains the only viable option that both sides will be prudent to carefully pursue if they want to avoid a potentially disastrous conflagration.

War: There are those who suggest that waging a war against Iran and destroying its nuclear facilities will bring Tehran to heel. This scenario is fundamentally flawed because of its ominous repercussions. Even under the best of circumstances, whereby Iran's nuclear installations are completely destroyed, Iran will still be in a position to unleash much of its conventional military arsenal against any real or even perceived enemies, especially Saudi Arabia, Israel, and the US.

Yes, under a war scenario, Iran could be devastated, but Iran would still be capable of inflicting incalculable damage on the attacker. We must remember that the clergy, with the backing of the military, would be fighting for their survival. And contrary to the views held by some American and Israeli hawks, there is little to no chance that such a war would bring an end to the mullahs' rule in Tehran.

Whereas a significant portion of the Iranian population rejects the reign of the clergy, as they seek more freedom and better job opportunities, they will not tolerate a foreign onslaught. Regardless of how a war ends, Iran is here to stay. Given time, Iran would become even more belligerent and resolute to acquire nuclear weapons while bolstering its determination to become the region's hegemon.

Maximum Pressure: The second scenario, which the Trump administration is currently pursuing, is to keep the crippling sanctions in place and impose new ones until Iran gives up in despair, as its economy continues to deteriorate and the public becomes increasingly restive. The worsening US-Iran relations since Trump withdrew from the JCPOA are only deepening the rift between the two sides. Nevertheless, although Iran is hurting badly from the effect of the sanctions, no one should underestimate its resiliency and capacity to cope under the worst of circumstances.

Iran has vast human and natural resources and the government can mobilize the masses in support of the government. It is also capable of ruthlessly cracking down on the demonstrators, as it is doing now and has done before. The Revolutionary Guard is committed to the clergy and will not falter to take brutal actions against any opponent to preserve the integrity of the regime, which best serves the Guard's interests.

Regime Change: The third scenario is regime change. Perhaps there is nothing more appealing to the US, Israel, Saudi Arabia, and others in Europe and the Middle East than to effect regime change in Tehran. Conversely, there is nothing more frightening to the clergy than forcible regime change.

The Trump administration has and continues to consider regime change in Tehran through a variety of means, including the support of public unrest, sanctions, and clandestine operations. In July 2017, when John Bolton was still the National Security Advisor, he called for regime change, stating that "the declared policy of the United States of America should be the overthrow of the mullahs' regime in Tehran."[43]

The problem here is that no one, including the CIA, knows what will follow sudden foreign-induced regime change, how loyalists will react, and what the domestic and regional ramifications will be. Besides, there is no doubt that there will be a serious disruption in oil supplies, as the Iranian government is perfectly capable of closing the Straits of Hormuz through which an average of twenty-one million barrels flow each day. That's the equivalent of about 21 percent of global petroleum liquids consumption—making it the world's most important oil chokepoint.[44] To be sure, forcible regime change is extremely risky, and the result may well be much worse than the conduct of the current one.

Containment: Iran is just about everywhere in the region—in Yemen, Iraq, Syria, and Lebanon—with a widespread network of extremist/terrorist organizations that are willing to follow Tehran's dictates and can cause havoc at a time and place of their choosing. The US military presence in Iraq and its meager remaining forces in Syria are not focused on Iran's entrenchment, but on fighting jihadist groups, especially ISIS and al-Qaeda.

Even under harsh sanctions, Iran still maintains and is further augmenting its presence in Syria by establishing permanent military bases and a strong foothold in the country, as they see it as central to their geostrategic objective to maintain a direct land corridor from Tehran to Lebanon. The Iraqi government still feels indebted to Tehran for providing a refuge to many Iraqi political leaders when they belonged to opposition groups fighting Saddam Hussein. At the present, no Iraqi politician can become prime minister without Iran's consent, and successive Iraqi governments have done nothing to reduce Tehran's influence in the country.

The desire for containment remains elusive at best. Other than imposing increasingly severe sanctions, and recent talks about a prospective US-Israel mutual defense treaty that could conceivably inhibit Iran from attacking Israel directly, there are no articulate plans for containing Iran in Iraq, Syria, Yemen, or Lebanon. The effort to contain is certainly not foolproof, as one single major miscalculation could lead to regional war. Thus, the inability to contain Iran has serious pitfalls, as Tehran feels free to destabilize the region to advance its national interests.

Face-to-face negotiations: The fifth and the only practical option that will spare blood and treasure by all sides is direct good-faith negotiations between the US and Iran. By now, both Israelis in the know and Americans have concluded that it was a bad mistake to withdraw from the JCPOA. Nearly a year and a half later, Iran has not been cowed; instead, it became increasingly aggressive, while openly and purposely violating certain elements of the original deal in retaliation against the US withdrawal.

French and German efforts to arrange for new negotiations between the US and Iran have not borne much fruit. An EU diplomat noted in November that any window to bring Iran and the US back to the table is now very small, stating "We're now entering a phase where Iran's actions have a serious impact on the breakout time."[45] But then, however small the prospect is to bring the US and Iran to the negotiating table, it must be continued.

The original Iran deal must still form the basis of new negotiations. The idea here is to build on that deal by addressing especially the sunset clauses, which were troublesome for Israel, and with which Trump agrees. In the search for a solution to the conflict, all major players must recognize the indisputable reality on the ground and make a realistic assessment of the assets that each player can bring.

The fact that the enmity and distrust between the US and Iran has lasted nearly two generations and the fact that the US after more than two years of arduous negotiations withdrew from the JCPOA make the search for and reaching a new agreement all the more difficult and complex. But then, there is no other sane and practical option.

A new deal with Iran would inhibit proliferation of nuclear weapons in the region, pave the way for finding a solution to the war in Yemen, and generally create a new positive atmosphere conducive to settling other regional conflicts.

2020 WILL BE MORE TURBULENT
THAN 2019, UNLESS...

December 19, 2019

U nless some drastic measures are taken, the various conflicts in the Middle East will become ever more intractable and exact a horrifying toll in blood and massive economic dislocation. The continuing severity of these crises and their repercussions will depend on whether the combatants assume a realistic posture, or new leadership rise and commit to finding equitable solutions that can endure. We must keep in mind though that the turmoil we experienced in 2019 may further intensify in 2020 because of the continuing global crisis of leadership and the challenges posed to the global order that was established in the wake of World War II. The following brief review of seven Mideast conflicts reflects these developments and raises the question as to what must be done to change the dynamics in the hope of solving some of these conflicts.

Betrayal

The Israeli-Palestinian conflict is the oldest and most intractable conflict that has consumed both people for more than seventy years and has been further impaired by their leadership's refusal to recognize each other's right to the same land. The leaders have betrayed their people by failing to appreciate each other's psychological, religious, and historic attachment to the land and being blind to the fact that the populations are interspersed, making coexistence inevitable. Israelis and Palestinians must now choose between endless violence or living in amity and peace. Given the crisis in leadership, the hour calls for new visionary and courageous leaders who recognize that their people's future security and prosperity still rests on the only viable option—a two-state solution.

Grandiose delusion

Following the revolution in 1979, Iran sought to become the region's hegemon equipped with nuclear weapons. The turmoil sweeping the Middle East points to Iran's complicity in most of the conflicts destabilizing the region, including Lebanon, Yemen, Iraq, and Syria, while enlisting, financing, and training jihadist and terrorist groups and threatening Israel's existence.

Although the US withdrawal from the Iran deal was a mistake, Iran's defiance led to crippling US sanctions. Seeking regime change and destroying Iran's nuclear facilities is not the answer. The resumption of US-Iran talks offers the only way out, provided Iran plays a constructive regional role and abandons its grandiose delusion to become a nuclear power and the region's hegemon.

Yearning for identity

Since Iraq was established in 1932, it has gone through frequent political turbulence, overshadowing its glorious history. Following the revolution in 1958, the Ba'ath Party, a nationalist and socialist regime, rose to power and was able to finance ambitious projects throughout the 1970s. In 1979, Saddam Hussein, a ruthless autocrat, assumed power and led the country to the disastrous Iran-Iraq and Gulf Wars. The 2003 war killed over 100,000 Iraqis, decimated the country, and invited Iran to exercise immense influence on all Iraqi affairs, while the people suffered from profound economic hardship. The current massive demonstrations demanding the ouster of Iran will ultimately prevail and restore Iraq's unique national identity, for which all Iraqis yearn.

Killing in God's name

The Yemen war will be remembered as perhaps the most horrific humanitarian disaster in modern history. It is a proxy war pitting the leader of Sunni Muslims—Saudi Arabia, which supports the internationally recognized government and is determined to prevent Iran from establishing a foothold in the Arabian Peninsula—against the leader of Shiite Muslims—Iran, which backs the Houthi rebels. Yemen became the battleground, and the Yemenis are killed in God's name. Tens of thousands have died, millions are starving, and over a million children are infected with cholera, all while the country lies in ruin. Five years later, the warring parties have finally realized the war is simply unwinnable. Ultimately, both sides must negotiate a solution.

The price of insatiable lust for power

Syria's civil war, which started in 2011, is hard to fathom. What began as a peaceful demonstration became the most devastating war of the twenty-first century. Had President Assad responded to his fellow citizens' demands by providing them with basic human rights, he might have averted a calamitous war that has killed at least 560,000 people, turned eleven million people into refugees or IDPs, and leveled half the country to the ground.[46] Now Assad is at the mercy of Russia, Turkey, and Iran, who are determined to maintain a permanent foothold in Syria. Syria may well become the battleground between Israel and Iran, while scores of militia, jihadist, and terrorist groups roam the country with no foreseeable end.

Erdogan's self-defeating dictatorship

Soon after Turkey's President Erdogan came to power in 2002, it was believed that under his stewardship Turkey would become the first functioning Islamic democracy. He embarked on socio-political reforms and extensive economic developments and engaged the Kurds to end a decades-long conflict while improving Turkey's prospective integration into the EU. But then he reversed gears. For him, democracy was only a vehicle to promote his Islamic agenda and lead the Sunni Muslim world. He pursued his religious and ideological rivals with vengeance, imprisoning tens of thousands of Gülen followers and Kurds, along with nearly two hundred journalists who are still languishing in jails. He will leave behind a legacy of a ruthless leader possessed with Ottoman revivalism who squandered Turkey's prospective brilliant future for a self-defeating dictatorship.

A preordained defeat

The Afghanistan war, the longest in American history, should have ended one year after it began in 2001. It was clear that the Taliban's initial defeat was temporary and that they would return to reclaim their inherent right to the millennium-old land of their ancestors. The US efforts to establish a democracy, coupled with a mounting build-up of American troops and escalating cost, bore little fruit. The Taliban relentlessly maintained their counteroffensive and, irrespective of their heavy losses, reestablished their central role. Under any negotiated agreement, the Taliban will eventually take over. All that the US can do is require the Taliban to fully adhere to human rights, and punish any violations with crippling punitive sanctions.

There are certainly many other countries in the Middle East and North Africa suffering from political instability, daunting economic hardship, violence, uncertainty, and fear. Sadly, the efforts that have been made by the UN, EU, and the US to quell or resolve many of these conflicts—be they in Lebanon, Libya, South Sudan, or many other countries—have largely failed.

The year 2020 will most likely be as turbulent if not more so than 2019 due mainly to the lack of American leadership and the rush of other powers, especially Russia, China, and, to a lesser extent, Turkey and Iran, to fill the vacuum the US has left behind. Beyond that, however, we are witnessing a global transformation where nationalism, extremism, and xenophobia are on the rise, millions of refugees are on the move, and poverty and economic dislocation are rampant, which together greatly contribute to instability and violence.

Sadly, these developments coupled with a worldwide crisis of leadership may well worsen before a new generation of leaders can rise up and try in earnest to resolve many of these conflicts humanely, passionately, and equitably to ensure their durability.

THE ABCs OF TRUMP'S PATH
TO IMPEACHMENT

December 23, 2019

F inally, Trump was impeached on December 18. It is a sad day for America because for the House of Representative to resort to such a historically rare punitive act suggests that Trump's transgressions have been so severe that the House was compelled to take such drastic measures. However, the two articles of impeachment—abuse of power and obstruction of Congress—hardly describe Trump's repeated blunders, lies, habitual abuse of the power of his office, and obstruction of justice. Indeed, the two articles of impeachment barely scratch the surface of his untamed behavior, which is devoid of any civility and moral responsibility.

In less than three years, the absurd has become the norm, ignorance has become a virtue, and lying has sadly become the order of the day. He brought shame and dishonor to the most prestigious office in the world—the American Presidency. His moral lapses, notoriety, vulgarity, and self-deceit are beyond the pale of human disorder.

As much as Trump must pay for the debased behavior that led to his impeachment, it is the corrupt Republican establishment that enabled him throughout the past three years to violate both the letter and the spirit of the Constitution. It is the Republicans—not the Democrats—that eventually precipitated his impeachment. Whether or not he escapes conviction in the Senate, the Republican party, as much as Trump himself, will be held responsible for the damage they have inflicted on America's democratic institutions, the rule of law, and its global leadership and moral standing.

To be sure, impeaching Trump is more than warranted because even a cursory review of his alarming misconduct suggests that there is more than one word for every letter of the alphabet—from A to Z—that describes one aspect of Trump's character, as he has brought nothing but shame and disgrace to his office.

Arrogant: To say that Trump is arrogant understates his propensity to show off his presumed skills as a negotiator, alleged business acumen, and supposed grasp of complex issues. He constantly claims that he is smarter than everyone around him, even insulting the US military by stating "There's nobody bigger or better at the military than I am," and "I know more about ISIS than the generals do. Believe me."[47] He feels empowered when he wakes up to "enlighten the world" with his early morning stream of twisted tweets, which only puts his arrogance and shallowness on full display.

Bigot: Many people refer to Trump as a bigot, a characterization that he owns and certainly makes no efforts to hide. No one has forgotten his outrageous attack on Mexican immigrants, stating: "When Mexico sends its people… They're bringing drugs. They're bringing crime. They're rapists."[48] His bigotry was even more pronounced when he belittled two Gold Star parents of a Muslim-American soldier who died in 2004 while serving in Iraq.[49] By now, Trump has earned the distinction of making bigotry synonymous with his name.

Crude: One does not need to know Trump well to quickly discern that he is a crude man with no scruples and a love of name calling and swearing. He continuously refers to Senator Elizabeth Warren as Pocahontas, going so far as to do so at an event honoring Navajo veterans. He regularly calls people "losers," "fools," and "lame," especially on Twitter. Speaking about his former Communications Director, Anthony Scaramucci, Trump decried him as a "nut job" he "barely knew."[50] This is the real Trump—behaving like a wild caveman who has long since forgotten the meaning of civility.

Demagogue: Being a demagogue is second nature to Trump; he will say anything, however contradictory and absurd, to arouse his base. He made a campaign and inauguration pledge to eradicate Islamic terrorism from the face of the earth, knowing that this will never happen.[51] In his inauguration speech, he stated: "Every decision ... will be made to benefit American workers and American families"[52]—a phony claim, as the tax bill shows. He craves pomp and circumstance, claiming "That military may be flying over New York City and Washington, D.C., for parades. I mean, we're going to be showing our military."[53] Demagoguery, to be sure, became Trump's staple diet on which he feeds.

Egomaniac: For Trump, being an egomaniac fits not only his persona, but also his perpetually revolting self-praise. Perhaps he still doesn't believe, for good reason, that he is the president and needs constant reinforcement. To show the enormity of his ego can best be expressed by his tweeting that "Time Magazine called to say that I was PROBABLY going to be named 'Man (Person) of the Year,' like last year, but I would have to agree to an interview and a major photo shoot. I said probably is no good and took a pass."[54] To this day, Trump continues to boast about the size of his inaugural crowd, insisting that he had a much larger turnout than Obama in 2009. He still can't digest that a smaller crowd attended his inauguration than that of a Black president, which irks him more than anything else.

Fraud: Trump is the only president who has committed fraud on such an unparalleled scale. Starting with Trump University, he violated NY laws by calling it a university and operating without an educational license. He charged students $35,000 a year, promising they would "learn from Donald Trump's handpicked instructors, and that participants would have access to Trump's real estate 'secrets.'"[55] No jobs were offered, and no secret information was shared or revealed because there was none. He has filed for bankruptcy four times (1991, 1992, 2004, and 2009) and has been repeatedly fined for breaking rules related to his casinos. He was found this year to have used his "charity," the Donald J. Trump Foundation, as an extension of his business and campaign; the foundation was shut down and ordered to pay $2 million in damages to eight legitimate charities.[56] The dictionary might as well define the word "fraud" by citing some of Trump's fraudulent business dealings.

Garbled: If nothing else, Trump is a master of garbled words. Despite his bragging about his own language skills, his garbled words and unscripted utterances are incoherent, such as his description of Napoleon, while visiting his tomb: "He did so many things even beyond. And his one problem is he didn't go to Russia that night because he had extracurricular activities, and they froze to death." He rambled on about foreign policy, stating "You know, he [Obama] can talk tough all he wants, in the meantime he talked tough to North Korea. And he didn't actually. You look at the red line in the sand in Syria. He didn't do the shot. I did the shot."[57] Yes, Trump did attack a Syrian airbase, but only after "receiving permission" from Putin.

Heartless: Putting his travel ban into immediate effect, stranding hundreds at airports, blocking off access to the US arbitrarily, and, more than anything else, putting children as young as two years old in cages is as heartless and cruel as can be imagined. He endorsed a proposed repeal of Obamacare without plans to provide aid to disadvantaged communities. He has made no effort to renew the Children's Health Insurance Program, ending care for nine million low-income children, while giving billions in tax cuts to the richest of the rich.[58] He callously ended DACA, which will affect almost 700,000 young adults who came to the US when they were children and don't have a home to return to if deported. Not to speak of the fact that terminating DACA would also lead to splitting up families—those who illegally immigrated but have children who were born in the US. If Trump needed a heart transplant, his body would reject any heart that has not already been infused with cruelty and malice.

Ignorant: Trump has repeatedly demonstrated that being ignorant is a virtue, especially when he pretends to know everything. He suggested that Frederick Douglass is still alive, offering "Frederick Douglass as an example of somebody who's done an amazing job and is getting recognized more and more, I notice."[59] He took pride in the fact that he was tutored by Chinese President Xi Jinping about Korean-Chinese relations at a dinner. That's how a quick learner he is. When discussing healthcare, he stated, "Nobody knew healthcare could be so complicated."[60] Of course not. Trump thought that repeating "repeal and replace" would be all it would take to resolve America's healthcare problem.

Juvenile: Trump talks, walks, and brags like a juvenile. He continuously tweets memes that no self-respecting adult would dream of doing—a meme with his head photoshopped onto Rocky Balboa's body, a meme with him awarding a fake medal to the dog injured in the raid on Abu Bakr al-Baghdadi, and a meme of him as the genocidal villain Thanos from the *Avengers* films wiping out his Democratic rivals, posted by his team. Offline, he left this month's NATO conference early after video circulated of other leaders venting about his erratic actions.[61] So, if you walk, talk, and brag like a juvenile, you are qualified to replace Trump.

Knavish: Knavishness is another characteristic that defines Trump as he has now become known: having no scruples and no principles. He insisted that his tax bill would benefit all Americans, when every study shows that the tax bill benefited the rich the most and will in fact harm middle-class and low-income families.[62] Since the bill was passed, Trump's biggest claims have been disproven by economists. He commonly mistreats his workers (many of whom were undocumented immigrants).[63] There are still many lawsuits against him for not paying his laborers.[64] Unfortunately for them, they will have to wait to sue him once he is out of office. Having been impeached is one frog leap toward the White House's exit.

Liar: If nothing else, Trump is known as a compulsive liar, and his political ascendance was built on lies. He really believes that if one repeats a lie time and again, it becomes the accepted truth and that is good enough for his base. *The Washington Post,* which tallies Trump's lies, reports that Trump has lied or made misleading statements over fifteen thousand times since becoming president (as of December 10, 2019). He lied about voter fraud, protesters being paid to oppose him, Obama wiretapping his phones, how many times he was on the cover of *Time*—the list goes on and on. His file in *Politifact* says he has outright lied over 50 percent of the time. At a rally in Pensacola, FL, he said "Black homeownership just hit the highest level it has ever been in the history of our country," but it's actually fallen almost yearly since 2004.[65] Trump is in his element when he is living in a world of colorful lies.

Manipulator: As a master manipulator, Trump uses language to galvanize voters; for instance, by using the marketable slogan "Make America Great Again," he made his politics an easy sale. He licensed and sold his name to give the appearance of success and stability. He used terrorist attacks in London and Egypt to push his travel ban.[66] He condemns others' actions in order to cover his own despicable delinquency (like his tweet in response to Al Franken's sexual misconduct,* when in fact he is the sexual predator-in-chief). For Trump, manipulation is a sort of twisted art form, and he should probably have his picture on the cover of *Time* magazine with caption "Manipulator of the Year."

Narcissist: When it comes to being a narcissist, Trump trumps them all— Putin, Erdogan, Netanyahu, and even Kim Jong Un. Everything Trump does is designed to make it solely about himself. When campaigning for failed Republican Senate candidate Luther Strange, he said, "I'm taking a big risk because if Luther does not make it, they are going to go after me."[67] Even in tragedy, he pulls attention back around to himself: "Appreciate the congrats for being right on radical Islamic terrorism."[68] On his desk, instead of having a Truman-esque plaque that reads "The Buck Stops Here," Trump's should read "It is me, me, me, all about me."

Obsessive: Trump's obsessive behavior spills out like waste from a corroded pipeline. He is obsessed with his looks, especially his thinning hair, and with people he hates, calling them by derogatory names. He refers to former VP Biden, who is likely to be his rival in 2020, "sleepy Joe." His obsession with image is tied up with his decades-long lust for being named *Time's* Person of the Year. He lashed out at this year's honoree, sixteen-year-old climate activist Greta Thunberg, decrying on Twitter: "So ridiculous. Greta must work on her Anger Management problem, then go to a good old-fashioned movie with a friend! Chill Greta, Chill!"[69] He never let go of Hillary Clinton's emails and wallows in conspiracy theories, such as the one claiming Ukraine interfered in the 2016 election on Clinton's behalf, not Russia on his own. In a competition for the title of the most obsessed person in the world, Trump would win handily.

Polarizing: When it comes to polarizing, you've got to give Trump an A+.

---

* "The Al Frankenstien picture is really bad, speaks a thousand words. Where do his hands go in pictures 2, 3, 4, 5 & 6 while she sleeps? .... And to think that just last week he was lecturing anyone who would listen about sexual harassment and respect for women. Lesley Stahl tape?" (Nov. 16, 2017)

His policies and behaviors polarize the public: the wall, the travel ban, his reactions towards the press, his treatment of immigrants .... Trump's name itself is polarizing. He sees everything in black and white, no middle ground, which has become increasingly painful for him in dealing with seriously complex issues. Since he came to office, the political and social divisiveness in the country grew ever wider, and "Us vs. Them" became the refrain of the day. The country has never been as divided politically as it has been since he came to office. To keep his base, Trump plays one group against another while enjoying the tension he creates.

Querulous: Another trait that distinguishes Trump is his querulous nature. He constantly picks fights on Twitter, makes wild statements like threatening to attack North Korea, and engages in disparaging statements to pick fights with senators, judges, football players, and many others, only to score a point. After Sen. Kirsten Gillibrand called for Trump to resign due to increasing sexual harassment, he showered her with insults and went as far as clearly implying that she had traded sexual favors for campaign contributions. His quarrel with the Democrats has become his staple of the day. He craves mean fights, which seem to energize him and give him that psychopathic satisfaction.

Racist: Trump is a racist man to the bone. Only a person who is disposed to white supremacy could draw a moral equivalence between white nationalists in the Charlottesville rallies and law-abiding counter-protestors, some of whom turned violent. His opposition to immigration is based totally on race and ethnicity. He made it clear that he wants to shut the border to immigrants from Central and South America precisely because they are Hispanic, while welcoming any white Europeans to immigrate. He claimed that one of the federal judges acting in the class action case against Trump University couldn't do his job because "he's a Mexican."[70] And no one can deny the fact that there was a notable difference between his response to Hurricane Maria (which devastated Puerto Rico) and his prompt and immediate generous aid to victims of Hurricanes Irma and Harvey (which affected Florida and Texas).[71] From Trump's perspective, white supremacy is only natural, as is the "inferiority" of minorities.

Showman: Being a showman is to a great extent the means by which Trump covers his shortcomings and lack of self-confidence. Everything, beginning with his candidacy announcement riding on a golden escalator, has been a performance. He has a predilection for props, from comparisons of Obamacare to its replacement, scores of folders purportedly containing plans to disentangle himself from his businesses, to giant stacks of paper adorned with red tape (to be cut with gold scissors) to symbolize his efforts to cut regulations.[72] To top it all, Trump lives and breathes for his rallies, which he continued from day one after his inauguration. He craves showing off his oratory skills, even though his messages are convoluted and often make no sense. In short, Trump lives on showmanship, and without a stage he feels empty—because he is.

Toxic: There has been a rise in hate crimes and antisemitism since Trump took office.[73] Trump's selfishness poisons the civilian and political atmosphere, infecting Congress and splitting the GOP. The list of current and past government officials, conservative media editors and columnists, and intelligence officials in opposition to Trump is incomparable to any of his predecessors. Trump's hatred toward anyone he views as opposed to him has long since become toxic. At his recent rally in Michigan, he viciously attacked Rep. Debbie Dingell, saying that her late husband, widely respected former Rep. John Dingell, may be "looking up" from hell, after her vote to impeach Trump.[74] Such a toxic and hateful statement was widely condemned from both sides of the aisle. Trump wanted to "drain the swamp" in Washington, but all he has done make the swamp larger, leaving toxic waste in his wake.

Unstable: Many people are concerned about Trump's unstable behavior, and even more are deeply troubled about its implications for his mental acuity. Time and again, Trump has demonstrated how unhinged he is. He is compulsive and reacts to matters unrelated to governance, getting into Twitter fights with people for no logical reason.[**] Trump is dangerously losing touch with reality. His erratic behavior and abrupt change of position about people and policy all point to a chronic mental disorder. Thousands of psychiatrists and psychologists from around the country who have been following his conduct and utterances strongly suggest that given his erratic behavior, he has a mental illness. Only an unstable person such as Trump would have penned the six-page letter he sent to Nancy Pelosi on the eve of his impeachment, full of lines such as "you know from the [Ukraine] transcript ... that the paragraph in question was perfect," "you have found

---

** Including model Chrissy Teigen, actress Debra Messing, Dayton, OH mayor Nan Whaley, and Senator Sherrod Brown (D-OH), among many, many others.

NOTHING!" in reference to the pre-impeachment hearings (which did in fact uncover a great deal of information), and referring to the last presidential election as "the great Election of 2016," among many other unhinged statements.[75]

Vulgar: The record on Trump's vulgarity is astounding. He seems to relish his vulgarity and the meanness that goes with it. It has been on full display since announcing his campaign, and has only continued three years into his presidency. He has continuously referred to Rep. Adam Schiff, head of the House Intelligence Committee and Trump's latest obsessive target, as Adam "Schitt," and in his attacks against former FBI attorney and agent Lisa Page and Peter Strzok, he imitated the sounds of an orgasm at a rally in reference to their (irrelevant) affair. For Trump, vulgarity is his drug of choice, on which he regularly overdoses.

Whiny: Trump himself openly and repeatedly admitted that he is whiny. In a statement to CNN's Chris Cuomo, he admitted: "I do whine because I want to win and I'm not happy about not winning and I am a whiner and I keep whining and whining until I win."[76] His excessive whining, however, did not help him to avert his impeachment in the House of Representatives. In fact, the more he kept whining that his conversation with Ukrainian President Zelensky was "perfect," thinking that he would eventually convince the public of the innocence of his call, he finally realized that his recipe to win through whining is just not working. In a typical show that everything must be about him, Trump even whined that he wasn't given enough credit for late Sen. John McCain's funeral, throwing a few lies in for good measure. "I didn't get a thank you," he said about his false claim that he had to approve McCain's state funeral.[77] Trump will soon realize that no matter how much he whines, in the future he will end up the loser because he has nothing to offer, other than whining.

Xenophobic: Trump was born xenophobic, a chauvinistic fool with no sense of what is right or wrong. He led an assault on immigrants—whether they be Muslim, Arab, or Hispanic—which he reinforced through his refugee and travel ban and "America First" campaign. He has attempted to cut off funding for sanctuary cities, which house thousands of immigrants, through Executive Order 13768. And through Attorney General Jeff Sessions and the Justice Department, he has been sending letters that attempt to harass jurisdictions that he feels have weak immigration policies into working with ICE.[78] Simply put, Trump's xenophobia is a consuming obsession based on illusions he often entertains, regardless of how far they might be removed from reality.

Yellow-Bellied: Trump is simply a yellow-bellied coward, which has been plain to see for decades. He dodged the draft in Vietnam and reacted to being gifted a veteran's Purple Heart by saying "I always wanted to get the Purple Heart. This was much easier."[79] His fear and trepidation about the Russia probe prompted him to fire FBI Director Comey. He was terrified of what Special Counsel Robert Mueller's investigation would eventually reveal, knowing that Russia's interference in the 2016 election and the potential collusion to help him win the presidency would be of focus. Deep down, Trump knows he did not earn the presidency and has been horrified by the idea that he might be impeached. Well, his nightmare has finally come true, because the writing was on the wall from the day he took office.

Zealot: Trump is an unbending zealot—not as much about his religious or ideological convictions, because he is neither a religious man nor prescribes to any ideology, but far more so about his possessions and the image he wants to project. To show his "conservative credentials" (although he would trade them for any self-serving interest), he nominated two extreme right-wing federal court judges to lifetime positions. One helped craft voter suppression laws in North Carolina, and the other professed that the promotion of transgender rights is "Satan's plan."**** Trump delivered a speech in Warsaw in July 2017 that was highly reminiscent of alt-right rhetoric, leaving the unmistakable impression that zealotry will guard his conservative white base.[80]

There is a touch of humor here and there to lighten up this alphabetic review of Trump's three years in office, but the subject matter is fateful to America's future. Trump is dangerous: his shortsightedness, mental instability, and ominous off-the-cuff statements could spark unintended horrifying consequences for America and the world.

The Republican Party, which is deeply engrossed in partisan politics, has become the enabler of Trump, ignoring the fact that they were elected not to protect the president but America's global and national security interests and the wellbeing of the American people. Every member of the Re-

---

*** Thomas Farr and Jeff Mateer; neither were confirmed by the Senate.

publican Party establishment will be held responsible for not rising up and stopping Trump from causing irreparable damage to the country's global leadership role and moral standing and for the social and political injury that he has inflicted on the nation.

Any individual, let alone the president, who praises Putin's Russia—America's foremost enemy—and in the same breath severely criticizes and disparages our most esteemed institutions, especially the intelligence agencies and the judiciary, is tantamount to treason. How could any Republican official who claims to put the country's security and safety first remain silent in the face of this unfolding perilous development? And worse yet, how could they continue to support a president who is unstable, unpredictable, and unfit to occupy the chair of the president? But then here we are. Trump will soon face trial in the Senate following his impeachment in the House, but there is hardly a single Republican member of Congress who has called for a fair trial and agreed to call witnesses and present documents that could potentially incriminate him.

This is the greatest travesty committed by the Party of Lincoln to whom the Constitution was a sacred document. Now the Republicans are unabashedly willing to toss it down the river. They put party and personal interest first and allow a lawless president to act like a monarch—a so-called president who has never been able to rise above the fray to determine the national security and wellbeing of the country. Judgment day is fast approaching.

Notes

1   Thomas Kaplan, "How the Trump Campaign Used Facebook Ads to Amplify His 'Invasion' Claim," *New York Times*, Aug. 5, 2019, https://www.nytimes.com/2019/08/05/us/politics/trump-campaign-facebook-ads-invasion.html.

2   Susan Miller, "El Paso, Dayton Make 251 Mass Shootings in the US in 216 Days, More Shootings than Days in the Year," *USA Today*, Aug. 3, 2019, https://www.usatoday.com/story/news/nation/2019/08/03/el-paso-walmart-shooting-250th-mass-shooting-this-year/1913486001/.

3   Phil Helsel and Kalhan Rosenblatt, "Horror in El Paso Another in a Long List of Mass Killings Plaguing the Nation," *NBC News*, Aug. 3, 2019, https://www.nbcnews.com/news/us-news/mass-shooting-el-paso-deadliest-2019-among-worst-modern-u-n1039016.

4   Peter Baker and Michael D. Shear, "El Paso Shooting Suspect's Manifesto Echoes Trump's Language," *New York Times*, Aug. 4, 2019, https://www.nytimes.com/2019/08/04/us/politics/trump-mass-shootings.html.

5   "Summary for Policymakers of IPCC Special Report on Global Warming of 1.5°C Approved by Governments," *Intergovernmental Panel on Climate Change*, Oct. 8, 2018, https://www.ipcc.ch/2018/10/08/summary-for-policymakers-of-ipcc-special-report-on-global-warming-of-1-5c-approved-by-governments/.

6   Simon Evans, "Why Fossil Fuel Divestment won't be Easy," Carbon Brief, Aug. 27, 2014, https://www.carbonbrief.org/why-fossil-fuel-divestment-wont-be-easy.

7   "Fossil Fuels Still Dominate U.S. Energy Consumption Despite Recent Market Share Decline," *US Energy Information Administration*, Jul. 1, 2016, https://www.eia.gov/todayinenergy/detail.php?id=26912.

8   Samantha Page, "The Most Villainous Act in History," *Cosmos*, Feb. 12, 2019, https://cosmosmagazine.com/climate/the-most-villainous-act-in-the-history-of-human-civilisation-tyler-prize-winner-michael-e-mann-speaks-out.

9   Ibid.

10   "Wildfires and Climate Change," *Center for Climate and Energy Solutions*, accessed Aug. 12, 2019, https://www.c2es.org/content/wildfires-and-climate-change/.

11   Edward Struzik, *Firestorm: How Wildfire Will Shape Our Future* (Washington, DC: Island Press, 2017), 238.

12   Frank Bierman and Ingrid Boas, "Preparing for a Warmer World: Towards a Global Governance System to Protect Climate Refugees," *Global Environmental Politics* 10, no. 1 (2010): 60–88.

13   "Within and Beyond Borders: Tracking Displacement in the Lake Chad Basin," *International Organization for Migration*, Displacement Tracking Matrix, March 2019, https://www.iom.int/sites/default/files/dtm/lake_chad_basin_dtm_201903.pdf.

14   "Population of Paradise down 90 Percent after Wildfire," *Associated Press*, Jul. 11, 2019, https://ktla.com/news/nationworld/population-of-paradise-down-90-percent-after-wildfire/.

15   "United States," *Internal Displacement Monitoring Centre*, accessed Aug. 12, 2019, https://www.internal-displacement.org/countries/united-states.

16   Tim McDonnell, "The Refugees the World Barely Pays Attention to," *NPR*, Jun. 20, 2018, https://www.npr.org/sections/goatsandsoda/2018/06/20/621782275/the-refugees-that-the-world-barely-pays-attention-to.

17   Letícia Casado and Ernesto Londoño, "Under Brazil's Far-Right Leader, Amazon Protections Slashed and Forests Fall," *New York Times*, Jul. 28, 2019, https://www.

nytimes.com/2019/07/28/world/americas/brazil-deforestation-amazon-bolson aro.html.

18   Annika Dean, "Deforestation and Climate Change," *Climate Council*, Aug. 21, 2019, https://www.climatecouncil.org.au/deforestation/.

19   John Weier, "Mapping the Decline of Coral Reefs," *NASA Earth Observatory*, Mar. 12, 2001, https://earthobservatory.nasa.gov/features/Coral.

20   Sylvia A. Earle, Facebook post, Oct. 13, 2017, 11:49 a.m., https://www.facebook.com/sylvia.a.earle/.

21   Leslie Hook, "World to Miss Paris Climate Targets by Wide Margin, Says UN Panel," *Financial Times*, Oct. 8, 2018, https://www.ft.com/content/353d0cac-ca52-11e8-9fe5-24ad351828ab.

22   "Blame Humans for Starting the Amazon Fires, Environmentalists Say," *CBS News Richmond*, Aug. 23, 2019, https://wtvr.com/2019/08/23/blame-humans-for-starting-the-amazon-fires-environmentalists-say/.

23   Joao Vitor Da Silva Marques and Orlando Crowcroft, "G7 Countries to Provide $20 Million in Emergency Funding to Combat Amazon Fires," *Euronews*, Aug. 26, 2019, https://www.euronews.com/2019/08/26/macron-g7-close-to-deal-on-am azon-fires-on-final-day-of-talks-in-biarritz.

24   Vasco Cotovio, "Amazon Destruction Accelerates 60% to One and a Half Soccer Fields Every Minute," *CNN*, Jul. 2, 2019, https://www.cnn.com/2019/07/02/americas/amazon-brazil-bolsonaro-deforestation-scli-intl/index.html.

25   Food and Agriculture Organization of the United Nations, *The State of Forests in the Amazon Basin, Congo Basin and Southeast Asia*. Report prepared for the Summit of the Three Rainforest Basins, Brazzaville, Republic of Congo, 2011, 61.

26   Fiona Maisels et al., "Devastating Decline of Forest Elephants in Central Africa," *PLOS ONE* 8, no. 3 (2013), https://doi.org/10.1371/journal.pone.0059469.

27   International Organization for Migration, *World Migration Report 2020* (Geneva, Switzerland: 2019), 45; "Asylum Statistics," *Eurostat*, May 26, 2020, https://ec.eu ropa.eu/eurostat/statistics-explained/index.php/Asylum_statistics.

28   Frank Biermann and Ingrid Boas, "Preparing for a Warmer World: Towards a Global Governance System to Protect Climate Refugees," *Global Environmental Politics* 10, no. 1 (2010).

29   John Vidal, "Global Warming could Create 150 Million 'Climate Refugees' by 2050," *The Guardian*, Nov. 2, 2009, https://www.theguardian.com/environment/2009/nov/03/global-warming-climate-refugees.

30   Weier, "Mapping the Decline of Coral Reefs."

31 Earle, Facebook post.

32 Compassion in World Farming, *Strategic Plan 2013-2017: For Kinder, Fairer Farming Worldwide* (UK: Godalming), 5.

33 "Livestock a Major Threat to Environment," *FAO Newsroom,* Nov. 29, 2006, http:// www.fao.org/newsroom/en/news/2006/1000448/index.html.

34 "Greenhouse Gas Emissions from Animal Agriculture," *The Humane Society of the United States,* accessed Sep. 24, 2019, https://www.humanesociety.org/sites/de fault/files/archive/assets/pdfs/farm/hsus-fact-sheet-greenhouse-gas-emissions-from-animal-agriculture.pdf.

35 Jonathan Safran Foer, *Eating Animals* (New York: Little Brown and Company, 2009), 194, Cloud Library edition.

36 Greta Thunberg, "Climate Action Summit 2019 - Morning Session," YouTube Video, 41:38, Sep. 23, 2019, New York, NY, https://www.youtube.com/watch?v=hae wHZ8ubKA&feature=emb_title.

37 "Turkey Syria Offensive: Dozens Killed as Assault Continues," *BBC News,* Oct. 11, 2019, https://www.bbc.com/news/world-middle-east-50011468.

38 "Turkey's Military Operation in Syria: All the Latest Updates," *Al Jazeera,* Oct. 13, 2019, https://www.aljazeera.com/news/2019/10/turkey-military-operation-syr ia-latest-updates-191011060434166.html.

39 Chris Dixon and Colby Itkowitz, "Sen. Graham Calls Trump Decision on Syria 'Biggest Blunder of His Presidency,'" *Washington Post,* Oct. 10, 2019, https:// www.washingtonpost.com/politics/sen-graham-calls-trump-decision-on-syria-biggest-blunder-of-his-presidency/2019/10/10/f693741c-eb95-11e9-9c6d-436a0df4f31d_story.html.

40 "Netanyahu Condemns 'Turkish Invasion of Kurdish Areas' in Syria," *Reuters,* Oct. 10, 2019, https://www.reuters.com/article/us-syria-crisis-israel-netanyahu/ netanyahu-condemns-turkish-invasion-of-kurdish-areas-in-syria-idUSKBN1W P1RC.

41 Fahrettin Altun, Twitter post, Oct. 10, 2019, 9:51 a.m., https://twitter.com/fahret tinaltun/.

42 Cristina Abellan Matamoros and Luke Hurst, "Macron: Turkey's Military Campaign in Syria Helping ISIS Build Caliphate," *Euronews,* Oct. 10, 2019, https:// www.euronews.com/2019/10/10/macron-turkey-s-military-campaign-in-syria-helping-isis-build-caliphate.

43 John Bolton, "Speech at Free Iran Gathering," YouTube Video, 4:17, Jul. 1, 2017, https://www.youtube.com/watch?v=hTMh24qlyQA&feature=youtu.be&t= 4m17s.

44 "The Strait of Hormuz is the World's Most Important Oil Transit Chokepoint," *US Energy Information Administration,* Jun. 20, 2019, https://www.eia.gov/todayinen ergy/detail.php?id=39932.

45 John Irish and Robin Emmott, "European Concerns Raise Prospect of Renewed U.N. Sanctions on Iran," *Reuters,* Nov. 12, 2019, https://www.reuters.com/article/ us-iran-nuclear-europe-analysis/european-concerns-raise-prospect-of-renewed- un-sanctions-on-iran-idUSKBN1XM2EB.

46 "Syria: 560,000 Killed in Seven Yrs of War," *Syrian Observatory for Human Rights,* Dec. 12, 2018, https://www.syriahr.com/en/108829/; Herve Verhoosel, "Syrian Crisis Enters Ninth Year with 11 Million Refugees Overseas & 6 Million Home," *ReliefWeb,* Mar. 15, 2019, https://reliefweb.int/report/syrian-arab-republic/syri an-crisis-enters-ninth-year-11-million-refugees-overseas-6-million.

47 Aaron Blake, "19 Things Donald Trump Knows Better than Anyone Else, Accord- ing to Donald Trump," *Washington Post,* Oct. 4, 2016, https://www.washington- post.com/news/the-fix/wp/2016/10/04/17-issues-that-donald-trump-knows- better-than-anyone-else-according-to-donald-trump/.

48 Donald Trump, "Presidential Campaign Announcement," YouTube Video, 3:34, Jun. 16, 2015, https://youtu.be/apjNfkysjbM?t=214.

49 Maggie Haberman and Richard A. Oppel Jr., "Donald Trump Criticizes Muslim Family of Slain U.S. Soldier, Drawing Ire," *New York Times,* Jul. 30, 2016, https:// www.nytimes.com/2016/07/31/us/politics/donald-trump-khizr-khan-wife- ghazala.html.

50 Donald J. Trump, Twitter post, Aug. 19, 2019, 9:19 a.m., https://twitter.com/real DonaldTrump/.

51 "'I Think Islam Hates Us,'" *New York Times,* Jan. 26, 2017, https://www.nytimes. com/2017/01/26/opinion/i-think-islam-hates-us.html.

52 Donald J. Trump, "Inaugural Address," Video, 37:33, Jan. 20, 2017, https://www. whitehouse.gov/briefings-statements/the-inaugural-address/.

53 Abby Phillip, "Trump Says He Wants a Massive Military Parade down Pennsylvania Avenue on July 4," *Washington Post,* Sep. 18, 2017, https://www.washingtonpost. com/news/post-politics/wp/2017/09/18/trump-says-he-wants-a-massive-mili tary-parade-down-pennsylvania-avenue-on-july-4/.

54 Donald J. Trump, Twitter post, Nov. 24, 2017, 5:40 p.m., https://twitter.com/real DonaldTrump/.

55 David A. Graham, "The Many Scandals of Donald Trump: A Cheat Sheet," *The Atlantic,* Jan. 23, 2017, https://www.theatlantic.com/politics/archive/2017/01/ donald-trump-scandals/474726/.

56 Luis Ferré-Sadurní, "Trump Pays $2 Million to 8 Charities for Misuse of Foundation," *New York Times*, Dec. 10, 2019, https://www.nytimes.com/2019/12/10/nyregion/trump-foundation-lawsuit-attorney-general.html.

57 "Excerpts from the Times's Interview with Trump," *New York Times*, Jul. 19, 2017, https://www.nytimes.com/2017/07/19/us/politics/trump-interview-transcript.html.

58 Eric Levitz, "Congress will not Renew the Children's Health Insurance Program this Year," *New York Magazine*, Dec. 20, 2017, https://nymag.com/intelligencer/2017/12/congress-will-not-renew-chip-this-year.html.

59 David A. Graham, "Donald Trump's Narrative of the Life of Frederick Douglass," *The Atlantic*, Feb. 1, 2017, https://www.theatlantic.com/politics/archive/2017/02/frederick-douglass-trump/515292/.

60 Kevin Liptak, "Trump: 'Nobody Knew Health Care Could be So Complicated,'" *CNN*, Feb. 28, 2017, https://www.cnn.com/2017/02/27/politics/trump-health-care-complicated/index.html.

61 Annie Karni and Katie Rogers, "Trump Abruptly Exits NATO Gathering after Embarrassing Video Emerges," *New York Times*, Dec. 4, 2019, https://www.nytimes.com/2019/12/04/world/europe/trump-video-nato.html.

62 John F. Wasik, "How the GOP Tax Plan Scrooges Middle Class, Retired And Poor," *Forbes*, Nov. 29, 2017, https://www.forbes.com/sites/johnwasik/2017/11/29/how-the-gop-tax-plan-scrooges-middle-class-retired-and-poor/#64fc95386c1e.

63 Charles V. Bagli, "Trump Paid over $1 Million in Labor Settlement, Documents Reveal," *New York Times*, Nov. 27, 2017, https://www.nytimes.com/2017/11/27/nyregion/trump-tower-illegal-immigrant-workers-union-settlement.html.

64 Steve Reilly, "USA TODAY Exclusive: Hundreds Allege Donald Trump doesn't Pay His Bills," *USA Today*, Jun. 9, 2016, https://www.usatoday.com/story/news/politics/elections/2016/06/09/donald-trump-unpaid-bills-republican-president-lawsuits/85297274/.

65 Louis Jacobson, "Donald Trump Wrong that Black Homeownership Rate is at a Record High," *Politifact*, Dec. 11, 2017, https://www.politifact.com/factchecks/2017/dec/11/donald-trump/donald-trump-wrong-black-homeownership-rate-record/.

66 Donald J. Trump, Twitter post, Sep. 15, 2017, 6:54 a.m.; Nov. 24, 2017, 1:49 p.m., https://twitter.com/realDonaldTrump/.

67 Bill Britt, "Moore Supporter Says, 'If Strange Wins Thank Trump if He Loses Thank God,'" *Alabama Political Reporter*, Sep. 25, 2017, https://www.alreporter.com/2017/09/25/moore-supporter-says-strange-wins-thank-trump-loses-thank-god/.

68   Donald J. Trump, Twitter post, Jun. 12, 2016, 12:43 p.m., https://twitter.com/real donaldtrump/.

69   Donald J. Trump, Twitter post, Dec. 12, 2019, 7:22 a.m., https://twitter.com/real donaldtrump/.

70   Lydia O'Connor and Daniel Marans, "Here are 13 Examples of Donald Trump Being Racist," *HuffPost*, Feb. 29, 2016, https://www.huffpost.com/entry/don ald-trump-racist-examples_n_56d47177e4b03260bf777e83.

71   Ron Nixon and Matt Stevens, "Harvey, Irma, Maria: Trump Administration's Response Compared," *New York Times*, Sep. 27, 2017, https://www.nytimes. com/2017/09/27/us/politics/trump-puerto-rico-aid.html.

72   Andrew Beaujon, "Donald Trump Keeps Using Stacks of Papers to Settle Arguments," *Washingtonian*, Mar. 7, 2017, https://www.washingtonian.com/2017/03/07/ donald-trump-stacks-of-papers/; Nolan D. McCaskill and Matthew Nussbaum, "Trump, Gold Scissors in Hand, Cuts Red Tape at White House," *Politico*, Dec. 14, 2017, https://www.politico.com/story/2017/12/14/trump-cut-red-tape-busi ness-regulations-296834.

73   Christopher Mathias, "Exclusive: New Report Offers Proof of US Hate Crime Rise in the Trump Era," *HuffPost*, Sep. 17, 2017, https://www.huffpost.com/entry/ hate-crime-rise-2016-united-states-trump_n_59becac8e4b086432b07fed8.

74   Brett Samuels and Morgan Chalfant, "Trump's Dingell Insults Disrupt GOP Unity amid Impeachment," *The Hill*, Dec. 20, 2019, https://thehill.com/homenews/ad ministration/475374-trumps-dingell-insults-disrupt-gop-unity-on-impeachment.

75   Donald J. Trump, letter to Nancy Pelosi, Dec. 17, 2019, https://www.whitehouse. gov/wp-content/uploads/2019/12/Letter-from-President-Trump-final.pdf.

76   Jeremy Diamond, "Donald Trump: 'I Keep Whining and Whining until I Win,'" *CNN*, Aug. 11, 2015, https://www.cnn.com/2015/08/11/politics/donald-trump- refutes-third-party-run-report/index.html.

77   Katie Galioto, "Trump Says He Never Got a Thank You for McCain's Funeral," *Politico*, Mar. 20, 2019, https://www.politico.com/story/2019/03/20/trump-mc cain-funeral-1230483.

78   "Justice Department Sends Letters to 29 Jurisdictions Regarding Their Compliance with 8 U.S.C. 1373," *United States Department of Justice*, Nov. 15, 2017, https:// www.justice.gov/opa/pr/justice-department-sends-letters-29-jurisdictions-re garding-their-compliance-8-usc-1373.

79   Nick Gass, "Trump: 'I Always Wanted to Get the Purple Heart. This was Much Eas- ier,'" *Politico*, Aug. 2, 2016, https://www.politico.com/story/2016/08/trump-pur ple-heart-226565.

80   Sarah Wildman, "Trump's Speech in Poland Sounded like an Alt-Right Mani-festo," *Vox*, Jul. 6, 2017, https://www.vox.com/world/2017/7/6/15927590/trump-alt-right-poland-defend-west-civilization-g20.

2020

STEPPING BACK FROM THE BRINK OF WAR

January 15, 2020

Trump's order to kill General Soleimani is one of the most reckless acts taken by a president, and he has once again put his personal political interest above the nation's security. Certainly, Soleimani deserved to meet his bitter fate. He was behind the killing of hundreds of American soldiers in Iraq while threatening and acting against American allies. However, killing him without considering the potentially dire regional repercussions and without a strategy, under the guise of national security concerns, is hard to fathom.

Republican members of Congress who praised the assassination of General Soleimani seem to be utterly blinded by their desire to see him eliminated. What will happen next, they seem to have no clue. Trump, who is fighting for his political life, appears to have cared less about the horrifying consequences as long as he distracts public attention from his political woes. He made the decision to assassinate Soleimani seven months ago, but he gave the order now to serve his own self-interest, especially in this election year, where he desperately needs a victory while awaiting an impeachment trial in the Senate.

During the Senate briefing on Iran led by Secretaries of State and Defense Pompeo and Esper and CIA Director Haspel, they produced no evidence that there was an imminent danger of an attack on four American embassies orchestrated by Soleimani, as Trump claimed. In fact, Esper said openly in a January 12 interview that he saw no evidence.[1]

Republican Senator Mike Lee labeled it as "probably the worst briefing I have seen, at least on a military issue .... What I found so distressing about the briefing is one of the messages we received from the briefers was, 'Do not debate, do not discuss the issue of the appropriateness of further military intervention against Iran,' and that if you do, 'You will be emboldening Iran.'"[2] Now, having failed to produce evidence of imminent danger, the Trump administration claims that the killing of Soleimani was part of a long-term deterrence strategy.

The assassination itself has certainly emboldened Iran's resolve to continue its nefarious activities throughout the region, but even then, the measure

Trump took to presumably make the US more secure has in fact done the complete opposite.

It has created new mounting problems and multiple crises. Trump danger-ously escalated the conflict with Iran; severely compromised the United States' geostrategic interest in the Middle East; intensified the Iranian threat against our allies, especially Israel; led Iran to double down in its support of terrorist and jihadist groups; badly wounded US relations with its Euro-pean allies; deemed the US untrustworthy by friends and foes; and pushed Iran to annul much of the nuclear deal, all while impressively advancing its anti-ballistic missile technology.

And contrary to Trump's claim that he made the right decision for the sake of American security, 55 percent of voters in a USA Today survey released on January 9 said he made the US less safe.[3] And we are still at the brink of war.

Although Iran has admitted to being behind the attack on the Asad air base in Iraq, it initiated the attack to save face in the eyes of its public and demonstrate its possession of precision missiles and willingness to stand up to the US. This retaliation was expected, but since Iran wants to avoid an all-out war, it was strategic and carefully calculated to inflict the fewest American casualties, if any, to prevent a vicious cycle of retaliatory attacks that could get out of control and lead to a war.

This, however, does not suggest that Iran will stop its clandestine proxy operations—employing its well-trained militia in Iraq, Yemen, and Syria to execute new attacks on American and allies' targets in the region while maintaining deniability. Similarly, the clergy can also pressure hawks in and outside the government to avoid any provocative acts against the US. Iran is patient and will carefully weigh its gains and losses before it takes the next step.

Following Iran's attack on the Asad base, Trump also showed restraint be-cause he too wants to prevent an all-out war, knowing that even though the US can win it handedly, it will be the costliest victory in blood, treasure, and certainly political capital.

The whole mess began when Trump withdrew from the Iran deal. What did Trump think he could accomplish? Withdrawing from the deal without having any substitute, without consultation with the European signatories, and with re-imposing sanctions, especially when Iran was in full compliance with all the deal's provisions, is dangerously reckless—undermining our national security interests and jeopardizing the security of our allies in the region. The Iran deal was not perfect, but the idea was to build on it, gradually normalize relations with Iran, and prevent it from acquiring nuclear weapons altogether as it works to become a constructive member of the community of nations.

To resolve the crisis with Iran, the US must demonstrate a clear understanding of the Iranian mindset. Iran is a proud nation with a long and continuing rich history; it has huge natural and human resources, is the leader of the Shiite world, occupies one of the most geostrategic locations in the world, and wants to be respected. The Iranians are not compulsive; they think strategically and are patient, consistent, and determined.

The revocation of the Iran deal simply reaffirms Iran's distrust of the US from the time the CIA toppled the Mosaddeq government in 1953 to the continuing sanctions, adversarial attitude, and open call for regime change.

Both Khamenei and Trump have their own domestic pressure to contend with and want to avoid war. The Iranian public is becoming increasingly restive. They are back in streets demanding immediate economic relief. Conversely, Trump calculated that further escalation of violent conflict with Iran will erode rather than enhance his political prospects, and would make defeat in November all but certain.

West European countries are extremely sensitive to any major escalation of violence, as it would lead to mounting casualties and destruction on all sides. Iran could resort to a wide range of hostile measures, including disrupting oil supplies from Saudi Arabia and other Gulf states, by mining the Straits of Hormuz through which twenty-one million barrels per day (21 percent of global oil consumption) pass, resulting in a massive economic dislocation in the Middle East and Europe in particular.[4]

The pause in hostilities offers a golden opportunity to begin a new process of mitigation. Germany, France, and Britain have already engaged the Iranians in an effort to ease the tension between Iran and the US and create conditions conducive to direct US-Iran negotiations. By now, Trump must realize that Iran cannot be bullied and the only way to prevent it from pursuing nuclear weapons is through dialogue.

Regardless of how flawed Trump views the Iran deal, it still provides the foundation for a new agreement, as many of its the original provisions remain valid and can be built on it. Other conflicting issues between the two sides, especially Iran's subversive activities, should be negotiated on a separate track.

In some ways, both Iran and the US need to lick their wounds and begin a new chapter, however long and arduous it may be, because war is not and will never be an option.

KILLING SOLEIMANI UNDERMINES GLOBAL ORDER

January 21, 2020

Those who applaud the assassination of General Soleimani seem to simply equate him to a terrorist who deserved to meet his fate. The question here is not whether he deserved to be killed, but whether his killing can be equated to those of Osama Bin Laden or Abu Bakr al-Baghdadi, the leaders of al-Qaeda and ISIS, respectively. They were the leaders of ferocious terrorist groups, stateless, and not associated with any international organization or recognized by a single country. The same cannot be said about Soleimani. Regardless of how vicious he was, he was also a very high-ranking government official in Iran, second only to Khamenei.

There are scores of other heads of state who are as brutal if not more so than Soleimani; are we now going to assassinate these individuals or their deputies because they are ruthless leaders? Are Turkey's Erdogan, Russia's Putin, China's Xi, North Korea's Kim, or the Philippines' Duterte less ruthless than Soleimani? These cruel leaders, who Trump openly admires, have committed unspeakable atrocities.

Just imagine what would have happened if Iran attacked a convoy escorting Vice President Pence and killed him just as he boarded his car near Riyadh airport. How would Trump have reacted? I venture to say that for Trump, this would have been tantamount to a declaration of war, just as Tehran viewed the attack on Soleimani. Trump would have retaliated in a massive way because an attack on a top US official by an adversary would simply be unacceptable to both Republicans and Democrats alike.

This begs the question as to what sort of global order we will have left if the leaders of one country eliminate the leaders of another simply because they deem them ruthless. Nothing but global chaos would ensue, destroying the very idea of an international order that governs the conduct of sovereign states toward one another. This would also defy the United Nations' founding principles and make it extraordinarily difficult for the community of nations to work together to solve bilateral and multilateral problems to make the world a safer place.

What is worse in the case of Soleimani is that he was assassinated at this particular time on the order of Trump, which was intended to distract public attention from Trump's political wounds and woes. Never mind that the Trump administration produced no shred of evidence of an imminent danger; nevertheless, he risked our national security strictly for his own personal political benefit. It is an election year, and he is now facing an impeachment trial in the Senate on charges of abuse of power and obstruction of Congress. If the past three years offer any indication, Trump would stop short of nothing, including obstruction of justice, cheating, lying, making misleading statements, threatening, bribing, and yes, killing foreign leaders to get reelected.

The Ukraine debacle, which blew up in his face and those of his top political advisors, pales in comparison to the assassination of Soleimani, which brought us to the verge of war with Iran—a war that would have made the Iraq war look like child's play. A war with Iran would exact thousands of American casualties at an astronomical cost while plunging the Middle East in an unending violent conflict that would spare none of our friends and allies.

Trump acted just like a dictator, and every single Republican member of Congress who demonstrates more loyalty to Trump than to the nation is complicit in his betrayal of the country. Senators, as jurors in his impeachment trial, have the opportunity to convict him based on the overwhelming evidence that he abused his power and obstructed Congress.

He must be stopped now because he is too dangerous and too reckless to be entrusted with national security and the wellbeing of the nation. Senators who exonerate him in his trial will be traitorous and will *put themselves* on trial come November.

Under any circumstances, Trump will leave office as an impeached president who made the world much less safe by playing into the hands of America's enemies. We and our allies will end up paying the price.

TRUMP'S DREADFUL FOREIGN POLICY

January 30, 2020

Recently, I met with a group of officials from different countries who came to the US to learn about our political system and the decision-making process regarding US foreign policy under the Trump administration. Had I been asked this question while Presidents Obama or Bush were in office, I could have answered with some specificity about certain US policies toward our allies and adversaries. However, Trump has no coherent foreign policy doctrine, no understanding of historical perspective, and no knowledge of the intricacies of various regional conflicts. He is dismissive of alliances, unbound by international agreements; he is erratic, unfettered, and issues policy directives based on "gut feelings." Here I provide a synopsis of Trump's foreign "policy" and the global disorder he has and continues to sow.

The Israeli-Palestinian conflict became more intractable than ever before, as Trump torpedoed the prospect of a two-state solution even before he unveiled his so-called "deal of the century." By moving the US embassy from Tel Aviv to Jerusalem in December 2017 and recognizing it as Israel's capital, declaring all settlements legal, giving the green light to annex the Jordan Valley, and freezing financial aid to the Palestinians, he deliberately left no room for the Palestinians to negotiate on the very issues that he granted to the Israelis. The Israeli right-wing celebration will be short-lived, as sooner than later this "deal" will explode in their faces. There is little prospect for peace left, and violence will be the order of the day.

Trump's abrupt withdrawal of US forces from Syria was nothing short of a disaster. He abandoned our most trusted ally in the fight against ISIS— the Syrian Kurds—to the mercy of Turkey's ruthless dictator Erdogan. Hundreds were killed and tens of thousands became refugees. Turkey has now established a foothold in Syria, and Russia became the sole power broker in the country. Iran became more determined than ever before to augment its military presence in Syria, which poses a constant threat to Israel and will make Syria the battleground between Israel and Iran. ISIS once again is on the rise, along with other jihadist groups, and violence between the conflicting parties will continue unabated. The US is left with no say about the country's future.

After three years of vacillation and uncertainty, **a new US-Iraq crisis ensued** immediately after the assassination of Iran's General Soleimani on Iraqi soil, ordered by Trump. Hundreds of thousands of Iraqis poured into the streets demanding the ouster of American troops, forcing the parliament to pass legislation to that effect. Trump's ill-fated decision further strained the already tense relations with Iraq, allowing Iran to further solidify its power and political influence in Iraq and severely undermine the United States' geostrategic interest in the country and the region. Although some US troops will remain in Iraq, as long as Iran dominates the Iraqi body politic, the US will increasingly be marginalized, which will adversely affect our allies in the Middle East.

The conflict with Iran is forty years old and has considerably worsened with Trump's hostile policy—first withdrawing from the Iran deal, then imposing crippling sanctions, threatening regime change, and most recently, assassinating General Soleimani. Instead of building on the nuclear deal, Trump destroyed any prospect of constructive relations with Iran, which has presently all but abandoned the deal. By all accounts, Iran can now produce any quantity and quality of uranium it chooses. Trump's misguided approach to Iran only increased the danger of proliferation of nuclear weapons and encouraged Iran to continue its nefarious activities in the Middle East. The new US-Iran conflict will destabilize the region, as the two countries remain at the precipice of war.

The effort to denuclearize North Korea was nothing but an illusion. Trump thought he could use his "unrivaled negotiating skills" to persuade Kim Jong Un to dismantle his nuclear weapons before the US would lift any sanctions. After three face-to-face meetings, Trump failed because he never understood that Kim would not denuclearize without an explicit, long-term plan. Furthermore, following Trump's withdrawal from the Iran deal, he gave Kim no reason to trust him. A plan to be implemented in stages over a period of seven to ten years while sanctions are gradually lifted, corresponding to denuclearization in stages, which would lead to normalization of relations, might have appealed to Kim. As a result of Trump's dismal failure, the tension in the Korean Peninsula has only risen and Kim resumed testing new ballistic missiles and nuclear weapons.

Since Trump came to power, Turkey has become increasingly more nationalist with a strong Islamist agenda. Under Erdogan, Turkey is willing to challenge Western values and is prepared to assert itself politically and militarily and to do so with impunity. Even though Erdogan cozied up to the United States' staunchest foes (Russia and Iran), defied NATO by buying Russia's S-400 air defense system, and threatened to prohibit the US from using the Incirlik Air Base, Trump conceded by giving Erdogan the green light to intervene in Syria and ravage the Syrian Kurds. Trump refrained from taking any punitive measures against Erdogan, even though he terrorizes his own people and has dismantled what's left of Turkey's democracy. Trump's accommodation of Erdogan's authoritarian conduct further emboldened Erdogan to interfere in the domestic affairs in Middle Eastern, Western Balkan, and North African countries while marginalizing the US.

The continuing disastrous war in Yemen will be remembered as one of Trump's most horrific failures, as he continues to directly contribute to the devastation by supplying Saudi Arabia with killing machines. Trump has made hardly any effort to end the war in Yemen. Tens of thousands of Yemeni civilians have been killed, millions are starving, and as many as one million children are infected with cholera. Although Iran and the Houthis are to blame just as much, Trump has said nothing and done less to bring this catastrophic war to an end. He puts his personal financial interest in Saudi Arabia first while ditching our moral responsibility, as he makes the US complicit in the Saudis' crimes against humanity under his watch.

Trump's failure to end the Afghanistan war is a continuation of both Bush and Obama's failure to realize that the Afghanistan war is unwinnable. While Trump criticized his predecessors for not ending the war, he followed their path while ignoring what has long been acknowledged—that the Taliban will ultimately wrest power from the current government. Trump's effort to reach an agreement was torpedoed just before it was finalized because a suicide bomber killed an American soldier. Instead of pausing the agreement temporarily, he scuttled it completely. The way to end the nearly two-decades-old war is by requiring the Taliban to commit to two vital provisions: preventing terrorist groups such as al-Qaeda and ISIS from using Afghanistan as a staging ground and fully adhering to human rights. Violating these commitments would trigger specific crippling sanctions.

Trump's policy toward the Libyan civil war hovered between neglect and indifference, leaving the country's fate to Russia and Turkey. Trump, who initially supported the UN-recognized Sarraj government, reversed course in support of Khalifa Haftar, who is determined to control the entire country. Secretary of State Pompeo, who attended the Berlin conference hoping to shape the deliberation about Libya's future, bore no fruit. Russia and Turkey, who have huge vested interests in Libya, have already established themselves as powerbrokers. Trump's ill-advised choice to steeply reduce US military presence in West Africa will only further weaken US influence not only in Libya, but also in the region as a whole, which has enormous geostrategic consequences for European allies in particular.

Trump has alienated our European allies to a degree that raises serious questions about his commitment to our trans-Atlantic ties. His embrace of Russia's Putin, and conversely his intense criticism of our allies, played directly into the hands of Putin, who is determined to weaken our alliances, especially NATO, which has enabled European collective security since World War II. Trump never understood the critically important bond between Europe and the US, treating them as business partners who must pay an equitable share on defense—failing to grasp that their security is pivotal to our own and serves our most vital geostrategic interests. His strong-arm tactics have increasingly alienated and antagonized both our friends and adversaries, making the US increasingly isolated, which inadvertently lessens American influence globally.

This is the plight of our foreign policy under Trump. Sadly, nothing is likely to change as long as he remains in power. Our only salvation is that even though Trump undermined America's image in the eyes of the international community, the US remains the singular superpower. It may take some time, but under new and enlightened leaders, America will regain its global leadership role and live up to its political and social values and moral principles.

TRUMP'S AND NETANYAHU'S FOLLY

February 5, 2020

Since the Second Intifada in 2000, Israel has been steadily moving to the right-of-center. Successive Israeli governments have made national security central to Israel's very survival, and linking it to the presumed existential threat posed by the Palestinians has become the national mantra. Thus, controlling Palestinian lives and territory has become synonymous with Israel's national security. Israel has, for all intents and purposes, given itself the license to do whatever it pleases in the Palestinian territories, including building settlements, erecting barriers and fences, demolishing Palestinian homes, and restricting their movement, and was poised to annex the Jordan Valley, all in the name of national security.

The unveiling of Trump's "deal of the century" (the Deal) was framed to fully support the Israeli scheme, yet it tragically condemned the next generation of Israelis and Palestinians to years, if not decades, of violence and wars while dangerously destabilizing the region, which is already plagued with widespread turmoil.

Do Trump and Netanyahu understand the implications of what they have done? Here we have an impeached president and a prime minister who is indicted and facing trial—two crooks facing new elections. Trump will drag himself through any gutter to be reelected, and pleasing his evangelical constituency is vital to that goal. Thus, releasing his decisively pro-Israel Deal at this particular juncture was meant to serve his immediate goal and that of Netanyahu, who is also seen as the conduit for the messianic mission of the evangelicals.

Netanyahu, whose zealotry and obscene lust for power matches only that of Trump, gladly embraced the Deal because it boosts his reelection prospects, realizes his life-long aspiration for a Greater Israel, and allows him to emerge as Israel's savior who restored much of the Jews' biblical "land of Israel" to its rightful owners.

To understand why the Deal puts Israel's future at risk, one need not go too far to find the answer. Even before the Deal was disclosed, the PA rejected it on the grounds that it denies the Palestinian right to statehood, legitimizes the settlements, allows for the annexation of nearly 30 percent of Palestinian land, and permits Israel to annex the Jordan Valley. This shatters any prospect of establishing a viable Palestinian state, regardless of what the deal stipulates.

By what logic then will the Palestinians accept such a deal that robs them of a more than seventy-year-old dream to establish an independent state? Whether or not they missed several opportunities in the past to realize their dream, their initial rejection of Israel's right to exist does not nullify their right to a state of their own that lives in peace with Israel.

The Deal has only justified the claim of extremist Palestinian groups, including Hamas and Islamic Jihad, and countries like Iran and others, that Israel has had all along no intention of allowing the Palestinians to have an independent state and that only continued violent resistance will force Israel's hands.

This will be the net outcome of the Deal. As the Palestinians lose hope and have little left to lose, violence and more violence will be the order of the day, which is precisely what Israel wants to avoid and what the Deal was presumably supposed to prevent.

This also begs the question as to who, in fact, poses an existential threat to Israel. Certainly not the Palestinians, who know only too well that Israel is a formidable military power that can take any security measure deemed necessary to protect itself. Moreover, there is not a single country in the Middle East, including Iran, that can challenge Israel militarily without sustaining horrifyingly unacceptable damage. Tehran especially knows that well.

What Trump and Netanyahu have cooked up is a recipe for perpetual violent conflict, and while Israel will always have the upper hand, it will not enjoy a day of rest. Israel will have to station thousands of additional troops and spend hundreds of millions of dollars more annually on security to protect the jigsaw puzzle of settlements scattered throughout the West Bank. The resentment and resistance of the Palestinians will only worsen, and any incident could trigger deadly violence.

Preventing the establishment of a Palestinian state and enshrining the dream of Greater Israel that Netanyahu championed will be the nightmare of the right-wing Israelis, as the "deal of the century" will blow up in their faces. Trump and Netanyahu will be remembered as the two leaders who betrayed Israel and subjected its citizens to live and die by the gun.

THE TRAVESTY OF THE CENTURY

February 12, 2020

After three years in office, one can hardly be surprised at what Trump is capable of saying, doing, or scheming. In the middle of his impeachment trial, Trump finally released his "deal of the century"—a deal that completely ignored several United Nations resolutions, accords that were sponsored by the European community and the United States, and bilateral agreements between Israel and the Palestinians. Trump assigned his "internationally recognized top expert on Middle Eastern affairs," Jared Kushner, to come up with a deal to solve a seven decades-old conflict that has eluded every American administration since 1948.

Whereas the US has over the years played a central role in the effort to solve the Israeli-Palestinian conflict, no American administration has provided such a detailed proposal, certainly not one that grants Israel its entire wish list. Every past administration knew full well that prejudicing the outcome would doom any prospective deal from the start, and thus settled on providing a general outline consistent with prior internationally recognized agreements.

When it comes to Trump though, prior interim agreements, UN resolutions, and numerous face-to-face negotiations between both sides simply do not matter. Instead, he relies on his "negotiating skills" and crude audacity to offer a solution that no one who has any deep knowledge of the history of the conflict, its intricacies, and its psychological and pragmatic dimensions would even contemplate.

It is important to note, however, that both Israel and the Palestinians have over the years denied each other's right to exist in an independent state, and to suggest that one side or the other is innocent and wholly wronged is a fallacy. Both have contributed to the impasse and both are guilty for failing to adhere to the numerous agreements sponsored by the international community, to which they initially subscribed. The following offers a synopsis of these resolutions and agreements.

On November 29, 1947, the United Nations General Assembly passed Resolution 181, stating that "independent Arab and Jewish States .... shall come into existence in Palestine ... not later than 1 October 1948."

On November 22, 1967 the UNSC passed Resolution 242 *"Emphasizing* ... respect for and acknowledgement of the sovereignty, territorial integrity and political independence of every State in the area ... to live in peace within secure and recognized boundaries."

On October 22, 1973 the United Nations Security Council Resolution 338 *"Calls upon* the parties concerned to start immediately after the cease-fire the implementation of Security Council resolution 242 (1967) in all of its parts."

On September 17, 1978 the Camp David Accords declared that "the agreed basis for a peaceful settlement is ... United Nations Security Council Resolution 242, in all its parts."

On September 13, 1993 the Oslo Accords aimed to establish principles of self-government, "leading to a permanent settlement based on Security Council resolutions 242 (1967) and 338 (1973)."

On March 28, 2002, the Arab Peace Initiative, which was unanimously endorsed by the Arab League and the international community, including a majority of Israelis, called for "Israel's acceptance of an independent Palestinian state with East Jerusalem as its capital."

On April 30, 2003, the Quartet's (US, EU, UN, and Russia) Road Map for Peace insisted that "a settlement ... will result in the emergence of a ... Palestinian state living side by side in peace and security with Israel and its other neighbors."

Trump in his wisdom, however, chose to completely ignore these prior resolutions and instead focused primarily on what he considers "best for Israel," although the deal will do more harm to Israel than he could possibly imagine. I dare say that he may well understand the dire implications for Israel, but cares less as long as it serves his interests.

Trump is known for violating international accords: he withdrew from the Paris Agreement on climate change; the JCPOA; and trade agreements with China, Canada, and Mexico and domestically revoked scores of regulations enacted by the Obama administration. To be sure, he wants to put his own mark on everything, whether he agrees or disagrees with the subject matter.

This raises the question by what logic Trump can assume upon himself the political, religious, and moral right to divide an occupied land between Israel and the Palestinians in defiance of all previous accords and internationally recognized agreements?

Whereas he consulted with the Israelis *ad nauseam* on every provision of his deal, he completely ignored the Palestinians. Notwithstanding the fact that the Palestinians severed direct talks with the US as a result of Trump's recognition of Jerusalem as Israel's capital, at a minimum he should have initiated back-channel contacts with Palestinian leaders and considered their requirements that could ensure some receptivity rather than outright rejection.

Moreover, Trump unveiling his grandiose deal standing side-by-side Netanyahu sent an unambiguous message as to where he really stands and to whom he is appealing. This scene alone was enough to disgust even moderate Palestinians, who otherwise would have at least paid lip service to the deal. But that was not on Trump's agenda. On the contrary, he did so deliberately for his targeted audience, Evangelical Christians in particular—and in that, he succeeded.

Like everything else, whatever Trump touches dies, and if there had been any hope for Israeli peace, it has now been deferred for years, if not decades. The Israelis will waste no time to act on all the provisions provided by the deal. Ganz, the leader of Kahol Lavan, has already stated that if he were to form the new Israeli government, he would annex all settlements and the Jordan Valley.

For Ganz, just like for Netanyahu, American political support is what matters, irrespective of any other internationally recognized accords that have granted the Palestinians the right to establish an independent state of their own.

To be sure, Trump's peace plan should be renamed "the travesty of the century" for which Israelis and Palestinians will pay with their blood.

"...I AM PROUD TO BE A SOCIALIST"

February 26, 2020

I t is sad, appalling, and outrageous that much of what Bernie Sanders is advocating is denigratingly labeled as socialist, as if it were a stigma detached from the day-to-day realities of life that affect every American man, woman, and child. I have and continue to be *apolitical*, but for me, anything to do with human rights matters, because in the final analysis, no one has any right whatsoever to undermine another person's right to be free, to believe, to feel secure, and to be treated humanely and equitably, as long as it does not infringe upon someone else's rights.

So, if the issues that address human rights are labeled "socialist", then I must proclaim that I am a socialist to the core, and I invite anyone to challenge the premise of my conviction.

If a woman's right to choose and decide her own reproductive future, chart a future for and with her family, and reject the status quo where largely white Republican men decide what women should be doing with their bodies is socialism, then I am proud to be a socialist.

If taking climate change seriously—which scientific evidence overwhelmingly confirms and is affecting the quality of life and livelihood of billions of people on the planet—and believing it must be tackled immediately is socialism, then I am proud to be a socialist.

If addressing the tragedy of child poverty, in a country that proclaims to be the richest yet is where more than twelve million children go to sleep hungry each night and little is done about it, is socialism, then I am proud to be a socialist.

If recognizing that the minimum wage must be raised to at least $15 per hour to allow people, at a minimum, to make ends meet and have a roof over their heads and live with some dignity rather than on the streets is called socialism, then I am proud to be a socialist.

If believing that healthcare is an absolute human right, that every American should have medical care, and that those who don't have it currently should be able to acquire it through a universal healthcare program is socialism, then I am proud to be a socialist.

If lowering the cost of prescription drugs, which can save the life of one individual, let alone the millions who cannot afford life-saving prescription drugs and are dying needless deaths as a result, is socialism, then I am proud to be a socialist.

If revitalizing the crumbling small towns and villages across America, which are rapidly becoming uninhabitable with rampant unemployment, to allow the people there to live a normal life and preserve their jobs is socialism, then I am proud to be a socialist.

If reforming the prison system, where nearly 2.3 million are imprisoned and 60 percent of the prison population is Black or Latino, the majority of whom are incarcerated for non-violent offences, especially drug charges,[5] is socialism, then I am proud to be a socialist.

If confronting the national opioid epidemic by providing the necessary medical help and cracking down on the pharmaceutical industry, which has heavily fueled this crisis while making billions in profit, is socialism, then I am proud to be a socialist.

If rectifying the immigration system and providing the approximately eleven million undocumented immigrants,[6] on whom many American industries, especially farming rely, with a path to citizenship is socialism, then I am proud to be a socialist.

If granting a pathway to citizenship for the 1.25-3.6 million DREAMers,[7] who came to the US as children, speak no other language than English, and are productive Americans in every way that matters, with pride in their families, is socialism, then I am proud to be a socialist.

If providing free tuition to all public colleges and universities, to give every young man and woman an opportunity to get an education and be productive citizens who contribute to the betterment of themselves and their family life, is socialism, then I am proud to be a socialist.

If forgiving the student loan debt of over forty-four million Americans (totaling more than $1.5 trillion[8])—a debt that is only increasing because of exorbitant interest rates, preventing them from progressing further in their lives—is socialism, then I am proud to be a socialist.

If tackling the problem of widespread homelessness, estimated at 568,000 in the United States[9]—the greatest shame of a country as rich and innovative as America—is socialism, then I am proud to be a socialist.

If dealing with the epidemic of corruption—starting with the White House and filtering down to many government officials and businesses who make exorbitant profits while riding on the backs of their employees—is social- ism, then I am proud to be a socialist.

If facing head-on the scourge of racism, Islamophobia, antisemitism, and the rise of white supremacy in America and seeking to become more inclu- sive regardless of race, religion, and ideology is socialism, then I am proud to be a socialist.

If the need to end the political polarization of the American people, which is instilling distrust, hate, and animosity and destroying the very social fab- ric of America as we know it, is socialism, then I am proud to be a socialist.

If addressing inequality of wages—between men and women, whites and people of color—in their place of work, for people performing the same job with the same responsibility, is socialism, then I am proud to be a socialist.

Enacting rules and regulations and fostering a sense of national unity while embracing the premise that human beings have equal rights, which the constitution provides, does not negate capitalism, but in fact enhances it. Capitalism thrives when there is a reason to believe that a better life and more opportunities await us, when despondency is replaced with hope, when equality and social justice prevail, and when national challenges are addressed with a unity of purpose.

This is the true meaning of the American dream: it is the solemn duty and responsibility of every Republican, Democrat, and independent alike to preserve and make America once again a light unto other nations.

TRUMP'S DISASTROUS DOMESTIC POLICY

March 5, 2020

S adly, we have become accustomed to Trump's lies and misstatements about the presumed progress the US made under his watch. It's time to take a hard look at his domestic policy, which is inflicting terrible damage and anguish on the majority of Americans. Trump knows that he lies regarding just about everything, but he continues to successfully sell his lies to his base, representing the 25 to 30 percent of Americans who still believe every word he says.[10] In my previous article[*] I addressed Trump's chaotic foreign policy, and in this article, I provide a brief review of Trump's dismal domestic failures and their implications.

Immigration: Trump's immigration policy has repeatedly disgraced this country, which was built by immigrants and has been a beacon of hope for those seeking a new life and new opportunities. The outrage began with his "Muslim ban" that targeted those from the Muslim-majority countries that he deemed a threat, followed by even more discriminatory executive orders and proclamations. In another ban, he targeted asylum seekers at the southern US border and shamelessly ordered the separation of children from their parents, placing them in cages unfit even for stray animals.

He refused to consider legislation that would grant citizenship to the approximately two million DREAMers, including nearly 700,000 DACA recipients, who know no other country.[11] They are hardworking, loyal, and have no place else to go. He insists on building a useless wall along the Mexican border that is costing billions of dollars, which by all accounts will be ineffective and will not stop a determined migrant from crossing it. Finally, he refused to grant a path to citizenship to nearly eleven million undocumented immigrants who are an integral part not just of American industries, but American culture.[12] He put in charge of immigration policy his ruthless, disdainful, and white supremacist advisor Steven Miller, whose narrow-minded approach to immigration is surpassed only by his bigotry and hollow soul.

Tax cuts: Trump's tax cut legislation far from benefits all Americans. In fact, every study shows that the tax bill benefits the rich the most, and is in fact

---

[*]   "Trump's Dreadful Foreign Policy," p. 189.

harming middle-class and low-income families.[13] While unemployment is at a record low, wages remain stagnant and an increasing number of families are often forced to choose between food and medicine.[14] He dishonestly equates the stock market's breaking records (before the outbreak of the coronavirus) to the health of the economy, when in fact the vast majority of Americans do not trade in the stock market and derive no benefit from the market's past repeated gains.

While Trump claimed that "Married couples won't pay a dime of income tax on their first $24,000 of income. A typical family of four earning $75,000 a year will see their tax bill slashed in half," the tax cut also increased the national debt by over $1 trillion, while poverty is on the rise.[15]

Failing to provide comprehensive healthcare: Since Trump tried and failed to repeal Obamacare, he has opted instead to gut it as much as possible, causing many millions to lose coverage. Trump constantly lies regarding his positions, especially about preexisting conditions. For example, he tweeted: "I was the person who saved Pre-Existing Conditions in your Healthcare, you have it now."[16] The reality is that healthcare for people with preexisting conditions was guaranteed by Obama's ACA; Trump's proposed alternative won't cover preexisting conditions and his claim to the contrary is a flat-out lie designed to bolster support from his base.

To prove his determination to gut federal support from safety net programs, including healthcare, Trump proposes cutting billions of dollars from these vital programs from his $4.8 trillion federal budget proposal for 2021. This includes $1 trillion in cuts to Medicaid and the ACA over a decade, which strongly contradicts his public statements.[17]

Child poverty: The National Center for Children in Poverty estimates that fifteen million children in the Unites States—21 percent of all American children—live in families with incomes below the federal poverty threshold, a measurement that has been shown to *underestimate* the basic needs of families.[18] It is estimated that 3.5 million Americans—including 1.25 million children—will suffer one or more episodes of homelessness over the course of this year.[19]

In 2019, the US spent more than $100 billion on the Child Tax Credit, the single largest federal expenditure meant to benefit children. The only problem, however, is that it fails to help those who need the tax credit the most. Twenty-three million children are ineligible for the full Child Tax Credit because their parents earn too little to qualify, as its current structure benefits higher income families. Over 50 percent of Hispanic and Black, non-Hispanic children are ineligible to benefit in full, and nearly one in five Black, non-Hispanic children do not benefit at all.[20]

Crumbling infrastructure: Another of Trump's gravest domestic failures is not proposing any significant legislation to address America's crumbling infrastructure, which he championed during his run for president in 2016. The American Society of Civil Engineers (ASCE) says that this country's infrastructure is in desperate need of investment. On its 2017 Infrastructure Report Card, which looks at sixteen different categories, the country received a D+, the same grade it received in 2013.[21]

The ASCE estimates that we need to spend roughly $4.5 trillion over the next five years to fix the country's roads, bridges, dams, and other infrastructure. In the past twenty years alone, there have been a number of catastrophic bridge failures leading to the deaths and injuries of hundreds, including the Minneapolis, MN bridge collapse in 2007, which killed thirteen and injured 145. The poor condition of America's roads, waterways, parks, and schools has affected cities and small towns across the country. The increasing number of floods, which is due in part to climate change, is made worse due to failing infrastructure. The Nebraska Department of Natural Resources reported in 2018 that "deficiencies exist which would lead to dam failure during rare, extreme events."[22] Even America's drinking water got a D, as many of the one million pipes in use are nearly one hundred years old and in dire need of repair.

Denial of climate change: Trump's denial of climate change is one of the most dangerous positions he has taken as president. His numerous actions, including withdrawing from the Paris Agreement on climate change, increasing environmental deregulation, and embedding climate change deniers in the EPA and Department of the Interior, are nothing but dangerous shams. The scientific evidence of climate change is overwhelming, but then Trump continues to claim that climate change is fiction, crying "Global warming is an expensive hoax!" and that "we must reject the perennial prophets of doom and their prediction of the apocalypse."[23] The unprecedented fires in the Amazon, Australia, and California, rising sea temperatures, and the intensity of hurricanes all point to the ominous danger of climate change that only a blind man like Trump can deny.

In August 2019, the Trump administration laid out plans to cut back on regulations for methane emissions, which are known to be a major contributor to climate change. The US is the second-largest polluter in the world after China, and more than any other country, it bears the responsibility to cut down on gas emissions. In addition, according to the *New York Times*, "Mr. Trump has sought to open millions of acres of public land and water to drilling, including the Arctic National Wildlife Refuge, and has lifted an Obama-era moratorium on new coal mining leases on public land."[24]

Opioid crisis: America's opioid crisis affects people from all walks of life and economic backgrounds—young and old, male and female. According to the National Institute on Drug Abuse, between 21 to 29 percent of patients prescribed opioids misuse them, 8 to 12 percent develop an addiction, and 4 to 6 percent who misuse prescription opioids eventually transition to heroin. In addition, roughly *130 people die every day after overdosing on opioids*—which include prescription painkillers, heroin, and synthetics such as fentanyl.[25]

Trump's response to the epidemic has been dismal, even though he likes to take credit for the overall drop in drug overdose deaths in 2018. Even with that drop, 2018 was still the second-highest year on record in terms of the overdose death toll—surpassed only by 2017.[26] The opioid crisis is at its heart a public health crisis, yet Trump continues to advocate pulling funding for Medicaid and repealing the ACA, programs that enable especially low-income Americans to access healthcare and have been shown to reduce opioid-related overdose deaths.[27]

Gun control: Trump's unwillingness to enact gun control laws makes him complicit in *the deaths of the more than one hundred Americans killed every day by firearms.* In 2017, gun deaths reached their highest level since 1968, with nearly forty thousand deaths by firearms. For every person killed in a gun homicide, there are six others injured in a gun assault. Additionally, as the Giffords Law Center reports, there is an average of one mass shooting every day in the US.

Even on background checks and assault rifles, Trump flip-flopped and has never committed himself genuinely to enact any effective gun control laws. Furthermore, Trump regularly ties mass shooting to mental illness alone and calls for more mental institutions rather than stricter gun laws. Trump has done virtually nothing to enact common sense gun legislation and has remained entirely in the pocket of the gun lobby and the NRA.

Trade wars: Despite Trump's claims to the contrary, his trade wars have done little to offset the gap between US imports and exports to China, which favor the latter. American farmers are angry over Trump's lies in his trade war with China. According to the *Washington Post*, China's tariffs are closing off the biggest export market for US agricultural products in the world.[28]

Trump's lies and misstatements about trade apply equally to NAFTA. Again, in one of his misleading remarks, he said: "We're taking NAFTA —one of the worst deals ever made in the history of trade – and we are redoing it .... We lost thousands of factories and millions of jobs because of NAFTA .... We're turning it around. Already, Chrysler is coming back with auto plants .... We're making incredible trade deals."[29] In fact, the newly negotiated United States-Mexico-Canada Agreement (USMCA) hardly differs from NAFTA, but leave it to Trump to boast about how much better the new trade deal is.

In sum, Trump's disastrous domestic policies will impact the lives and well-being of most Americans for years to come. His failures must be exposed for all to see, and drastic corrective measures must be taken to address them systematically. The cost will certainly be astronomical, but then, with a clear vision, determination, responsible budgeting, and equitable taxation over a period of five to seven years, much of America's domestic ills could be addressed on a continuing basis.

America's future national security and global leadership is intertwined, as it has always been, with its domestic health and vitality. Any Republican or Democratic president who fails to grasp this reality will do so at their peril.

TRUMP'S PANDEMIC FAILURE:
A MISSED OPPORTUNITY

April 10, 2020

For a self-absorbed, power hungry narcissist who wants to be recognized as one of the greatest presidents of the United States while desperately trying to be reelected, Trump has failed miserably to rise to the occasion precipitated by the unfortunate advent and spread of the novel coronavirus. Rather than minimizing the ominous danger of the virus and ignoring the warning of top scientists about the prospective disastrous consequences it could unleash, he could have mobilized from the onset of this pandemic every national resource to tackle the virus head on. This includes the military, the National Guard, and thousands of companies and medical institutions to produce critical equipment and testing on a national scale and creating an aggressive national program to fight this virus as a war on all fronts.

Had he done that, he could have realized just about everything he wanted. In fact, he would have been able to emerge from this tragic outbreak as a hero. The public would have forgiven him for his incessant lies, deliberate misleading statements, idiosyncrasies, and corruption. I also believe that Trump would have been able to handedly beat any prospective Democratic nominee, including Joe Biden, come November.

The question is: why didn't Trump pursue this logical course of action? There are a number of reasons that explain his bizarre behavior, although none should have obscured the gravity of the situation—if he only wasn't so immersed with himself. From his vantage point, everything starts first and foremost with what can serve his personal interests.

From the onset, Trump sought to disassociate himself from the outbreak of the virus by denying that he failed to prepare the country for such epidemic, when in fact he greatly contributed to the country's unpreparedness. In the spring of 2018, he dismantled the team in charge of responding to pandemics, including the departure of its head, Rear Adm. Timothy Ziemer. In addition, he cut funding for the CDC and continues to push for reducing US funding of the World Health Organization.[30] Moreover, he seems to be unwilling to embrace testing on a national scale because he does not want to show that the number of those infected is exponentially increasing, leaving the country more vulnerable that it has ever been.

Trump's concern with the economy was first and foremost in his mind. As he sees it, the continuing economic boom was central to his reelection campaign, and he rebuffed anything that could adversely impact the health of the economy. Thus, he had to minimize the dire implications of the coronavirus, even though he knew about the virus early in January and dismissed the scientific evidence that suggested that the impact of the virus would be catastrophic if the country was not fully mobilized to deal with the epidemic.

As customary for Trump, he never takes responsibility for anything that turns sour and rushes in and relishes taking credit for anything good, perceived or real, like the record-breaking stock market or the lowest unemployment rate in a generation, which, in fact, was largely precipitated by Obama's economic recovery plans. In this case, he put blame for the lack of essential medical supplies squarely on the Obama administration, and various governors who were told that they are on their own: not only because it was convenient, but because it would also distinguish himself from the "failings" of his predecessor, whom he intensely disliked.

Being totally consumed by his reelection campaign is an understatement. For Trump, nothing else matters. He was determined to treat COVID-19 as a distraction and not allow the rapid spread of the virus to interfere in his reelection efforts. Having finally realized the severity of the pandemic, as the number of deaths and those infected rose exponentially, Trump was quick to capitalize on it by conducting a daily press conference, which has become a replacement for his campaign rallies.

Finally, Trump was quick to take full credit for the passage of the largest economic stimulus bill, to the tune of $2.2 trillion. For him, the bill is essential in order to keep unemployment—which has exploded in recent weeks—as low as possible and allow the stock market to regain some of its substantial losses. To be sure, Trump wants to present himself as the savior of the economy, knowing that short of a significantly improved economic outlook in the immediate future, his reelection prospects will be dim at best.

While Trump was focusing on what serves his personal interests, COVID-19 claimed the lives of tens of thousands of Americans and infected hundreds of thousands more (14,696 deaths and 427,460 cases at the time of writing). Much of this tragic infliction could have been prevented had his administration been better prepared, and had Trump himself acted in good faith. Instead, he sought to push unproven and under-tested pharmaceuticals in the hopes that they would prove beneficial, so that he could present it to the nation as another sign of his great success in handling the pandemic.

The problem with Trump is his obsession with himself, which blinds him from seeing the larger picture. Trump's ignorance prevented him from realizing that one can engender a breakthrough from a breakdown. Had he been honest with himself and with the American public, he could have simply admitted that the country was unprepared and that he will fight this deadly virus with all of America's might. He could have also offered assistance to other countries in need, restoring some of America's global leadership.

Indeed, assuming responsibility and rising to the occasion to right the wrongs would have put Trump in a completely different light. He could have emerged from this historic pandemic a truly decisive, strong, and visionary leader—attributes that have only eluded him when they were within his very grasp.

THE PANDEMIC UNDERLINES
AMERICA'S INGRAINED RACISM

June 2, 2020

The murder of George Floyd by a police officer in broad daylight came amid a high point in the continuing rampage of the coronavirus throughout the country, which has killed over 100,000 and infected nearly two million (at the time of this writing), while more than forty-five million have lost their jobs. The death of Floyd is no longer seen merely as an act of police brutality but the final crack in the dam, revealing the insidious socioeconomic and healthcare malaise that continues to be inflicted disproportionately on the African American community.

A paper in the *Annals of Epidemiology* reports that while disproportionately Black counties make up only 30 percent of the US population, they are the location of 56 percent of all COVID-19 deaths. According to NPR's analysis, Blacks are dying at higher rates relative to their total proportion of the population in thirty-two states plus Washington, DC.[31]

Dr. Marcella Nunez-Smith, director of the Equity Research and Innovation Center at Yale School of Medicine, says, "We know that these racial ethnic disparities in COVID-19 are the result of pre-pandemic realities. It's a legacy of structural discrimination that has limited access to health and wealth for people of color."[32]

What made matters worse is Trump's overt racism, the muted leadership of the Republican Party, and its antipathy toward the Black community, all of which added fuel to the simmering fire of the centuries-long history of slavery, discrimination, and hopelessness. They know that their plight will not be allayed any time soon, not as long as Trump is the president and his party follows him like sheep that blindly graze in the meadows of discontent while the country is unraveling at the seams. They have betrayed the country by putting their party's interests above that of the nation.

We are now reaping the harvest of the seeds of racism and discrimination: the devaluation of Black life in job opportunities, in buying and lending, and in wages, positions, and treatment. The whole socioeconomic and cultural system is lopsided, as it lacks the fundamentals of justice and equality. The pandemic provided a wakeup call that pointed out the ugly tradition of subjugation of the Black community, which sadly did not stop with the end of slavery, but continued in the wanton indifference to their pain and agony, our uncanny negligence, and our failure to understand what they are really experiencing.

Time is not our ally; neither concerned white nor Black people should now be satisfied with words of sympathy toward the plight of African Americans. It is not merely changing the police culture and practices in the way they handle Black versus white suspects. What is needed is a fundamental change from our innate desire to apply slavery to Black people as deserving nothing more than bare necessities.

Little has changed since the birth of the civil rights movement more than a half-century ago. Although the majority of white Americans may not be white supremacists, they certainly hold onto their privileges in all walks of life as they view their relation with Black people and other people of color as a zero-sum game, as if a Black man's gain invariably chips away from a white man's privileges. The insidious, learned biases pitting white against Black Americans directly leads to the treating of Black Americans as second-class citizens and suppression (whether conscious or unconscious) by white Americans—a necessary ingredient that satisfies their ego and elevates their self-worth.

The week-long demonstrations throughout the country suggest not only the obvious—that Black lives matter, that inequality is rampant and must be addressed, that racism is consuming America from within, that injustice affects the perpetrators just as much as the victims, that enough is enough—the demonstrations also reveal the deep sense of frustration with a president who fans the flame of racism, who sees the country as his own enterprise, who can do whatever serves his own interests. He is cruel, cunning, and careless about the pain and suffering of Black America; he cannot count on their political support and hence his complete rejection of their outcry.

As has been widely observed, there have been instances of looting and destruction of property—much of it by opportunistic individuals trying to take advantage of the situation and also by bad-faith actors attempting to delegitimize the protests. These acts are succeeding in drawing the attention of the media away from the importance and relevance of the majority of demonstrations that have been peaceful.

This is exactly what Trump wants to see happening. He wants the country divided between us and them. He wants to blame the Democrats and liberal-minded people for the mayhem, while cowering in fear in the White House basement. He refuses to address the nation, knowing that regardless of what he says, nothing will hide his demagoguery and disdain for people of color.

I wish to see tens of millions of Americans demonstrate **peacefully** day in and day out and send a clear message to this corrupt Trump administration that they will not rest until a fundamental change occurs. They must demand bipartisan legislation that will address discrimination against all people of color under any circumstances: in particular in affordable housing, healthcare, job opportunities, equal pay, and anti-bias training for police and national bans on the use of force.

I also wish to see the Republican leadership wake up and halt their blind subservience to a president who has lost his way and dangerously degraded America here at home and abroad. If nothing else, the pandemic has demonstrated his utter ineptitude and the huge disparity between white versus Black America, topped with his demonstrable racism in which he takes pleasure.

I am not naïve enough to assume that my wishes will come true. But it should serve as a warning to every Republican member of Congress that the murder of George Floyd and the horrifying injustice it confirmed is the poison they will have to swallow just before Election Day if they fail to act.

THE REPUBLICANS' TREASONOUS
BETRAYAL OF THE AMERICAN PEOPLE

June 8, 2020

T here is nothing that Trump says or does that will surprise me anymore, no matter how shocking or outrageous. After three and a half years in office, he has ushered America to the brink of anarchy, a political condition that I now believe he has sought all along. But what is even more treacherous than Trump's behavior is the way the Republican Party has followed him, worrisomely akin to blind sheep following a lost shepherd grazing in the meadows of national outrage. I wonder how many Republican governors and members of Congress look themselves in the mirror and ask: "why I am supporting a president who has sacrificed the country's wellbeing on the altar of his ego, a man with a dangerous authoritarian instinct, a man who has divided rather than united the country, and one who will stoop to any low or ignore any law to satisfy his lust for power and personal gain?"

There is hardly a Republican leader who can answer this question publicly with honesty, because if they were honest, they would have raised their voices in defiance of Trump's alarming behavior long ago. We would have heard them publicly stating—without fear of reprisal—where they stand, or watched them quit the Republican party, resign from office in protest, or refuse to run again as long as Trump remains in power.

Sadly, such actions by Republican leaders have been exceptionally rare, allowing Trump to do essentially whatever he wants. The most critical question then is not how far Trump will go to promote his treasonous agenda, but for how long Republican leaders will silently accept and subserviently enable Trump to destroy the basic moral tenets and values on which this Union was founded, and which they swore to uphold and protect.

Republican leaders excuse their willfully blind support for Trump in a variety of ways that appear to relieve them of any sense of guilt, shame, or responsibility. They often pretend to have not heard or analyzed Trump's acts or statements at issue. Indeed, at other times they claim it is not their place to comment, when in fact, it is their voices America needs to hear from most of all.

Unfortunately, those Republicans who stand for reelection dare not oppose Trump on any ground, fearing his wrath and vindictiveness. It has become abundantly clear that Republican leaders' concerns about the wellbeing of the country are secondary to their political survival and hunger for power. They lie to themselves—and to us—perhaps thinking they can still do some good for the country, even while it is tearing apart in front of their eyes.

There are other Republican leaders who truly believe in their party's conservative platform, and that as long as Trump backs their legislative scheme, they will support him regardless of his mischiefs, misconduct, and delinquency. Notwithstanding the harm to the country, they believe that what is good for the party is good for the nation, and those who disagree are simply uninformed and shortsighted. They view bipartisanship on any issue as a necessary evil as long as they can continue to promote the policies they espouse.

And then there are those bigot rejectionist Republicans who always see eye-to-eye with Trump; they defy, detest, and degrade any democratic initiative, regardless of how well-meaning or how well it might serve the country. For them, Trump is the savior who has been ordained by a higher authority to "drain the swamp that Obama left in his wake."

One of those Republicans is the fascist Senator Tom Cotton, who in a *New York Times* editorial advocated that the Army should quell demonstrations. He and other degenerate Republicans represent the intransigent constituency, the so-called base—narrow-minded evangelicals, zealous conservatives, and white supremacists, who stick to and hail Trump because he is anti-Democrat, sufficiently conservative, and racist.

There exists a symbiotic relationship between Trump and the Republican leadership. Republican leaders want Trump to sign-off on their highly conservative agenda, including opposing new gun control laws, appointing conservative judges, rejecting women's reproductive rights, denying climate change and promoting environmental deregulation, passing tax cuts mostly for the rich, drilling and fracking for oil and gas, privatizing healthcare, and, in principle, rejecting any initiative Democrats propose.

Although Trump is far more opportunist than political, he is willing to coddle the party as long as Republican leaders accommodate his tendencies and enable him to pursue his self-indulgent agenda. They have swallowed his nineteen thousand (and growing) lies and misrepresentations,[**] his profiteering, bigotry, misuse of power, indecency, mendacity, meanness, rancorous nature, and perhaps most of all, his divisive policies pitting American against American.

No Republican has criticized Trump for his tragic mishandling of the coronavirus pandemic that still ravages the country, his defunct foreign policy toward our allies and adversaries alike, his disjointed immigration policies, his nepotism, his threat to deploy the military to "defend the life and property of their [city and state] residents," and his parading of military hardware in Washington, DC.[33]

During the ongoing historic pandemic outbreak and the widespread protests throughout the country, Senate Republicans blocked a Democratic resolution condemning Trump for using tear gas and rubber bullets on peaceful protesters near the White House. Senate Majority Leader McConnell objected, saying "It just indulges in a myopic obsession with President Trump that has come to define the Democratic side."[34]

Only a handful of Republicans leaders spoke, though feebly, against Trump's actions regarding the protests: "He needs to make more unifying comments." "The country is looking for healing and calm. And I think the president needs to project that in his tone." "The president should help to heal the racial divisions." "I do think some of his tweets have not been helpful."[35]

Of course, shame on us if we continue to be surprised by Republicans' continuing silence, because as we all know, even when presented with overwhelming evidence that Trump committed crimes against the American people, Trump's Republican stooges in the Senate exonerated him following impeachment almost unanimously.

Although Trump deserves much of the blame for the calamitous state of the nation, many of his transgressions and disastrous domestic and foreign policies could have been avoided had Republican leaders actually acted like leaders, stood their ground, protected the Constitution, and refused to bow to Trump's whims. Their collective failure has caused the country immea-

---

[**] As tabulated by *The Washington Post*; as of July 9, 2020, it is 20,055 false or misleading claims.

surable and perhaps irreparable damage, for which the American people must hold the Republican Party accountable.

The Republican leadership, to be sure, has made its bed. It has committed moral suicide. History will judge them harshly for their treason and betrayal of the nation, including all of those who have lived and died throughout our history to foster and protect our safety, integrity, and freedom.

THE PANDEMIC OF RACISM IN AMERICA

The continuing demonstrations throughout the country suggest not only the obvious—that Black lives matter—but that racism is consuming America from within, that injustice affects the perpetrators just as much as the victims, that enough is enough.

July 16, 2020

The rage, desperation, and determination that continue to bring tens of thousands of Americans to the streets in protest against racism and injustice hopefully will be just the beginning. They are sick and tired of systemic racism against Black people, bigotry at the top, crude discrimination, police brutality, a prejudiced criminal justice system, economic disparity, and society's robbing Black people of experiencing real freedom and equality. Hypocritically, white people blame the victims of racism for their own plight, claiming that Black people would do better in life if they were only willing to work harder.

We are now reaping the harvest of the seeds of racism and discrimination—the devaluation of Black life. The whole socioeconomic and cultural system is lopsided, as it lacks the fundamentals of justice and equality. The pandemic provided the wakeup call that pointed out the ugly tradition of subjugation of the Black community, which sadly did not stop with the end of slavery, but continued in the wanton indifference to their pain and agony, our uncanny negligence, and our failure to understand what they are really experiencing.

Ingrained Racism

The fact that Black people were slaves, and the carefully cultivated myth that slaves were always obedient and happily served their white masters, left an indelible imprint on white people that has lasted generations. They maintain that African Americans were born to servitude and hence they do not qualify for equal treatment, equal opportunity, or equal status.

Films such as D.W. Griffith's immensely influential *Birth of a Nation* (1915), which helped to reestablish the Ku Klux Klan, also reinforced the racist stereotype that Black men are unintelligent and an inherent danger to the white community—specifically white women. When on May 25 (the same day George Floyd was killed) a white woman, Amy Cooper, called the cops on a Black man, Christian Cooper, who was bird watching in Central Park, she was tapping into the long history of that racist trope. To put it plainly, Black lives are simply not valued the way white lives are, as white people consciously or subconsciously view Black man as both sub- and supra-human, threatening, and expendable.

Thus, due to this entrenched prejudice, any activity, however innocent, in which a Black man is engaged in invites suspicion, alarm, and often puts the life of Black men in danger—such as twenty-five-year-old Ahmaud Arbery, who was shot and killed by white residents of the suburban Georgia neighborhood he was jogging in. The mayor of Minneapolis bluntly said, "Being black in America should not be a death sentence."[36] Racism, to be sure, is so ingrained that it flows in the veins of many Americans without notice.

The insidious, learned biases pitting white against Black Americans directly leads to the treating of Black Americans as second-class citizens and suppression by white Americans—a necessary ingredient that satisfies their ego and elevates their self-worth. Although the majority of white Americans may not be white supremacists, they certainly hold onto their privileges in all walks of life as they view their relation with Black people (and other people of color) as a zero-sum game, as if a Black man's gain invariably chips away at a white man's privileges.

Wanton discrimination

Racial prejudice in America takes a heavy toll on African Americans, which translates to discrimination in all walks of life, including education, job opportunities, professional advancements, and medical treatment, especially maternal health. Black workers receive 22 percent less in salary than whites with the same education and experience; Black women receive even less—34.2 percent.[37] According to a University of Chicago/Duke 2016 study, when factoring in all African American and white men (inclusive of those incarcerated or otherwise out of the workforce), the racial wage gap is the same as it was in the 1950s.[38] Even where racial discrimination should not occur, such as medical treatment, when Black patients access medical care, doctors regularly prescribe fewer pain medications and believe Black patients feel less pain than white patients, even among veterans seeking care.[39]

Whereas Black men have served in the military and fought and died along-side white soldiers in every war since the Revolutionary War (when five to eight thousand Black soldiers fought against the British[40]), they had to face discrimination and segregation while still serving in the military, hardly recognized for acts of bravery. Indeed, until 1948—*after* the end of WWII—the US military was entirely segregated. While the top brass of the military, who are mostly white, like to claim that military institutions are "colorblind," the reality is that "racism and discrimination remain extensive problems even in the U.S. military."[41]

Police brutality

Although police brutality against Black men in particular, which instigated the current protests, is a known phenomenon, police killings of Black men continue unabated. It can and has taken different forms historically—including harassment and intimidation, assault and battery, torture and murder, and even complicity with the KKK. Often, police officers approach any situation connected to a Black man with apprehension and fear. White police officers see threats where they do not exist; they are too quick to draw and as quick to fire to kill.

Here are just a few glaring examples. A Black man taking a nap in a car in a parking lot was shot dead. Another pulled over in a traffic stop was shot and killed in front of his girlfriend and her daughter. A Black man sitting in his home eating ice cream was shot dead by his neighbor, an off-duty white police officer. A Black woman playing video games with her nephew was shot and killed through her window. A Black woman (and EMT) sleeping in her home was shot eight times when officers entered her apartment executing a no-knock warrant.***

It is rare for a prosecutor to decide to charge a police officer, especially because they often know each other and have developed close working relationships. Even Internal Affairs divisions of police departments, which ostensibly exist to investigate and report misconduct among officers, have widely conducted sub-standard investigations and failed to identify problem officers who commit wanton abuse.[42]

*** Rayshard Brooks, Philando Castile, Botham Jean, Atatiana Jefferson, and Breonna Taylor.

This cultural pattern enables police officers like Derek Chauvin, Daniel Pantaleo, and Nathan Woodyard to commit the heinous crime of slowly squeezing the life out of George Floyd (MN), Eric Garner (NY), and Elijah McClain (CO). As troubling is the fact that police officers have been known to give false testimony in court, whether to avoid punishment for their own criminal and/or unconstitutional actions, to ensure a conviction, or for other reasons.[43]

Disproportionate incarceration

Although the US judiciary is considered to be just and impartial, in most court hearings race is present albeit it is not spelled out. It is as though Black men inherently have no equal rights and to this day, 230 years since the constitution was written, injustices still exist in both federal and state courts.

Blacks are incarcerated at more than five times the rate of whites—while they are 13 percent of the total US population, they constitute 40 percent of the total male prison population.[44] The mass incarceration of African Americans in this country has created what sociologist Becky Pettit, citing the novelist Ralph Ellison, calls "invisible men"—the millions of Black men in the American penal system. Prison inmates are not included in most data collecting national surveys, so these men are effectively invisible to social institutions, lawmakers, and most social science research. It is almost as if they do not exist, they do not count; their reality is ignored, neglected, and brushed aside.

Thirty-three percent of young Black men—one in three—will be imprisoned at some point in their lives.[45] These statistics can only begin to convey the enormity of the injustice that is being compounded day after day. Pettit's book reveals that "penal expansion has generated a class of citizens systematically excluded from accounts of the American populace. This exclusion raises doubt about the validity of even the most basic social facts and questions the utility of the data gathered for the design and evaluation of public policy and the data commonly used in social science research. As a consequence, we have lost sight of the full range of the American experience."[46]

Economic disparity

Economic disparity between white and Black Americans is glaring and reverberates through generations of Black families. Economic exclusion is the source of inequality. It is caused by a confluence of factors, beginning with nearly 250 years of chattel slavery (during which Black families were torn apart, let alone able to accumulate wealth), to sharecropping and unrestrained lynchings, to ninety years of Jim Crow laws, to redlining neighborhoods on demographic lines. All of these factors are manifested today in hiring decisions, property valuation, mortgage applications, interest charges, and even how credit scores are tabulated. The average white family's net worth is more than ten times that of a Black family.[47] Economic disparity, to be sure, is the "mother of all evil" in the lives of Black people.

A poor Black man cannot pay for decent housing, cannot pay for healthcare, and cannot afford to send his kids to higher education, which directly impacts his social standing and professional competency. Thus, he has to settle for menial jobs, low wages, and little or no prospect of ever climbing out of the vicious cycle. The saddest thing of all is that he is blamed for his own dilemma, as if the conditions and lack of opportunities in which he lives has nothing to do with his sorry state of affairs.

The bigotry of the leadership

During the past four years, racism in America has been on the rise and in no small measure Trump, the Racist-in-Chief, has made race a campaign issue from the very start. He began his political campaign by branding Hispanics as rapists; during his presidency, he banned Muslims from entering the US, cruelly separated children from their parents at the borders, described white supremacists in Charlottesville as "very fine people," and celebrated this Fourth of July by defending Confederate statues.

Trump's racism against Blacks in particular is nothing new. It was there in 1973 when Trump Management Inc. was sued by the Department of Justice for housing discrimination against African-American renters. We could see it in 1989, when he took out a full-page advertisement in four New York City newspapers calling for the reinstatement of the death penalty over the Central Park Five, who were wrongfully convicted and sent to prison. Trump refuses to apologize for that, even though, as Innocence Project founder Barry Scheck said, "by calling for the reinstitution of the death penalty, it contributed to an atmosphere that deprived these men of a fair trial."[48] He also refused to apologize for his persistent perpetuation of the "birther" lie that Obama was not born in the US.

Trump's Independence Day speech at Mount Rushmore was laden with racially divisive and partisan rhetoric, but that makes no difference to many conservative Republican leaders and his misguided supporters who follow him blindly. They wrap themselves with the flag as a sign of American patriotism, when in fact their patriotism is defined by their racism and intolerance of people of color.

Although some Republican leaders disagree with him on race, they are fearful of his anger to say anything publicly, lest they risk losing their power or position. Sadly, their silence suggests consent, which only reinforces Trump's racism. With Trump, as with much of the country, racism is deeply ingrained, something he refuses to admit.

Although racism did not start when Trump came to power—as it is imbued into America's history and culture—and it will not end with his departure from office, his overt racism brought to focus racism in America. The persistent protests reveal the deep sense of frustration with a president who fans the flame of racism, who sees the country as his own enterprise, who does whatever he wants to serve his own interests. He is cruel, cunning, and careless about the pain and suffering of Black America; he cannot count on their political support and hence completely rejects their outcry.

Unlike any other protests in the past against racism, this year's protests have had a greater impact in part due to the spread of the coronavirus and its disproportionate impact on Black people, who are being infected and dying at higher rates than whites. That, in conjunction with a presidential election, provides a rare opportunity to start a process of mitigating racism in earnest. What will be necessary, however, is for the protests to persist through Election Day in the hopes that the Racist-in-Chief will be ousted. Only then we stand a better chance that a new day will dawn and a new administration will commit to relentlessly addressing the plight of Black people for the sake of all Americans, especially because the day when America will have a majority of people of color is fast approaching.

Although there are scores of measures that must be taken and many years and huge financial resources to make a discernible change for the better in the life of Black Americans, we have no choice but to start, regardless of how insurmountable the obstacles and the culture of resistance to change. It will take the collective efforts, determination, and consistency of local, state, and federal authorities to begin this process if we ever want to reach a modicum of equality.

The work to change the culture of innate racism in America will be long and hard, but we must not shy away from it. As a small start, the immediate focus should be on educating students about Black history, changing the police culture and training, investing in housing in Black neighborhoods, offering educational support for young Black boys and girls starting at elementary age, up to providing free education for them to attend college or professional schools, and providing job opportunities and equal pay to give them the chance to climb up over time the social ladder.

The continuing demonstrations throughout the country suggest not only the obvious—that Black lives matter—but that racism is consuming America from within, that injustice affects the perpetrators just as much as the victims, that enough is enough.

TRUMP THE WANNABE DICTATOR

Trump is unlike any of his predecessors; he is corrupt to the core and his self-interest comes before the nation. He will stoop to any low, cheat, lie, threaten, viciously attack his opponents, suppress voting rights, and continue to delegitimize the upcoming elections even before they take place.

July 22, 2020

I, like many of my fellow Americans, am extremely concerned about Trump's dictatorial tendencies. Given his behavior—what he said and did over the past four years—he may well act on some of these tendencies, especially if he loses the election by a narrow margin. The concerns I have are not numerous, but are extremely critical. What if he challenges the results of the election and remains adamant on calling for a recount or a new election entirely? What if he refuses to leave the White House and prevents the peaceful transition of power? What if he calls on the military to occupy all major American cities while he still is the Commander-in-Chief between Election Day and the inauguration of the new president? And what if he prompts his supporters to take up arms, converge in the streets, and violently confront the likely massive number of protesters who would demand Trump's removal from the White House, which could lead to some kind of a civil war?

Although many Democratic leaders, including Joe Biden, and scores of journalists and others have spoken about their concerns in this regard, there is still no rife discussion about the above unthinkable scenarios. Besides, does Congress—the House and/or the Senate—have the constitutional power to take action in such a situation, or does the Supreme Court have the authority to intervene? Is there anything else in the constitution that would address these troubling issues?

The Twentieth Amendment says that "The terms of the President and the Vice President shall end at noon on the 20th day of January." But what if he doesn't leave? I posed this question to Erwin Chemerinsky, Dean of the UC Berkeley School of Law and one of the country's foremost constitutional scholars. "After all," he said, "that has happened elsewhere in the world. My hope is that the courts would quickly rule that Joe Biden is the President and has all of the powers of the office… Every incumbent president who has lost a reelection bid, starting with John Adams in 1800, has left office without incident."

In my view, however, Trump may well be an aberration. And what if Trump still will not leave the White House? Chemerinsky said, "I doubt that the military would stick with him in that circumstance. Of course, if it did, we would then have a military dictatorship, as other countries have experienced. What if some of the military with the right-wing militias support Trump. Then we would have some kind of a civil war."

While many Republicans and Democrats may think that any of these scenarios are farfetched, the fact remains that Trump has dictatorial tendencies and occasionally acts on them by testing the ground to gauge the public reaction and weigh how his base responds to his moves. Here is what he displays, and how much in common he shares with dictators in general.

President for life: Trump has said on many occasions that he will be president for life—in March of 2018, he played around with the idea after praising Xi Jinping for granting himself precisely that term extension.[49] Trump also retweeted an absurd meme showing him remaining president for 88,000 years—*slightly* longer than the human lifespan.

I can do whatever I want: Like many despots, on Tuesday July 23, 2019, Trump suggested that the constitution gives him the power to do "whatever I want as president." But I don't even talk about that."[50] However, he often tries to do just that to see if he can get away with it.

Defies reality: Trump notoriously lies and creates his own reality just like many dictators do. Bob Woodward reports in his book *Fear* that John Kelly described Trump as unhinged: "He's an idiot. It's pointless to try to convince him of anything. He's gone off the rails. We're in crazytown. I don't even know why any of us are here."[51] According to *The Atlantic*, in a conversation with journalist Sharon Begley in May 2017 psychologist Ben Michaelis—an analyst of speech for cognitive assessments—said that "Trump has exhibited a 'clear reduction in linguistic sophistication over time' with 'simpler word choices and sentence structure.'"[52]

Presents himself as infallible: Authoritarian leaders never admit that they made a mistake, and neither does Trump. For example, in a tweet he refused to back down from his "forecast" that Alabama was going to be hit by Hurricane Dorian, which was false. Trump went so far as to alter the National Weather Service's map of Dorian's trajectory to include part of Alabama to "prove" that he was right.[53] Despite the FDA's warning against its use and the number of scientific studies disproving its usefulness, he continues to tout hydroxychloroquine as an effective treatment for COVID-19. He has also continued to refuse responsibility for any failings of himself or his administration; in response to criticism over the lack of coronavirus testing, he bluntly said, "I don't take responsibility at all."[54]

Vindictive: Vindictiveness is second nature to all dictators. Following his impeachment acquittal, Trump was characteristically vindictive towards his perceived enemies. They were "evil, vicious, corrupt 'dirty cops.'"[55] He is habitually mean-spirited and spiteful. Trump's cruelty is often gratuitous, without any explanation. At a fundraiser with Chris Christie, who had just endorsed his presidential run, he cruelly said to the crowd, "I'm not eating Oreos anymore, you know that—but neither is Chris. You're not eating Oreos anymore. No more Oreos. For either of us, Chris. Don't feel bad."[56] It is just who he is.

Narcissist: We have yet to know one despot who is not self-centered to the core. Trump, in fact, is a textbook narcissist. Sander Thomaes, developmental psychologist at Utrecht University, maintains that Trump is "a prototypical narcissist."[57] According to Ian Hughes, author of *Disordered Minds: How Dangerous Personalities Are Destroying Democracy* and Senior Research Fellow at MaREI Centre, University College Cork, "It is long past time to acknowledge the truth that has been staring us in the face all along —Donald Trump is clearly mentally disordered and poses a grave danger to us all."[58] He has grandiose visions of himself and the need to be admired and envied.

Domestic military intervention: Trump is quick, like all tyrants, to resort to the military to show his strength and authority. On June 1, 2020, Trump deployed the military to intervene during the protests in DC, and further declared in a Rose Garden statement, "If a city or a state refuses to take the actions that are necessary to defend the life and property of their residents, then I will deploy the United States military and quickly solve the problem for them."[59] He dispatched federal troops with no identification to quell the protests in Portland a few weeks ago against the will of the mayor, which continue to haul peaceful protesters off in unmarked cars, akin to the Gestapo. He is further threatening to send more federal law enforcement officers to major US cities, particularly where the mayor just happens to be a Democrat. "We're not going to let this happen in our country," he said, "all run by liberal Democrats."[60]

Praises dictators: Trump's affinity for dictators, whom he envies for doing whatever they please without accountability, is well known. On September 7, 2016, Trump said on NBC: "If [Putin] says great things about me, I'm going to say great things about him. I've already said, he is really very much of a leader."[61] Even when the intelligence community concluded that Russia offered bounties to Taliban fighters in Afghanistan to kill American soldiers, he called the findings fake news and refused to raise the issue with Putin, with whom he has spoken six times since March.[62] His failure as the Commander-in-Chief to even raise the question with Putin suggests how much he does not want to upset Putin, whom he admires and wants to emulate.

About the ruthless Turkish President Erdogan, he stated in October 2019 "He's a friend of mine ... he's a hell of a leader, and he's a tough man."[63] A month later, he followed up his praise with "I'm a big fan of the president."[64]

Attacking media: Free media is the biggest threat to authoritarian regimes. Trump's attacks on the media are routine, calling it the "enemy of the people." In a Twitter screed last September, he wrote that the media "take good news and make it bad. They are now beyond Fake, they are Corrupt ... our primary opponent is the Fake News Media. In the history of our Country, they have never been so bad!"[65] During last year's trip to the G20 summit in Japan, Trump said to Putin regarding the media present: "Get rid of them. Fake news is a great term, isn't it?"[66]

Conspiracy theorist: Trump is a master in conspiracy theories. They are what despots often concoct to punish their enemies. Among the many conspiracies he promotes, Trump has called climate change a Chinese hoax, stating, "The concept of global warming was created by and for the Chinese in order to make U.S. manufacturing non-competitive."[67] He also claims that Ukrainians, not Russians, interfered in the 2016 election and were working against him (despite overwhelming agreement from intelligence agencies that Russians hacked the DNC server).[68]

Withdrawal from international agreements/organizations: Authoritarian leaders often defy international agreements when it serves their interests to appeal to their political base. Trump has withdrawn from the Paris Agreement on climate change in June 2017, the Joint Comprehensive Plan of Action in May 2018, the UN Human Rights Council in June 2018, among many others. In addition, in February 2019, he withdrew the US from the Intermediate-Range Nuclear Forces Treaty with Russia, claiming that Russia has failed to comply with it.[69] However, this has had another side effect of greatly worrying the United States' European allies, as the agreement was a major centerpiece of European security since World War II.

Trump's attacks on critics: Dictators do not tolerate any criticism. In January 2017, in response to criticism from Rep. John Lewis, Trump said "Congressman John Lewis should spend more time on fixing and helping his district, which is in horrible shape and falling apart (not to mention crime infested) rather than falsely complaining about the election results."[70] He said about Mitt Romney—once under consideration as his Secretary of State—in October 2019, in response to condemnation of Trump's actions regarding Russia, Ukraine, and Hunter Biden, that "He is a fool who is playing right into the hands of the Do-Nothing Democrats!"[71]

Surrounding himself with yes-men: Like any despot, Trump retains only those who agree with him. As a former National Security Council official told *Politico*, "I feel like you already don't have an A Team or B Team. You're really getting down to who's left that will say 'yes.'"[72] Defense Secretary Mattis and national security adviser John Bolton are just two of the many advisers Trump has fired or forced out over policy disagreements.

I do not believe that Democrats and responsible Republican leaders should simply dismiss any of the above alarming scenarios only because they have not happened before. Trump is unlike any of his predecessors; he is corrupt to the core and his self-interest, as he perceives it, comes before the nation. He desperately wants to cling to power, in whatever way he can. Just like any dictator, he will stoop to any low, cheat, lie, threaten, viciously attack his opponents, and suppress voting rights (especially of the Black and Hispanic communities).

Moreover, the president's casual suggestion that the November election should be delayed is nothing less than a chilling reminder of the significant threat to American democracy that Trump poses. The crucial point is not that Trump does not have the authority to change the date of the election. The mere proposal from a sitting president is unheard of, because it clearly represents a direct attempt to undermine the sanctity of our democratic institutions and processes. Trump is only getting started—he will continue to sow distrust regarding the integrity of the election, and will undoubtedly become even bolder in his claims of fraud and a rigged election, even though such claims are baseless lies of the most shameless kind. American democracy is going to be tested as it has never been in modern times.

His enablers, the leadership of the Republican Party, stood idly by all along and allowed him to run wild, to jeopardize the country's domestic security and global standing, for which they will likely pay dearly come November.

I am hopeful that none of the above scenarios will occur. But can we be certain that, given his disturbing behavior and consistent efforts to emulate dictators, Trump would simply concede if he loses the election and peacefully vacate his office come January 20, 2021?

We can only hope so, but it will be a grave mistake not to take these clear warning signs seriously. Be aware America, and be prepared to act.

HOW DID WE GET TO THIS
DIRE STATE OF AFFAIRS?

We are in desperate need of unity, public engagement, and spiritual renewal to rediscover the faith in our ability to overcome any adversity and prevail.

July 30, 2020

A s I survey the state of our union, I feel deeply troubled and dismayed, wondering why and how we here in America got to this dire state of affairs in which we find ourselves. The federal government is in complete disarray, the country is alarmingly polarized, the coronavirus continues to spread like wildfire, discrimination against the Black and Hispanic communities is widespread, the economy is in shambles, the gulf between the poor and the rich is deepening, unemployment is staggering, our national debt is skyrocketing, our infrastructure is crumbling, our international standing is at an all-time low, and the American dream has been replaced by hopelessness and despair.

It is hard to fathom how the country richest in human and natural resources—the greatest military power on earth, the most advanced technologically, the harbinger in all sciences and discoveries, the center of cultural diversity, the champion of human rights, with unparalleled global outreach and influence—has descended to this sorry state of affairs.

Although the decline of the American enterprise did not begin with the rise of Trump to power, he, with the support of misguided Republican leaders, has perilously mismanaged the affairs of the country and inflicted severe damage not only on our democratic institutions, but also on the very soul of America.

Trump has polarized the country beyond recognition and made it nearly impossible to reach a consensus on any issue regardless of how detrimental it may be to the national interests. He and his party leadership have cynically convinced themselves that their interest converges with that of the nation, and when it doesn't, that the party's interest supersedes that of the nation—for example, Republicans consistently try to restrict voting ostensibly to prevent voter fraud, but politicians have spoken the truth. In regards to Democrats' efforts to expand vote-by-mail in the midst of the COVID-19 pandemic, Trump openly stated, "if you'd ever agreed to it, you'd never have a Republican elected in this country again."[73]

It will take years to heal the nation's wounds, but we cannot begin the healing process until Trump, who has betrayed his oath of office, is democratically removed from power and takes down with him many of his treacherous stooges who brought the country to its current disastrous environment.

If Joe Biden is elected to be the next president, it will certainly raise a renewed hope that a new day is dawning in America and potentially help alleviate some of the woes we are experiencing today. With the best of intentions, however, and regardless of how committed Biden may be, he alone cannot shoulder the awesome task that lies ahead. He needs a Congress with a unity of purpose to get things done. He needs an engaged citizenry ready to rise and fight for what's right to remedy many of the country's social and political ills. And he needs spiritual renewal to restore America's moral standing, credibility, and values, which have hit rock bottom notably during the past four years.

Trump, with the tacit approval of the Republicans, has pursued an economic agenda that has harmed most Americans financially, threatened the freedoms of speech, assembly, and a free press, undermined healthcare affecting millions of Americans, intensified discrimination, and aggravated inequality. All of these actions have laid bare Trump's incompetence and dismal failure. He and the Republican leadership have further weakened our democratic institutions, skewed our judiciary, abandoned the poor, and catered to the rich. Like the blind leading the blind, they have followed their aspiring despot by focusing only on what they perceive to be in their best interest—and to hell with the country.

Reaching out to the Republicans

If elected, Joe Biden's first item on his agenda as president should be to mitigate the polarization that has plagued both parties and paralyzed the country. He needs the support of both chambers of Congress and can foster that by reaching across the aisle to Republicans, which will be central to effectuate his domestic and foreign agendas.

As written in a speech that John F. Kennedy intended to give on the day of his assassination, "our duty as a party is not to our party alone, but to the Nation, and, indeed, to all mankind .... So, let us not be petty when our cause is so great. Let us not quarrel amongst ourselves when our Nation's future is at stake. Let us stand together with renewed confidence in our cause – united in our heritage of the past and our hopes for the future."[74]

To demonstrate his determination to end polarization, Biden should invite moderate Republicans to join his administration, perhaps in Cabinet positions. In doing so, Biden will send a clear message that he is not looking to settle the score with the party's antagonists but to ensure that moderate Republicans feel that they have contributed to any successful outcome of the new administration's policies for the country's sake.

Without Trump in the White House, many Republican moderates who have disagreed with him on a host of issues but were afraid to speak out will now be free to cooperate with the Democrats, even if Republicans retain control of the Senate. They don't want only to redeem themselves; they understand the dire need and the urgency to act to put the country on the path of recovery and healing.

Engaged citizenry

The second critical component of the recovery is an active and engaged citizenry who must make their voices heard and remain relentless until the federal and state governments develop a clear road map to address much of the country's ills. The impressive protests that continue to sweep the country over police brutality, sparked by the tragic death of George Floyd, offers one important example of how responsible citizenry must act to force a change—in this case, reforming police departments to bring an end to discrimination and brutality, especially against Black people.

That said, we cannot address much of what ails America today before we eliminate completely the coronavirus and begin the slow and painful process of economic recovery. Millions of young and old Americans should pour into the streets demanding that the Trump administration mobilize all national resources and produce scientifically based comprehensive plans to stop the scourge of the virus.

Even though Trump is unlikely to come up with any such plan, massive **peaceful protests** will further galvanize the public rejection of his dismal failure (demonstrated by his denying the virus's velocity and pervasiveness), which cost the lives of 150,000 Americans and counting. I emphasize peaceful protest because we do not want to give Trump any excuse to send federal troops to quell the protests under the pretext of protecting federal property, *à la* the unfolding horror in Portland, Oregon.

Just the same, Biden as president will need public backing to pass any comprehensive bill that may require the support of some Republicans in either chamber. Given our experience over the past four years, the American public cannot afford to be passive. In the final analysis, the real power rests with the people, and only the American people can oust Trump from power and begin the process of renewal.

Spiritual renewal

The third component, which is just as vital as our socioeconomic and political recovery, is spiritual renewal to restore America's moral standing, as it has dramatically ebbed since Trump came to power. Indeed, what made America great is its commitment to human rights regardless of color, creed, religion, or race; to freedom; to democratic principles; and to its strong moral standing.

These are the values that have sustained America. Yes, economic, military, and technological prowess matter greatly, but they are not enough to maintain America's greatness. Historically, empires have collapsed because of pervasive corruption and moral decadence at the top. Trump, who came to power with the slogan of "make America great again," instead dangerously weakens the very pillars on which America's greatness rests.

During the campaign, issues of healthcare, climate change, wages, infrastructure, taxes, and many others of concern to every American will be debated; Biden has advanced several comprehensive plans that address these issues. But ultimately the election is about the soul of America, and to that end, Trump's defeat is a prerequisite. "Let us stand together," John F. Kennedy observed, "with renewed confidence in our cause – united in our heritage of the past and our hopes for the future."[75]

We are in desperate need of unity, public engagement, and spiritual renewal to rediscover the faith in our ability to overcome any adversity and prevail.

Notes

1   Robert Burns, "Esper Says He's Seen no Hard Evidence Embassies under Threat," *Associated Press*, Jan. 12, 2020, https://apnews.com/5a168a5d8f560e928f3924f 7af10f1d8.

2   Aaron Blake, "The Most Troubling Part of Mike Lee's Broadside against the Trump Administration's Iran Briefing," *Washington Post*, Jan. 8, 2020, https://www.wash ingtonpost.com/politics/2020/01/08/most-disturbing-part-mike-lees-broad side-against-trump-administrations-iran-briefing/.

3   Susan Page, "Exclusive: Americans Say Soleimani's Killing Made US Less Safe, Trump 'Reckless' on Iran," *USA Today*, Jan. 9, 2020, https://www.usatoday.com/ story/news/politics/2020/01/09/killing-soleimani-made-us-less-safe-trump-reckless-iran-poll/2835962001/.

4   "The Strait of Hormuz is the World's Most Important Oil Transit Chokepoint," *US Energy Information Administration,* Jun. 20, 2019, https://www.eia.gov/todayinen ergy/detail.php?id=39932.

5   "United States Profile," *Prison Policy Initiative,* accessed Feb. 24, 2020, https://www. prisonpolicy.org/profiles/US.html#disparities.

6   Elaine Kamarck and Christine Stenglein, "How Many Undocumented Immigrants are in the United States and Who are They?," *Brookings Institution,* Nov. 12, 2019, https://www.brookings.edu/policy2020/votervital/how-many-undocumented-immigrants-are-in-the-united-states-and-who-are-they/.

7   "MPI Estimates the Number of DREAMers Potentially Eligible to Benefit Under Different Legalization Proposals in Congress," *Migration Policy Institute,* Oct. 20, 2017, https://www.migrationpolicy.org/news/mpi-estimates-number-dreamers-potentially-eligible-benefit-under-different-legalization.

8   John Thune and Mark Warner, "Americans are Drowning in $1.5 Trillion of Student Loan Debt. There's One Easy Way Congress could Help," *Time*, Aug. 27, 2019, https://time.com/5662626/student-loans-repayment/.

9   Hannah Knowles, "Homelessness in the U.S. Rose for a Third Year, Driven by a Surge in California, HUD Says," *Washington Post*, Dec. 21, 2019, https://www. washingtonpost.com/nation/2019/12/21/homelessness-us-rose-third-year-driv en-by-surge-california-hud-says/.

10 E.J. Dionne Jr., "Trump's Base is Smaller than He Thinks," *Washington Post*, Oct. 6, 2019, https://www.washingtonpost.com/opinions/trumps-base-is-smaller-than-he-thinks/2019/10/06/0826a842-e6dd-11e9-a6e8-8759c5c7f608_story.html.

11 "MPI Estimates the Number of DREAMers."

12 "Profile of the Unauthorized Population: United States," *Migration Policy Institute,*

accessed Mar. 3, 2020, https://www.migrationpolicy.org/data/unauthorized-im migrant-population/state/US.

13 John F. Wasik, "How The GOP Tax Plan Scrooges Middle Class, Retired and Poor," *Forbes*, Nov. 29, 2017, https://www.forbes.com/sites/johnwasik/2017/11/29/ how-the-gop-tax-plan-scrooges-middle-class-retired-and-poor/#6b22c0b26c1e.

14 Jeff Cox, "That 50-Year Low in Unemployment isn't Helping Worker Paychecks," *CNBC*, Oct. 7, 2019, https://www.cnbc.com/2019/10/07/that-50-year-low-in-unemployment-isnt-helping-worker-paychecks.html.

15 "Remarks by President Trump on Tax Cuts for American Workers," *The White House*, Apr. 12, 2018, https://www.whitehouse.gov/briefings-statements/remarks-presi dent-trump-tax-cuts-american-workers/; Jim Tankersley, "Budget Deficit Topped $1 Trillion in 2019," *NPR*, Jan. 13, 2020, https://www.nytimes.com/2020/01/13/ business/budget-deficit-1-trillion-trump.html.

16 Donald J. Trump, Twitter post, Jan. 13, 2020, 8:39 a.m., https://twitter.com/real DonaldTrump/.

17 Peter Sullivan, "Trump Budget Calls for Cutting Medicaid, ACA by about $1 Trillion," *The Hill*, Feb. 10, 2020, https://thehill.com/policy/healthcare/482378- trump-budget-calls-for-cutting-medicaid-aca-by-about-1-trillion.

18 "Child Poverty," *National Center for Children in Poverty*, accessed Mar. 3, 2020, http://www.nccp.org/topics/childpoverty.html.

19 Nick Hanauer, "Trickle-Downers Created the Homelessness Crisis. Now They Want You to Believe They can 'Solve' It.," *The Nation*, Feb. 20, 2020, https://www. thenation.com/article/society/homelessness-crisis-trickle-down-economics/.

20 Sophie Collyer, David Harris and Christopher Wimer, "Left Behind: The One-Third of Children in Families Who Earn Too Little to Get the Full Child Tax Cred-it," *Poverty and Social Policy Brief* 3, no. 6 (2019).

21 "2017 Infrastructure Report Card," *American Society of Civil Engineers*, accessed Aug. 5, 2020, https://www.infrastructurereportcard.org/.

22 Irwin Redlener, "The Deadly Cost of Failing Infrastructure in Historic Midwest Floods," *The Hill*, Apr. 5, 2019, https://thehill.com/opinion/energy-environ ment/437550-ignoring-warning-signs-made-historic-midwest-floods-more-dan gerous.

23 Donald J. Trump, Twitter post, Jan. 29, 2014, 1:27 a.m., https://twitter.com/real-DonaldTrump/; Matthew Rozsa, "Trump Rebukes Greta Thunberg and Climate Activists: 'We must Reject the Perennial Prophets of Doom,'" *Salon*, Jan. 21, 2020, https://www.salon.com/2020/01/21/trump-rebukes-greta-thunberg-and-cli mate-activists-we-must-reject-the-perennial-prophets-of-doom/.

24 Lisa Friedman and Coral Davenport, "Curbs on Methane, Potent Greenhouse Gas, to be Relaxed in U.S.," *New York Times*, Aug. 29, 2019, https://www.nytimes.com/2019/08/29/climate/epa-methane-greenhouse-gas.html.

25 "Opioid Overdose Crisis," *National Institute on Drug Abuse,* May 27, 2020, https://www.drugabuse.gov/drug-topics/opioids/opioid-overdose-crisis.

26 Holly Hedegaard, Arialdi M. Miniño and Margaret Warner, "Drug Overdose Deaths in the United States, 1999–2018," *NHCS Data Brief* no. 356 (Jan. 2020), https://www.cdc.gov/nchs/products/databriefs/db356.htm.

27 Nicole Kravitz-Wirtz et al., "Association of Medicaid Expansion with Opioid Overdose Mortality in the United States," *JAMA Network Open* 3, no. 1 (2020), https://doi.org/10.1001/jamanetworkopen.2019.19066.

28 Greg Sargent, "Trump is Lying to Farmers' Faces, and They're Finally Getting Angry about It," *Washington Post*, Aug. 27, 2019, https://www.washingtonpost.com/opinions/2019/08/27/trump-is-lying-farmers-faces-theyre-finally-getting-angry-about-it/.

29 "Remarks by President Trump on Tax Cuts for American Workers."

30 Robbie Gramer and Colum Lynch, "Trump Seeks to Halve U.S. Funding for World Health Organization as Coronavirus Rages," *Foreign Policy*, Feb. 10, 2020, https://foreignpolicy.com/2020/02/10/trump-world-health-organization-funding-coronavirus-state-department-usaid-budget-cuts/.

31 Maria Godoy and Daniel Wood, "What do Coronavirus Racial Disparities Look Like State by State?," *NPR*, May 30, 2020, https://www.npr.org/sections/health-shots/2020/05/30/865413079/what-do-coronavirus-racial-disparities-look-like-state-by-state.

32 Ibid.

33 "Statement by the President," *The White House,* Jun. 1, 2020, https://www.whitehouse.gov/briefings-statements/statement-by-the-president-39/.

34 Richard Cowan, "Senate Republicans Block Bill Condemning Trump over Protesters," *Reuters*, Jun. 2, 2020, https://www.reuters.com/article/us-minneapolis-police-congress/senate-democrats-ready-bill-condemning-trump-on-protesters-idUSKBN2392L0.

35 Burgess Everett, Marianne Levine and Andrew Desiderio, "As Trump Rages, Republicans Plead for Calm," *Politico*, Jun. 1, 2020, https://www.politico.com/news/2020/06/01/republican-senate-trump-protest-294900; Christal Hayes, "'Some of his Tweets have not been Helpful': GOP Senators Criticize Trump's Floyd Protest Rhetoric," *USA Today,* Jun. 1, 2020, https://www.usatoday.com/story/news/politics/2020/06/01/george-floyd-protests-gop-senators-criticize-president-trumps-rhetoric/5312463002/.

36   "'Being Black in America should not be a Death Sentence': Officials Respond to George Floyd's Death," *CBS Minnesota,* May 26, 2020, https://minnesota.cbslocal.com/2020/05/26/being-black-in-america-should-not-be-a-death-sentence-officials-respond-to-george-floyds-death/.

37   Valerie Wilson and William M. Rodgers III, "Black-White Wage Gaps Expand with Rising Wage Inequality," *Economic Policy Institute,* Sep. 20, 2016, https://www.epi.org/publication/black-white-wage-gaps-expand-with-rising-wage-inequality/.

38   Elizabeth Austin, "Black-White Earnings Gap Remains at 1950s Levels for Median Workers," *University of Chicago Harris School of Public Policy,* Dec. 14, 2016, https://harris.uchicago.edu/news-events/news/black-white-earnings-gap-remains-1950s-levels-median-worker.

39   Shari Eli, Trevon Logan and Boriana Miloucheva, "Physician Bias and Racial Disparities in Veteran Health," *Vox EU | CEPR,* Aug. 20, 2019, https://voxeu.org/article/physician-bias-and-racial-disparities-veteran-health.

40   Colette Coleman, "7 Black Heroes of the American Revolution," *History,* Jun. 15, 2020, https://www.history.com/news/black-heroes-american-revolution.

41   David Barno and Nora Bensahel, "Reflections on the Curse of Racism in the U.S. Military," *War on the Rocks,* Jun. 30, 2020, https://warontherocks.com/2020/06/reflections-on-the-curse-of-racism-in-the-u-s-military/.

42   "Internal Affairs Units," in *Shielded from Justice: Police Brutality and Accountability in the United States* (New York: Human Rights Watch, 1998), https://www.hrw.org/legacy/reports98/police/uspo25.htm.

43   Joseph Goldstein, "'Testilying' by Police: A Stubborn Problem," *New York Times,* Mar. 18, 2018, https://www.nytimes.com/2018/03/18/nyregion/testilying-police-perjury-new-york.html.

44   Wendy Sawyer and Peter Wagner, "Mass Incarceration: The Whole Pie 2020," *Prison Policy Initiative,* Mar. 24, 2020, https://www.prisonpolicy.org/reports/pie2020.html.

45   "Mass Incarceration," *American Civil Liberties Union,* accessed Aug. 7, 2020, https://www.aclu.org/issues/smart-justice/mass-incarceration.

46   Becky Pettit, *Invisible Men: Mass Incarceration and the Myth of Black Progress* (New York: Russell Sage Foundation, 2012), 9.

47   Kriston McIntosh et al., "Examining the Black-White Wealth Gap," *Brookings Institution,* Feb. 27, 2020, https://www.brookings.edu/blog/up-front/2020/02/27/examining-the-black-white-wealth-gap/.

48   Jan Ransom, "Trump will not Apologize for Calling for Death Penalty over Central Park Five," *New York Times,* Jun. 18, 2019, https://www.nytimes.com/2019/06/18/nyregion/central-park-five-trump.html.

49   "Trump Just Joked about being President for Life - For the 6th Time," *The Week*, July 11, 2019, https://theweek.com/speedreads/852099/trump-just-joked-about-being-president-life--6th-time.

50   Michael Brice-Saddler, "While Bemoaning Mueller Probe, Trump Falsely Says the Constitution Gives Him 'The Right to do Whatever I Want,'" *The Washington Post*, Jul. 23, 2019, https://www.washingtonpost.com/politics/2019/07/23/trump-falsely-tells-auditorium-full-teens-constitution-gives-him-right-do-whatever-i-want/.

51   Bob Woodward, *Fear: Trump in the White House* (New York: Simon and Schuster, 2018), 286.

52   James Hamblin, "Is Something Neurologically Wrong with Donald Trump?," *The Atlantic*, Jan. 3, 2018, https://www.theatlantic.com/health/archive/2018/01/trump-cog-decline/548759/.

53   Sonam Sheth, "Trump may have Broken Federal Law by Altering Hurricane Dorian's Path on a Map to Validate his False Claim That It Could Hit Alabama," *Business Insider*, Sep. 4, 2019, https://www.businessinsider.com/trump-may-have-broken-law-by-altering-hurricane-dorian-map-2019-9.

54   Caitlin Oprysko, "'I don't Take Responsibility at All': Trump Deflects Blame for Coronavirus Testing Fumble," *Politico*, Mar. 13, 2020, https://www.politico.com/news/2020/03/13/trump-coronavirus-testing-128971.

55   David A. Graham, "Charity toward None, Malice toward All," *The Atlantic*, Feb. 6, 2020, https://www.theatlantic.com/ideas/archive/2020/02/trumps-vindictiveness/606214/.

56   Conor Friedersdorf, "Donald Trump's Cruel Streak," *The Atlantic*, Sep. 26, 2016, https://www.theatlantic.com/politics/archive/2016/09/donald-trumps-cruel-streak/501554/.

57   "Donald Trump: Textbook Narcissist," *Faculty of Social and Behavioural Sciences, Utrecht University*, accessed July 20, 2020, https://www.uu.nl/en/node/541/donald-trump-textbook-narcissist.

58   Ian Hughes, "Joining up the Dots Shows the True Depths of Trump's Dangerous Narcissistic Pathology," *Euronews*, Apr. 23, 2020, https://www.euronews.com/2020/04/22/joining-up-the-dots-shows-the-true-depths-of-trump-s-dangerous-narcissistic-pathology-view.

59   "Statement by the President," *The White House*, June 1, 2020, https://www.whitehouse.gov/briefings-statements/statement-by-the-president-39/.

60   "Portland Protests: Trump Threatens to Send Officers to More US Cities," *BBC News*, July 21, 2020, https://www.bbc.com/news/world-us-canada-53481383.

61   Domenico Montanaro, "6 Strongmen Trump Has Praised - And the Conflicts It Presents," *NPR*, May 2, 2017, https://www.npr.org/2017/05/02/526520042/6-strongmen-trumps-praised-and-the-conflicts-it-presents.

62   Charlie Savage, Michael Crowley and Eric Schmitt, "Trump Says He did not Ask Putin about Suspected Bounties to Kill U.S. Troops," *New York Times*, Jul. 29, 2020, https://www.nytimes.com/2020/07/29/us/politics/trump-putin-bounties.html; David Smith, "Trump's Ties to Putin under Fresh Scrutiny in Wake of Russia Bounty Reports," *The Guardian*, Jun. 30, 2020, https://www.theguardian.com/world/2020/jun/30/trump-putin-russia-afghanistan-us-soliders-bounty.

63   Brett Samuels, "Trump Praises Turkey's Erdogan after US Announces Cease-Fire Deal," *The Hill*, Oct. 17, 2019, https://thehill.com/homenews/administration/466334-trump-praises-turkeys-erdogan-after-us-announces-ceasefire-deal.

64   Dave Lawler, "Trump Praises Turkey's Erdogan as "Great Ally" Despite Syria Tensions," *Axios*, Nov. 13, 2019, https://www.axios.com/trump-erdogan-press-conference-syria-washington-79b29300-a573-44f6-8d85-8d8933f22267.html.

65   Donald J. Trump, Twitter post, Sep. 2, 2019, 8:22 a.m., https://twitter.com/realDonaldTrump/.

66   Julian Borger, "Trump Jokes to Putin They should 'Get Rid' of Journalists," *The Guardian*, Jun. 28, 2019, https://www.theguardian.com/us-news/2019/jun/28/smirking-trump-jokes-to-putin-dont-meddle-in-us-election-g20.

67   Donald J. Trump, Twitter post, Nov. 6, 2012, 2:15 p.m., https://twitter.com/realDonaldTrump/.

68   "The Problems with Trump's Claims of Ukrainian Election Interference," *PBS Newshour*, Dec. 6, 2019, https://www.pbs.org/newshour/show/the-facts-behind-trumps-claims-of-ukrainian-election-interference.

69   Zachary B. Wolf and JoElla Carman, "Here are All the Treaties and Agreements Trump has Abandoned," *CNN*, Feb. 1, 2019, https://www.cnn.com/2019/02/01/politics/nuclear-treaty-trump/index.html.

70   Maeve Reston, "While America Mourns John Lewis, Trump Continues to Divide the Nation," *CNN*, Jul. 19, 2020, https://www.cnn.com/2020/07/19/politics/us-election-donald-trump-john-lewis-death/index.html.

71   Donald J. Trump, Twitter post, Oct. 5, 2019, 3:06 p.m., https://twitter.com/realDonaldTrump/.

72   Nahal Toosi, "Trump's NSC Rocked by Ukraine Scandal," *Politico*, Oct. 5, 2019, https://www.politico.com/news/2019/10/05/trumps-national-security-council-ukraine-030564.

73   Sam Levine, "Trump Says Republicans would 'Never' be Elected Again If It was

Easier to Vote," *The Guardian*, Mar. 20, 2020, https://www.theguardian.com/us-news/2020/mar/30/trump-republican-party-voting-reform-coronavirus.

74   John F. Kennedy, "Remarks Intended for Delivery to the Texas Democratic State Committee [Undelivered]," Nov. 22, 1963, Austin, TX, https://www.jfklibrary.org/archives/other-resources/john-f-kennedy-speeches/austin-tx-undelivered-19631122.

75   Ibid.

CONCLUSION

TRUMP IS THE ANTITHESIS OF AMERICA'S GREATNESS

To summarize Trump's mishaps in domestic and foreign poli-
cy, here are 12 areas where Trump has inflicted a severe injury
on the American public, on the country as a whole, and on
America's reputation abroad. Unless measures are taken by a
new president to reverse the consequences of Trump's reckless
actions and policies, they will permanently erode America's
global standing, degrade our democracy, tear apart our social
fabric, and compromise our constitution which has held the
country together for two and a half centuries.

Donald Trump ran for office using the slogan "Make America Great Again." America was great before he came to office, but sadly nearly four years later under his leadership, America's greatness appears to be in the distant past. In less than one term in office, Trump systematically chipped away brick by brick at America's greatness and made the office of the presidency a laughing stock in the eyes of small and major powers alike. Whereas countries around the world used to show tremendous respect and admiration for America as a country, for its social and political values, cultural riches, scientific innovation, and commitment to human rights, under Trump America's star has dimmed precipitously and ominously to a point from which it may take years to recover. Electing Trump for another four-year term in office will set America too far back, causing major damage on many fronts that may well be irreversible.

Diminishing America's global leadership

On a number of occasions, Trump intensely criticized our European allies while praising our adversaries, and undermined the importance of NATO—an alliance that constitutes the security bedrock of the Western hemisphere while serving the US' national security interests in the European continent. In a Twitter rant during the 2018 NATO summit, Trump whined "What good is NATO if Germany is paying Russia billions of dollars for gas and energy? Why are there only 5 out of 29 countries that have met their commitment? The U.S. is paying for Europe's protection, then loses billions on Trade. Must pay 2% of GDP IMMEDIATELY, not by 2025."[1] As such, Trump has played directly into the hand of Russia's President Putin, which is precisely what Putin was hoping for. Trump's withdrawal from the internationally-negotiated JCPOA only deepened the already adversarial relations with Tehran. He abruptly decided to withdraw American forces from Syria, and although some American troops remained behind, he has weakened the US' influence in the region, which further strengthened Russia's and Iran's foothold in Syria to the dismay of our Middle Eastern friends and allies.

Furthermore, Trump failed miserably to denuclearize North Korea, naïvely thinking that he could use his "magical negotiating skills" to persuade its dictator Kim Jong Un to dismantle his nuclear arsenal. Instead, by meeting the North Korean despot three times, he legitimized him and left him free to resume testing nuclear warheads and ICBMs.

Trump's trade war with China was defunct from the start, as it mostly punished American farmers who could not export their produce to China.[2] He proposed the "deal of the century" presumably to forge an Israeli-Palestinian peace without any Palestinian input, which died on arrival. Recently he gave Israel, through Secretary of State Pompeo, the green light by stating that it was up to Israel to decide on annexing more Palestinian territories, but then he changed his mind again. He has only scuttled any prospect for an Israeli-Palestinian peace based on a two-state solution.

By his actions or inactions on major foreign policy issues, by his misleading statements and failure to work closely and consult with our allies in Europe, the Middle East, and Asia, and by largely disengaging from world affairs, Trump lost his credibility. As a result, he squandered the US' international leadership role, which had been central to the relative global stability since World War II.

Political polarization under Trump

Party polarization has certainly increased drastically under Trump. According to Gallup data, Trump faces the highest degree of political polarization than any post-WWII president, especially during his second and third years in office.[3] He played a major role in dividing the country on a number of critical issues, including climate change, the appointment of hyper-conservative judges (some of whom have been rated "not qualified" by the American Bar Association[4]), and women's reproductive rights. Political partisanship under Trump became the norm in Washington regardless of the issue at hand, which often led to Congressional paralysis.

"Us vs. them" became the mantra that governed nearly every encounter between Republican and Democrats. The saddest aspect is that political polarization seeped into the public domain, instigating intense personal loathing, often destroying friendships and even estranging family members from one another. The use of demeaning and dehumanizing language in Trump's public rallies and disgraceful tweets has served to engender hatred and further polarize the nation, poisoning the atmosphere between many Democrats and Republicans in general, and especially among members of Congress.

However, given that this is an election year, he will remain a divisive figure because he still believes that dividing the country gives him the best chance of winning, through bolstering his base and sowing distrust of the Democrats. To be sure, Trump will deliberately continue to contribute to the social and political divide as a means by which to advance the Republicans' conservative agenda. Notwithstanding the fact that some Republican Congressional leaders, especially those who are running for reelection, will keep some distance away from him, the party as a whole has become captive to his whims and will continue to support him and keep his base happy, irrespective of the harm being inflicted on the general public and the nation.

Deregulating climate change

The scientific evidence of climate change is incontrovertible as it manifests itself in massive forest fires, rising sea levels and temperatures, unprecedented hurricanes, the destruction of coral reefs and marine life, and growing contamination of air and water resources. Leave it to Trump and company, however, to deny the clear signs of anthropogenic global warming and claim that "occasional" severe change of "weather" is not a new phenomenon. Trump mistakenly conflates the weather and the climate, which are not the same. While weather fluctuations are natural, the severity of climate change which we are now witnessing is not normal and is directly tied to human activities. Sadly, Trump remains oblivious to the long-term repercussions of the climate crisis, which will make the coronavirus pandemic and its terrible toll pale in comparison.

Trump's willful blindness to the reality of climate change led to the US withdrawal from the Paris Agreement, citing economic concerns. Although he promised to negotiate a new deal, he never followed through. He claimed disingenuously that "The United States, under the Trump administration, will continue to be the cleanest and most environmentally friendly country on Earth"[5], but then he removed a significant number of environmental regulations in the United States.

He dismantled the 2015 Sage Grouse Conservation Plans to open up more habitats for fossil fuel extraction, issued an executive order to increase logging of forests on federal lands, and allowed offshore gas and oil wells to be drilled in the Arctic. In 2018, he disbanded the EPA's Particulate Matter Review Panel, which could make it easier to roll back pollution standards, and ended NASA's Carbon Monitoring System, which dramatically weakened auto emissions standards. He dropped climate change from the list of national security threats.[6] He weakened the Endangered Species Act by decreasing the amount of habitat they need to survive.[7] Finally, his proposed 2021 budget calls for a 26 percent cut to the EPA, eliminating 50 EPA programs and massively cutting research and development.[8]

Trump will be criticized for years if not decades to come for many of his failings on multiple fronts, but the most intense criticism and condemnation he deserves will be about his dismissive position on climate change and its effect on generations to come, which diminishes America's greatness rather than makes it great again.

Crumbling infrastructure

Despite it being one of Trump's campaign pledges in 2016, he has done nothing to significantly address America's crumbling infrastructure. The American Society of Civil Engineers (ASCE), which is the nation's oldest engineering society, rated the US' overall infrastructure D+ on their quadrennial Infrastructure Report Card in 2017—the same grade it received in 2013. Of the 16 categories the Report Card analyzes, not one received an A; only one category (Rail—including passenger and freight) received a B.[9]

The status of the country's roads and bridges in particular, which are used daily by everyone alike—rural, suburban, urban—is dismal and puts people's lives at risk. ASCE found that one in ten bridges across the country are structurally deficient, distributed fairly evenly across the country. In the past 20 years alone, there have been a number of catastrophic bridge failures leading to the deaths and injuries of hundreds, including the 2007 bridge collapse in Minneapolis, MN, which killed 13 and injured 145.[10] The scenes from these incidents are more akin to a disaster film than a bustling city in the world's richest country.

With Trump bragging about the US being the "greatest economy in the world" under his watch, one might think that America's wealth would not only be reflected in its GDP, but in how such wealth is used on behalf of the country's people, including on the infrastructure which has been in disrepair for decades, and has not gotten better during the past four years. Having failed to deliver on infrastructure in his first term, Trump is now mute on the subject for his second run. America did not become a great country because of unkept pledges, but because previous leaders have largely delivered on their promises.

Deepening poverty

Trump has sought to change how the federal poverty level is calculated, which will reduce the number of individuals and families eligible for government benefits—the poverty level is used to determine eligibility for over 40 government social programs, including SNAP and Medicaid.[11] Trump decided to close a "loophole" whereby in most states, families that qualify for Temporary Assistance for Needy Families (TANF) automatically qualify for SNAP, without having to go through a separate application process.[12] This puts another hurdle in the path of struggling families that need assistance.

Moreover, Trump's tax cuts, touted to benefit all Americans, actually benefited the wealthiest Americans the most. More than 60 percent of tax savings went to only the top 20 percent of earners.[13] Trump claimed that because of the tax cuts, working families would receive on average $4,000 more per year, but according to census data, those families only received on average $500.[14] Now Trump is proposing a 10 percent tax cut on the middle class as part of his "Tax Cuts 2.0" plan, which will be released in September[15]—a blatant ploy to pander to voters close to the election, as he well knows how unpopular his first round of tax reform was.

To be sure, poverty in America has increased over the past four years from which children in particular have suffered the most. It is estimated that over

11 million children face hunger on a daily basis, with an increasing number who drop out from school, as prolonged hunger causes developmental impairment and leads to behavioral problems.[16] Sadly the coronavirus, which has removed children from schools, where the poorest can receive free or reduced-cost lunches, is only causing this number to rise. Sixteen percent of American children under age 18 live in poverty—two times higher than adults over 65[17]. While Trump did not create the problem of poverty, he has done nothing to address it—he cannot "make America great" while allowing this kind of pervasive poverty to destroy an entire generation.

A whole generation that could have a brilliant future is being completely neglected, which is a terrible loss of human resources for America. That these disheartening if not tragic conditions are to be found in the richest country on earth does not make America great. Trump's claim rings hollow, as he could not demonstrate in any starker terms his indifference toward the poor and the despondent, which puts America to shame under his morally bankrupt leadership.

Inspiring the rise of racism

Racism in America is not a new phenomenon, as over the years African Americans, Hispanics, and other non-white citizens suffered from discrimination. Under Trump though, racism is on the rise because his bigotry is constantly on display, infecting millions of his followers who blindly emulate him with pride. He misses no words to express his disdain against people of color. In January 2018 he said: "Why are we having all these people from shithole countries come here?" "Why do we need more Haitians? Take them out."[18] He also refused to extend Temporary Protected Status to people from Haiti, El Salvador, Honduras, Nicaragua, Nepal, and Sudan, which would force those taking refuge in the US to return to their home countries or face deportation. While multiple court injunctions have prevented the status terminations from being implemented, the Trump administration continues to fight for the deportation of those from these six countries.[19]

A study from the Center for the Study of Hate and Extremism at CSU San Bernardino found that hate crimes had increased by 12.46 percent in 2017 from the previous year in an analysis of the 10 largest US cities; 2017 was also a record high in their 7-year analysis.[20] In its 2019 report, it notes regarding antisemitism specifically that "Jews were the direct target of half of the bias/extremist homicides in 2018, in the *worst year ever for anti-Semitic killings in the United States*."[21]

White nationalists have become more active, and more violent, with 17 instances of white nationalist/far right-motivated homicides in 2018 (up from 13 in 2017). The Center's 2019 report states: "Hate crimes overall have spiked over the last decade around political events and rhetoric. The expansion of white nationalism has created a coalesced movement and a violent extremist fringe." It further states that "August 2017, the month of the violent Charlottesville rally ... was tied for the second worst month since November 2008, even though the homicide and assaults there were not reported as hate crimes."[22]

While the overall percent of hate crimes based on anti-Black bias dropped (from 50.2 percent in 2016 to 47.1 percent in 2018), the total number of hate crimes motivated by race/ethnicity/ancestry has increased (4,426 in 2016 to 5,155 in 2018), with Black victims facing the largest segment of targeted violence (FBI Uniform Crime Report 2016, 2018).

In short, Trump is a racist through and through, and could never hide his penchant against non-white Americans regardless of their positions and daily contribution to the wellbeing of the country. What he said about a federal judge overseeing class-action suit against Trump University sums up his bigotry: "He's a Mexican. We're building a wall between here and Mexico. The answer is, he is giving us very unfair rulings—rulings that people can't even believe."[23] A president who promotes racism is not making America great again, he is debasing the greatness of America, and for that he will be remembered with scorn and contempt.

Impairing immigration policy

Since entering office, Trump proposed or implemented policies against immigration which run contrary to the US' history as a country made up of immigrants. Initially Trump called for massive deportations to "remov[e] the millions of illegal aliens" from the US "as fast as they come in."[24] To stop illegal immigration, Trump insisted on building a wall along the Mexican border that so far has cost over $11 billion,[25] regardless of the fact that such a physical wall will not stop a determined migrant from entering the US— in fact, most undocumented people in the US are those who overstayed their visas (typically traveling by plane), not those crossing the southern border (700,000 visa overstays in 2017, versus 300,000 crossing the Mexican border, which was also a record low).[26]

In January 2020, the Trump administration further expanded its "Muslim ban", targeting in particular people of color. Furthermore, he refused to provide a path for citizenship to nearly 700,000 DACA recipients and to the more than 11 million undocumented immigrants, the majority of whom have been living in America for decades with children born in the US. Finally, he insisted that asylum seekers should remain in Mexico while stopping pregnant women from entering the US to prevent them from giving birth on American soil, which would automatically make the newly born child an American citizen.

What Trump has sadly forgotten is that this country was built by immigrants from all over the world. Millions of immigrants came to the US to realize the American dream, from the workers who built America's railroads to the millions who today farm American land, the tens of thousands of scientists, artists, and writers, and many others from all walks of life that have made far-reaching contributions to the advancement of America, which made the country the forerunner in just about every field of endeavor.

It is the tradition of generally welcoming and embracing these immigrants that made America great in the first place, but leave it to Trump to stop the flow of immigrants in the name of making America great again, when in fact his immigration policy is depriving the US from attracting the talents needed to sustain America's greatness.

Violating human rights

Human rights violations under Trump have crossed many red lines, raising serious questions about the US' commitment to human rights, an area that America has historically championed the world over. Trump's violations of human rights are too long to numerate; it will suffice to mention only a few to demonstrate the seriousness of these offenses. To begin with, in June 2018 Trump withdrew the US from the UN Human Rights Council, the world's most important human rights body, in protest of its frequent criticism of Israel's treatment of Palestinians.

He worked to roll back protections for LGBTQ individuals. One of his first acts as president was to revoke Obama's transgender student guidance for schools; not long after, he declared that transgender people could no longer serve in the military.[27] His administration on the whole generally refuses to recognize gender identity as a protected class under the Civil Rights Act, and particularly Title VII.

Human rights violations are also manifested in the behavior of police officers and immigration agents toward minority and vulnerable populations, influenced by how Trump addresses these transgressions. As of August 6, police reportedly shot and killed 985 people in the US over the past year. Black Americans are shot at a disproportionate rate—twice the rate of white Americans, while only making up 13 percent of the population.[28] He has endorsed police brutality[29], and his enthusiastic pardon of former Sheriff Joe Arpaio, who was convicted of criminal contempt related to his treatment of immigrants, highlights his vicious streak.

To inflict severe pain on immigrants, in May 2018 Trump ordered the separation of more than 2,500 children from their parents, and were held in cages unfit for even stray animals at the US border by Customs and Border Patrol, under an explicit Trump policy. Staff of the Office of Refugee Resettlement was found to be giving psychotropic medication—sometimes forcibly—to migrant children at a Texas facility.[30]

Human rights abuses, however, are not limited to deliberate acts that violate any individual's given rights. Millions of American children going to sleep hungry, inaccessibility of medical treatment, homelessness, inequity in pay, and racial discrimination are all human rights violations, which Trump has only aggravated because of his policies. Indeed, no matter how many times he repeats his empty slogan of making America great again, the precise opposite is occurring.

Violating women's rights

As a womanizer and adulterer, Trump has shown little respect for women, treating them as second-class citizens at best. Trump ended an Obama-era rule that required companies with more than 100 employees to report how much workers are paid by race and gender, which was intended to close both gender and race wage gaps through greater transparency in pay.[31]

Trump does not believe that women have the right to determine their own reproductive plans or family planning, and his administration even called for the elimination of discussion of sexual and reproductive health from United Nations documents. His administration claims that the terms promote abortion, saying "there is no international right to an abortion."[32] In this regard the US was joined by Russia, Saudi Arabia, Sudan, Yemen, Egypt, Libya, and others—all infamous for their attitudes against women.

Trump reinstated the Global Gag Rule, which prevents international aid groups that receive US funding from even educating people about safe abortion.[33] Clinics must make the impossible choice of giving safe and accurate information to their clients but lose US funding, which makes it extremely difficult to keep operating clinics and providing services; or keep US funding but deny essential services to the communities they serve. However, in this regard, Trump simply followed precedent, as the Global Gag Rule is repealed under Democratic presidents and reinstated under Republican presidents.

For a president who brags about making America great again, exhibiting this much disrespect and disregard for more than 50 percent of the population is a return to the medieval era which certainly defies greatness—a legacy that Trump is cursed to live with.

Depriving millions of healthcare

Whereas in every advanced country health care is considered a human right, Trump has attempted numerous times to undermine or outright end Obama's ACA, which he has pledged to do. Republicans removed the individual mandate penalty in 2017 in an attempt to undermine the health bill.

In the midst of the COVID-19 pandemic, Trump refused to instate an open enrollment period for healthcare under the ACA at a time when many people lost health insurance, which in the United States is usually tied to one's employment. While people can still apply under special enrollment due to losing their jobs (and thus their employer-provided health insurance), creating a special open enrollment period would have eased the burden for millions of Americans whose need for health insurance is critical at this time, especially when up to 40 million Americans are expected to be uninsured (an increase from the 29 million uninsured from before the pandemic).[34]

Although states who run their own health exchanges can and, in many instances, did run their own special open enrollment, nearly two thirds of states' health exchanges are run by the federal government.[35] Furthermore, in another appalling decision, Trump ended funding for the WHO in the midst of the global COVID-19 pandemic.

In his proposed budget for 2021, he called for nearly $1 trillion in cuts to the ACA and Medicaid over the next 10 years. This includes $150 billion in Medicaid cuts due to imposing work requirements, which would cause people to lose coverage. In 2015, Trump had promised: "I'm not going to cut Medicare or Medicaid. Every other Republican is going to cut it."[36]

In fact, if it were not for Democrats who sternly objected to any cut in Medicare or Medicaid, Trump would have certainly gone along with Republican Congressional leaders. Trump kept calling for repealing and replacing the ACA, but he failed miserably to find a replacement. Millions of Americans must choose between paying the high cost of healthcare insurance or putting food on the table. Healthcare is not a luxury, it is a necessity, and no country can claim greatness when millions of its citizens fall sick, cannot meet the cost medical treatment, and end up financially bankrupt. Indeed, in which way can Trump reconcile his campaign slogan of making America great again with the reality that tens of millions are without accessible healthcare?

Mishandling the coronavirus pandemic

By all accounts, had Trump took the coronavirus seriously and employed all the necessary measures to tackle it at the onset, instead of deliberately dismissing its potential deadly spread, he could have dramatically minimized the horrifying consequences that we are witnessing today. In his second year in office, he dismantled the task force responsible for pandemics,[37] and in his 2018 budget request to Congress he proposed a massive 17 percent cut ($1.2 billion) for the Centers for Disease Control.[38]

As early as January 2020 Trump was briefed regularly about the virus and its potential dreadful spread, but he simply ignored the warning. On February 25th, Trump said that "We have very few people with it, and the people that have it are ... getting better. They're all getting better .... As far as what we're doing with the new virus, I think that we're doing a great job"[39], which of course could not have been further from the truth. Obsessed with the stock market and the health of the economy which, from his perspective, are central to his reelection, Trump missed no opportunity to make light of the virus. On February 28 he stated that "It's going to disappear. One day, it's like a miracle, it will disappear."[40]

Sadly for him, as of this writing there are nearly five million confirmed cases and 160,000 deaths, which continue to increase, while over 30 million Americans lost their jobs and many millions joined the poverty line.[41] The pandemic has also highlighted racial disparities in this country. Black, Indigenous, and other Americans of color are dying at disproportionate rates to whites; Black Americans are dying from COVID-19 at the most disproportionate rate, 2.3 times higher than whites.[42] It is due largely to systemic issues which have created more poverty and lower access to health care among Black communities. While the White House has called its response to the pandemic a "great success story", more Americans have died from this crisis than all its wars since World War II.*

Two months ago, in one of his infamous press conferences, Trump mused about potential "cures" for COVID-19 using things which are not meant and were never meant to be consumed by a human person—like disinfectant. Injecting disinfectants, as Trump pondered, would cause a very painful death. What is so sad is that our so-called president is stupid enough to voice that proposition aloud. Indeed, this is so grossly irresponsible that it staggers the imagination.

As the economy continues to decline, Trump wants to reopen the economy, but in the absence of adequate testing and without an available vaccine, he will be putting American lives at risk simply so he can boost his chances for re-election. His decisions have already led to hundreds of thousands of American deaths, his irresponsible and reckless comments and musings have brought embarrassment, shame, confusion, and danger into American homes. And now in his desperation to keep the office, Trump is preparing to sacrifice potentially tens of thousands more American lives on the altar of his ego.

To this day, whereas experts say the US may need to do 20 million tests per day to combat the spread of the virus, only 59 million have been run during the entire period of the pandemic (averaging at slightly more than 400,000

---

* As of August 7, the COVID-19 death toll per the CDC is 157,631 total deaths; the Department of Veterans Affairs' death toll encompassing the Korean War, Vietnam War, and Desert Shield/Desert Storm is 146,414, inclusive of battle deaths, other deaths in the theater of war, and other non-theater service deaths.

per day).[43] Moreover, there is still not enough PPE to protect medical personnel who are putting their lives on the line to save the lives of others. If Trump reopens the economy, as he is so eager to do, in the absence of adequate testing and without an available vaccine for all Americans, he will be putting millions of American lives at risk for no reason other than to boost his chances for re-election.

To be sure, the US was entirely unprepared to provide healthcare workers with the equipment they need to fight this deadly disease and faced a complete failure to take charge on the federal level; instead Trump left states hanging with little or no help from his administration.

Dangerously eroding our democracy

From the day he announced his candidacy, Trump began to systematically undermine the fundamental principles of our democracy. His affinity for dictators and insatiable lust for power have been clear to see for some time, and he has tried in every which way he can to strip away the democratic rules enshrined in the Constitution and the norms of political conduct that have been largely respected and followed by his predecessors for over two centuries.

To stifle the media's criticism of his policies and positions on various domestic foreign issues, Trump made his attacks on the media routine, calling the press in general "fake news" and the "enemy of the people". Freedom of speech and freedom of the press are constitutionally protected, and yet Trump freely undermines those guarantees and tramples on the fourth estate wantonly, violating one of the central pillars of American democracy.

Trump has made no secret of his disdain of peaceful protesters. The right to protest peacefully is guaranteed constitutionally, and no president has the prerogative to impede the people from exercising this freedom. Yet Trump tries to do just that, most recently in dispatching federal troops to protests in Portland, OR and threatening to do the same in other Democrat-led cities and states.

Trump's only response to protests during his president is to denigrate the protesters as well as their causes. He has called NFL players "disgraceful" for kneeling during the national anthem in protest of racial inequality and remarked that he is "ashamed" of the protesters[44]; he threatened that protesters outside of the White House in the wake of George Floyd's death "would have been greeted with the most vicious dogs, and most ominous weapons, I have ever seen", relishing the idea of Secret Service agents jumping in for "good practice"[45]; he called the proposed painting of "Black Lives Matter" on Fifth Avenue in New York a "symbol of hate"[46]; he tried to discredit 75 year old Martin Gugino, a long-time Buffalo, NY peace activist involved in the Catholic Worker movement, who suffered a fractured skull after being pushed to the ground by police, by calling him an "ANTIFA provocateur."[47]

Through his political appointees, Trump continues to undermine the rule of law on just about every level. From the beginning of his presidency he has politicized and tried to exploit the office of the Attorney General. His first attorney general, Jeff Sessions, recused himself from overseeing the Russia investigation launched against Trump in order to protect the rule of law; this only sparked Trump's ire, leading to Sessions' undignified firing after months of public, verbal abuse. Sessions' replacement, William Barr, has proved to be a loyal sycophant of Trump, acting more as Trump's personal attorney and lapdog than the nation as a whole's top lawyer.

The present crisis has revealed that Trump is simply unfit to be president; he is utterly incompetent and fails consistently to meet the challenges of the office of the presidency. His decisions have already led to the deaths of tens of thousands of Americans; his irresponsible and reckless comments and musings have brought embarrassment, shame, confusion, and danger into American homes.

The greatness of any country is measured by the moral principles it stands for – including its protection of human rights, its adherence to the rule of law, the equitable treatment of its citizens regardless of ethnicity, religion, or race, the ingenuity and creativity of its people, and the opportunities the government provides its citizens to grow and prosper.

The one thing that can harness the country's human and material resourcefulness to meet any challenge for the good of the multitude is leadership. Leaders who are enlightened, visionary, courageous, selfless and above all honest and fully dedicated to the wellbeing of the country. These are the hallmarks of what make a country great. Trump betrayed the principles on which this country was founded. He is the antithesis of American greatness, and America will not be great again as long as Trump occupies the office of the presidency.

Notes

1   Donald J. Trump, Twitter post, Jul. 11, 2018, 1:07 p.m., https://twitter.com/real
    DonaldTrump/.

2   Karl Plume and P.J. Huffstutter, "U.S. farmers see another bleak year despite Phase
    1 trade deal", *Reuters*, Jan. 3, 2020, https://www.reuters.com/article/us-usa-trade-
    china-agriculture-insight/u-s-farmers-see-another-bleak-year-despite-phase-1-
    trade-deal-idUSKBN1Z20CK.

3   Jeffrey M. Jones, "Trump Third Year Sets New Standard for Party Polarization", *Gal-
    lup*, Jan. 21, 2020, https://news.gallup.com/poll/283910/trump-third-year-sets-
    new-standard-party-polarization.aspx.

4   Ariane de Vogue and Alex Rogers, "'Not qualified' rating and accusation from
    American Bar Association moves Trump nominee to tears", *CNN*, Oct. 31, 2019,
    https://www.cnn.com/2019/10/30/politics/american-bar-association-nomi
    nees-vandyke/index.html.

5   "Statement by President Trump on the Paris Climate Accord", The White House,
    Jun. 1, 2017, https://www.whitehouse.gov/briefings-statements/statement-presi
    dent-trump-paris-climate-accord/.

6   Michael Greshko, Laura Parker, Brian Clark Howard, Daniel Stone, Alejandra Bo-
    runda, and Sarah Gibbens, "A running list of how President Trump is changing en-
    vironmental policy", *National Geographic*, May 3, 2019, https://www.nationalgeo
    graphic.com/news/2017/03/how-trump-is-changing-science-environment/.

7   Darryl Fears, "The Trump administration weakened Endangered Species Act rules -
    17 state attorneys general have sued over it", *Washington Post*, Sep. 25, 2019, https://
    www.washingtonpost.com/climate-environment/2019/09/25/trump-admin
    istration-weakened-endangered-species-act-rules-today-state-attorneys-general-
    sued-over-it/.

8   Rebecca Beitsch and Rachel Frazin, "Trump budget slashes EPA funding, environ-
    mental programs", *The Hill*, Feb. 10, 2020, https://thehill.com/policy/energy-en
    vironment/482352-trump-budget-slashes-funding-for-epa-environmental-pro
    grams.

9   "2017 Infrastructure Report Card."

10 David Schaper, "10 Years After Bridge Collapse, America Is Still Crumbling", *NPR*,
    Aug.1, 2017, https://www.npr.org/2017/08/01/540669701/10-years-after-
    bridge-collapse-america-is-still-crumbling.

11 Susan J. Demas and Allison Winter, "Trump's poverty line changes could crush
    Michiganders 'barely getting by'", *Michigan Advance*, Feb. 17, 2020, https://www.
    michiganadvance.com/2020/02/17/trumps-poverty-line-changes-could-crush-
    michiganders-barely-getting-by/.

12 Nathalie Baptiste and Jessica Washington, "Trump Isn't Waging a War on Poverty. He's Waging a War on Poor People.", *Mother Jones*, Feb. 14, 2020, https://www.motherjones.com/politics/2020/02/trump-isnt-waging-a-war-on-poverty-hes-waging-a-war-on-poor-people/.

13 Scott Horsley, "After 2 Years, Trump Tax Cuts Have Failed To Deliver On GOP's Promises", *NPR*, Dec. 20, 2019, https://www.npr.org/2019/12/20/789540931/2-years-later-trump-tax-cuts-have-failed-to-deliver-on-gops-promises.

14 "Opinion: Trump tax cuts are a broken promise to the middle class", *Los Angeles Times*, Jan. 1, 2020, https://www.latimes.com/opinion/story/2020-01-01/donald-trump-tax-cut-deficit.

15 Brian Faler, "Trump weighing 10 percent middle-class tax cut plan", *Politico*, Feb. 14, 2020, https://www.politico.com/news/2020/02/14/trump-middle-class-tax-cut-115262.

16 "Facts About Child Hunger in America", Feeding America, accessed May 3, 2020, https://www.feedingamerica.org/hunger-in-america/child-hunger-facts.

17 "The State of America's Children 2020", Children's Defense Fund, accessed Aug. 4, 2020, https://www.childrensdefense.org/policy/resources/soac-2020-child-poverty/.

18 Josh Dawsey, "Trump derides protections for immigrants from 'shithole' countries", *Washington Post*, Jan. 12, 2018, https://www.washingtonpost.com/politics/trump-attacks-protections-for-immigrants-from-shithole-countries-in-oval-office-meeting/2018/01/11/bfc0725c-f711-11e7-91af-31ac729add94_story.html.

19 "Temporary Protected Status", U.S. Citizenship and Immigration Services, accessed Aug. 4, 2020, https://www.uscis.gov/humanitarian/temporary-protected-status.

20 Center for the Study of Hate & Extremism, *Hate Crimes in Los Angeles 2017-2018: A Comparative Analysis With Other Major Cities* (San Bernardino, CA: 2018), https://www.csusb.edu/sites/default/files/LA%20City%20Hate%20Crime%20v8.pdf.

21 Center for the Study of Hate & Extremism, *Factbook on Hate & Extremism in the U.S. & Internationally* (San Bernardino, CA: 2019), 3, https://www.csusb.edu/sites/default/files/CSHE%202019%20Report%20to%20the%20Nation%20FINAL%207.29.19%2011%20PM_0_0.pdf.

22 *Factbook on Hate & Extremism in the U.S. & Internationally* 3, 14.

23 Lydia O'Connor and Daniel Marans, "Trump Condemned Racism As 'Evil.' Here Are 20 Times He Embraced It.", *HuffPost*, Jan. 12, 2018, https://www.huffpost.com/entry/trump-racism-examples_n_5991dcabe4b09071f69b9261.

24 Nick Miroff and Maria Sacchetti, "Trump vows mass immigration arrests, removals of 'millions of illegal aliens' starting next week", *Washington Post*, Jun. 17, 2019, https://www.washingtonpost.com/immigration/trump-vows-mass-immi

gration-arrests-removals-of-millions-of-illegal-aliens-starting-next-week/2019/06/17/4e366f5e-916d-11e9-aadb-74e6b2b46f6a_story.html.

25 John Burnett, "$11 Billion And Counting: Trump's Border Wall Would Be The World's Most Costly", *NPR*, Jan. 19, 2020, https://www.npr.org/2020/01/19/797319968/-11-billion-and-counting-trumps-border-wall-would-be-the-world-s-most-costly.

26 Sean McMinn and Renee Klahr, "Where Does Illegal Immigration Mostly Occur? Here's What The Data Tell Us", *NPR*, Jan. 10, 2019, https://www.npr.org/2019/01/10/683662691/where-does-illegal-immigration-mostly-occur-heres-what-the-data-tell-us.

27 Selena Simmons-Duffin, "'Whiplash' Of LGBTQ Protections And Rights, From Obama To Trump", *NPR*, Mar. 2, 2020, https://www.npr.org/sections/health-shots/2020/03/02/804873211/whiplash-of-lgbtq-protections-and-rights-from-obama-to-trump.

28 "Police shootings database 2015-2020", *Washington Post*, accessed Aug. 7, 2020, https://www.washingtonpost.com/graphics/investigations/police-shootings-database/.

29 Cleve R. Wootson Jr. and Mark Berman, "U.S. police chiefs blast Trump for endorsing 'police brutality'", *Washington Post*, Jul. 30, 2017, https://www.washingtonpost.com/news/post-nation/wp/2017/07/29/u-s-police-chiefs-blast-trump-for-endorsing-police-brutality/.

30 Samantha Schmidt, "Trump administration must stop giving psychotropic drugs to migrant children without consent, judge rules", *Washington Post*, Jul. 31, 2018, https://www.washingtonpost.com/news/morning-mix/wp/2018/07/31/trump-administration-must-seek-consent-before-giving-drugs-to-migrant-children-judge-rules/?fbclid=IwAR2z_BTzdgaiuH2zRw54TKI2HxBXVQCOLmbMi4MvDyNall3ZV2z6AoBn8Qo.

31 Suzy Khimm, "Trump Halted Obama's Equal Pay Rule. What it Means for Working Women", *NBC News*, Aug. 31, 2017, https://www.nbcnews.com/politics/white-house/trump-killed-obama-s-equal-pay-rule-what-it-means-n797941.

32 "Trump's anti-woman push puts America in the pantheon of human rights offenders", *Washington Post*, Sep. 27, 2019, https://www.washingtonpost.com/opinions/trumps-anti-woman-push-puts-america-in-the-pantheon-of-human-rights-offenders/2019/09/27/e8428a56-e12c-11e9-b199-f638bf2c340f_story.html.

33 "Trump's Global Gag Rule a blow for women's rights and lives", Amnesty International, accessed May 3, 2020, https://www.amnestyusa.org/74153-2/.

34 "COVID-19 Impact on Medicaid, Marketplace and the Uninsured, by State", Health Management Associates, Apr. 3, 2020, https://www.healthmanagement.

com/wp-content/uploads/HMA-Estimates-of-COVID-Impact-on-Coverage-public-version-for-April-3-830-CT.pdf.

35   Susannah Luthi, "Trump rejects Obamacare special enrollment period amid pandemic", *Politico*, Mar. 31, 2020, https://www.politico.com/news/2020/03/31/trump-obamacare-coronavirus-157788.

36   Peter Sullivan, "Trump budget calls for cutting Medicaid, ACA by about $1 trillion", *The Hill*, Feb. 10, 2020, https://thehill.com/policy/healthcare/482378-trump-budget-calls-for-cutting-medicaid-aca-by-about-1-trillion.

37   Deb Riechmann, "Trump disbanded NSC pandemic unit that experts had praised", *Associated Press*, Mar. 14, 2020, https://apnews.com/ce014d94b64e98b7203b8 73e56f80e9a.

38   "Overview of the CDC FY 2018 Budget Request", Centers for Disease Control and Prevention, May 21, 2017, https://www.cdc.gov/budget/documents/fy2018/fy-2018-cdc-budget-overview.pdf.

39   "Remarks by President Trump in Press Conference", The White House, Feb. 25, 2020, https://www.whitehouse.gov/briefings-statements/remarks-president-trump-press-conference-4/.

40   Stephen Collinson, "Trump seeks a 'miracle' as virus fears mount", *CNN*, Feb. 28, 2020, https://www.cnn.com/2020/02/28/politics/donald-trump-coronavirus-miracle-stock-markets/index.html.

41   Erica Werner and Rachael Bade, "Coronavirus relief talks collapse on Capitol Hill as Trump readies executive actions", *Washington Post*, Aug. 7, 2020, https://www.washingtonpost.com/us-policy/2020/08/07/congress-coronavirus-stimulus-trump/.

42   "The Color of Coronavirus: COVID-19 Deaths by Race And Ethnicity in the U.S.", APM Research Lab, Jul. 22, 2020, https://www.apmresearchlab.org/covid/deaths-by-race?fbclid=IwAR2AG0midfKG49dgup9qjm0o-LWyB_oR00qEM C0sWxT5WFXAc_5yJM1jmG4.

43   Charlotte Jee, "The US needs to do 20 million tests a day to reopen safely, according to a new plan", MIT Technology Review, Apr. 20, 2020, https://www.technolo gyreview.com/2020/04/20/1000228/the-us-will-need-to-do-20-million-tests-a-day-to-reopen-safely/; "COVID-19 Dashboard", Center for Systems Science and Engineering at Johns Hopkins University, accessed Aug. 7, 2020, https://coronavi rus.jhu.edu/map.html.

44   "Trump: NFL anthem kneeling protesters 'disgraceful'", *BBC*, Sep. 26, 2017, https://www.bbc.com/news/world-us-canada-41407176.

45   Donald J. Trump, Twitter post, May 30, 2020, 8:41 a.m., https://twitter.com/real DonaldTrump/.

46 Donald J. Trump, Twitter post, Jul. 1, 2020, 9:48 a.m., https://twitter.com/real
    DonaldTrump/.

47 Geoff Herbert, "Buffalo protester Martin Gugino released from hospital nearly 4
    weeks after poice shoved him", *Syracuse.com | Post-Standard*, Jul. 1, 2020, https://
    www.syracuse.com/state/2020/07/buffalo-protester-martin-gugino-released-
    from-hospital-nearly-4-weeks-after-police-shoved-him.html.